AF323678

Law and Society
Recent Scholarship

Edited by Melvin I. Urofsky

A Series from LFB Scholarly

American Public Religion in Frankfurter and Scalia's Opinions

David C. Meadors

LFB Scholarly Publishing LLC
El Paso 2014

Library of Congress Cataloging-in-Publication Data

Meadors, David C., 1966- author.
  American public religion in Frankfurter and Scalia's opinions / David
C. Meadors.
     pages cm
  Based on author's thesis (doctoral - Baylor University, 2012).
  Includes bibliographical references and index.
  ISBN 978-1-59332-748-4 (hardcover : alk. paper)
  1. Church and state--United States--Cases. 2. Religious observances
on public property--Law and legislation--United States--Cases. 3.
Religious law and legislation--United States--Cases. 4. Scalia,
Antonin--Views of Church and state 5. Frankfurter, Felix, 1882-1965--
Views on Church and state I. Title.
  KF4865.M39 2014
  342.7308'52--dc23
                                            2014030256

ISBN 978-1-59332-748-4

Manufactured in the United States of America.

Table of Contents

Acknowledgments and Dedication

The author wishes to thank the following scholars for shaping my thoughts throughout my study of American Public Religion and the jurisprudence of the First Amendment religion clauses: Dr. Barry G. Hankins, Professor Sanford Levinson, Professor Tim Hall, and Dr. Robert N. Bellah.

I dedicate this book to my incredible wife, Carrie K. Meadors, and to our wonderful children: Beth Anne, Emma, Causey, and Paul Thomas. Their patience and love has encouraged me throughout my study of Justices Frankfurter and Scalia, and their religion clause opinions.

CHAPTER 1

American Public Religion in the Opinions of Felix Frankfurter and Antonin Scalia

INTRODUCTION

The First Amendment religion clause jurisprudences of two United States Supreme Court justices—Felix Frankfurter (1939-1962) and Antonin Scalia (1986-present)—find different forms of American public religion constitutional.[1] Frankfurter's jurisprudence applied the Free Exercise Clause weakly, but the Establishment Clause strictly as exemplified in the cases *Minersville School District v. Gobitis*, 310 U.S. 586 (1940) and *McCollum v. Board of Education*, 333 U.S. 203 (1948). Scalia, on the other hand, has interpreted both clauses with deference to government action in most cases, and this is evident in *Employment Division v. Smith*, 494 U.S. 872 (1990) and *McCreary County v. ACLU*, 545 U.S. 844 (2005).

---

[1] Steven B. Epstein's article, "Rethinking the Constitutionality of Ceremonial Deism," *96 Columbia L. Rev. 2083, 2094-2098* (1996) provides a lengthy definition of ceremonial deism more fully delineated below, and uses the terms American public religion and American civil religion without distinction. He does, however, distinguish between different types of American public religion, especially American public religion that includes a belief in God and American public religion that does not. Ibid., 2096-2097.

The originalist interpretive methodology applied by both judges to the religion clauses relies for authority upon leaders from America's founding era such as Thomas Jefferson and George Washington, especially in Establishment Clause cases. Yet, Frankfurter and Scalia do not cite the same founders as authority, and they do not interpret the Establishment Clause in the same manner since Frankfurter has applied it strictly whereas Scalia applied it weakly. In addition, Scalia has defended his originalist interpretive methodology of textualism in extrajudicial sources whereas Frankfurter's rationale for the originalism he applies to the religion clauses appears in his official opinions. Moreover, Frankfurter's Free Exercise Clause opinions also defer to government action because of his arguments in favor of judicial restraint, and both judges agree that religious liberty is best protected when cherished and protected by citizens in the democratic process before resort to judicial review.

The American public religion found constitutional by Frankfurter is also more secular in nature than Scalia's in that it does not include belief in God. Yet, there are elements in it similar to religious faith such as the secular need for a day of rest,[2] veneration of the American flag, and an appeal to the need for unifying beliefs in society, or what Frankfurter called "cohesive sentiment."[3] Frankfurter reasoned in the *McCollum* case, however, that more specifically religious education programs in public schools were unconstitutional because they would likely create social conflict.[4] Scalia, to the contrary, has found more specifically theistic public religious expressions such as graduation prayers and displays of the Ten Commandments constitutional. This is not only because Scalia finds these expressions of American public religion consistent with an American tradition allowing preference for monotheistic faiths in public acknowledgements of deity, but also

---

[2] *McGowan v. Maryland*, 366 U.S. 420, 459-543 (1961) (FRANKFURTER, J., concurring).

[3] *Minersville School District v. Gobitis*, 310 U.S. 586, 591-600 (1940).

[4] *McCollum v. Board of Education*, 333 U.S. 203, 231f, (1948) (FRANKFURTER, J., concurring).

because he argues that relatively generic prayers at graduation ceremonies will enhance religious tolerance and civility.[5]

AMERICAN PUBLIC RELIGION: FRANKFURTER AND SCALIA

Frankfurter and Scalia's treatment of American public religion in their opinions is important because the debate about originalist[6] interpretive methodology continues, and because the Supreme Court has not reached a consensus regarding how to apply the founding era's history to interpretation of the First Amendment religion clauses. The author will document the debate concerning originalism, and how the Supreme Court has used founding era history to interpret the religion clauses in its review of the literature relevant to this book's argument before more specifically engaging Frankfurter and Scalia's religion clause opinions. The book will limit review of the Supreme Court's use of founding history, though, to cases decided after that Court applied the religion clauses to state and local governments through the doctrine of incorporation in the 1940s.[7] Incorporation refers to application of the First Amendment's religion clauses to state and local government via the Fourteenth Amendment.

As the author began research about the jurisprudences of both of these Supreme Court justices it became evident that both handled religion clause questions within a frame of reference as to the proper nature of American democracy, the place of religion within that democracy, and from the perspective of a particular reading of

---

[5] *Lee v. Weisman*, 505 U.S. 577, 631-646 (1992) (SCALIA, J., dissenting); and *McCreary County v. ACLU*, 545 U.S. 844, 886-898 (2005) (SCALIA, J., dissenting).

[6] Originalism, or originalist interpretive methodology, refers to attempts to find the original meaning of the United State's Constitution as compared to its "current" meaning today. Antonin Scalia, *A Matter of Interpretation: Federal Courts and the Law* (Princeton, NJ: Princeton University Press, 1997), 38-39.

[7] The Free Exercise Clause was incorporated in the case of *Cantwell v. Connecticut*, 310 U.S. 296 (1940), and the Establishment Clause in the case of *Everson v. Board of Education*, 330 U.S. 1 (1947).

American history.[8] Justice Frankfurter was the child of immigrant Jewish parents from Austria who was educated in public schools in New York City, and became very successful in an atmosphere, which he felt gave little preference to sectarian faiths to the benefit of those committed to secular democratic values. Frankfurter developed interpretations of the Free Exercise Clause and the Establishment Clauses that appealed to America's founding history, and especially the views of Thomas Jefferson and James Madison. Yet, in free exercise cases Frankfurter also grounded his interpretation in arguments for judicial restraint attributable to one of his mentors, James Bradley Thayer, who taught him at Harvard Law School. In several instances Frankfurter also made explicit remarks declaring his faith in American democracy, and stated his belief that public schools should serve as fountains of democratic values and behavior.[9]

Kathleen M. Sullivan has argued that Frankfurter was a "secularist" meaning that he had a strong view with regard to the Establishment Clause, but a weak free exercise view as expressed in the *Gobitis* and *West Virginia v. Barnette* cases.[10] The *Gobitis* and *Barnette* cases involved public school ceremonies that prescribed salute to the American flag in the context of Word War II. Jehovah's Witnesses objected to these ceremonies based on their understanding of the Bible, and sought legal relief pursuant to the Free Exercise Clause of the First Amendment. When the two cases reached the United States Supreme Court on appeal Frankfurter authored opinions in each reasoning that the Free Exercise Clause did not provide the relief sought by the Jehovah's Witnesses. He cited the importance of religious freedom for America's founders, with particular reference to Thomas Jefferson, but then reasoned further that the founders did not authorize exemptions to laws generally unrelated to religion in the free

---

[8] Michael E. Smith, "The Special Place of Religion in the Constitution," *1983 Sup. Ct. Rev. 83* (1983).

[9] Ibid., 110-113.

[10] Kathleen M. Sullivan, "Justice Scalia and the Religion Clauses," *22 U. Haw. L. Rev. 449, 452* (2000). *Minersville School District v. Gobitis,* 310 U.S. 586 (1940); *West Virginia State Board of Education v. Barnette,* 319 U.S. 624 (1943).

exercise context. His *Gobitis* and *Barnette* opinions also appealed to the need for judicial restraint where the legislature had a rational basis for the law at issue, and stated that the need for "cohesive sentiment" cultivated by the flag salute ceremonies at issue was as important in the American scheme of government as religious liberty.[11]

Scalia used similar logic to that of Frankfurter in the *Gobitis* opinion, and in fact relied upon *Gobitis* in his *Smith* opinion for a majority of the Court, even though *Gobitis* had subsequently been overruled in the *West Virginia v. Barnette* case in 1943 in a landmark opinion by Justice Robert Jackson.[12] This piqued the author's interest in a comparison between the religion clause jurisprudences of the two justices. Review of Scalia's approach to free exercise and no establishment cases revealed that he has been labeled an "assimilationist" by Professor Kathleen Sullivan, and that he has interpreted the Free Exercise Clause similarly to Frankfurter in most of his opinions, but Scalia has articulated an extrajudicial "textualist" methodology for interpreting the Constitution. Moreover, Scalia has applied a much weaker approach to the Establishment Clause than Frankfurter, and he has relied on America's founders and its founding history in a manner that is distinct from Frankfurter in no establishment cases. Additionally, the American public religion deemed constitutional in their respective religion clause jurisprudences is different in that Frankfurter found American public religion constitutional which did not include belief in God, but contained elements similar to religious faith such as the secular need for a day of rest, veneration of the American flag, and an appeal to "cohesive sentiment" in the *Gobitis* case.[13] To the contrary, Scalia has found more specifically theistic public religious expressions such as graduation prayers and displays of the Ten Commandments constitutional. This is confirmed when one examines the secondary literature about their jurisprudences including the scholarship of

---

[11] *Gobitis*, 310 U.S. at 594, and *Barnette*, 319 U.S. at 646-672.

[12] Judge and First Amendment scholar Michael McConnell has criticized Scalia's *Smith* opinion at length in "Free Exercise Revisionism and the *Smith* Decision," *57 U. Chicago L. Rev. 1109, 1124-1125* (1990).

[13] *Minersville School District v. Gobitis*, 310 U.S. 586, 594 (1940).

Sanford Levinson, Timothy L. Hall, H.N. Hirsch, Ralph Rossum, Christopher Smith, David A. Schulz, James Brian Staab, Richard Brisbin, Joseph Lash, and Melvin I. Urofsky.[14]

These issues are important because debates about interpretation of the religion clauses, appropriate use of history in religion clause opinions, and the constitutionality of American public religion and ceremonial deism continue to agitate commentators, and because the approaches adopted by Frankfurter and Scalia exemplify at least two of the basic approaches to the religion clauses that have been labeled "secularist" and "assimilationist."[15] The scholarship of Derek Davis, Donald L. Drakeman, John Witte, Jr., Michael McConnell, Thomas J. Curry, Leonard L. Levy, John M. Murrin, Steven K. Green, Steven Smith, and Edwin Gaustad, who have studied and debated originalist methodology and the historical roots and context of the First Amendment, serves as a source of reference with which to evaluate the present relevance of Frankfurter and Scalia's distinct religion clause

---

[14] Please see the Bibliography and review of these scholars herein for detailed information for these sources, which will form part of the scholarly base for the author's argument.

[15] Barry Adamson, *Freedom of Religion, the First Amendment and the Supreme Court: How the Court Flunked History* (Gretna, LA: Pelican Publishing Co., 2008); Frank S. Ravitch, *Masters of Illusion: The Supreme Court and the Religion Clauses* (New York: New York university Press, 2007). Professor Sullivan identifies four basic approaches in an article on Scalia: separationism (strong Free Exercise Clause and strong Establishment Clause), secularism (weak FE and strong EC), accomodationism (strong FE and weak EC), and assimilation (weak FE and weak EC). Kathleen M. Sullivan, "Justice Scalia and the Religion Clauses," *22 U. Haw. L. Rev. 449, 452* (2000). Also, Justices Scalia and Stephen Breyer recently continued their public debate about originalism and the "living" Constitution in the United States Senate. See Mike Sacks, "Justices Breyer and Scalia Take Their Constitutional Show to the Senate," October 5, 2011; available from http://www.huffingtonpost.com/2011/10/05/supreme-court-stephen-breyer-antonin-scalia-senate-hearing_n_997156.html; Internet; accessed 18 October 2011.

methodologies as well as their different treatments of American public religion.[16]

IS AMERICAN PUBLIC RELIGION STILL RELEVANT?

Challenges the author has faced in researching American public religion in the opinions of Frankfurter and Scalia included, first, the potential problem that scholarly study of American civil religion had diminished in the late 1990s as compared to the volume of scholarship following Robert Bellah's initial article on the subject in the 1960s.[17] Moreover, commentator Charles Lippy has argued that the idea of American civil religion may not have continuing viability or relevance.[18] Lippy's argument seems to indicate that previous attempts

---

[16] Historians tend to see the question as to the original intent or meaning of the religion clauses as being much more complex than judges do. Edwin Gaustad finds seven different views on the religion question as prevalent during the founding era in *Faith and of the Founders: Religion and the New Nation 1776-1826*, 2d ed. (Waco, TX: Baylor university Press, 2004), 3-10. Emeritus Professor of history at Princeton University John Murrin comes to a similar conclusion in his "Fundamental Values, the Founding Fathers, and the Constitution," in *To Form a More Perfect Union: The Critical Ideas of the Constitution*, eds. Herman Belz, Ronald Hoffman, and Peter J. Albert (Charlottesville, VA: The University Press of Virginia, 1992), 1-37. See also historian Alfred H. Kelly's article on the Supreme Court's alleged abuses of history in "Clio and the Court: An Illicit Love Affair." *1965 Sup. Ct. Rev. 119* (1965).

[17] Robert Bellah, "Civil Religion in America," *Daedalus: Journal of the American Academy of Arts and Sciences* (Winter 1967): 1-21. Yet, the scholarship of sociologist Robert Wuthnow offers some fairly recent examples of engagement with issues related to American public religion and civil religion, especially his *The Restructuring of American Religion: Society and Faith Since World War II* (Princeton, NJ: Princeton University Press, 1988), 241-267. See also, Steven B. Epstein, "Rethinking the Constitutionality of Ceremonial Deism," *96 Columbia L. Rev. 2083, 2083-2174* (1996).

[18] Charles H. Lippy, "American Civil religion: Myth, Reality, and Challenges," in *Faith in America: Changes, Challenges, New Directions, vol. 2, Religious*

to define American public religion and how it may or may not shape religious life in America were limited to previous historical contexts. Yet, a recent law review article by Steven B. Epstein has presented an extensive treatment of ceremonial deism,[19] and noted that ceremonial deism is closely related to American public religion and American civil religion.[20] Also, John F. Wilson's argument that American public religion is ad hoc and episodic supports the notion that American public religion can wax and wane in American public life.[21] Recent legal controversy surrounding the language "under God" in the Pledge of Allegiance to the American flag also evidences a recent example of a constitutional dispute over American public religion. In the case of *Elk Grove United School District v. Newdow,* 542 U.S. 1 (2004) an extensive list of public interest groups filed *amicus curiae,* or friend of the Court, briefs with the Supreme Court both in support and opposition to the religious reference in the pledge. They included: the Christian Legal Society, the Rutherford Institute, the American Legion, the Eagle Forum, American Atheists, the American Civil Liberties Union, the American Humanist Association, the American Jewish Congress, Americans United for Separation of Church and State,

---

Issues Today, ed. Charles H. Lippy (Westport, CT: Praeger Publishers, 2006), 19-36.

[19] Epstein defined ceremonial deism as follows: "all practices including: 1) actual, symbolic, or ritualistic; 2) prayer, invocation, benediction, supplication, appeal, reverent reference to, or embrace of, a general or particular deity; 3) created, delivered, sponsored, or encouraged by government officials; 4) during governmental functions or ceremonies, in the form of patriotic expressions, or associated with holiday observances; 5) which, in and of themselves, are unlikely to indoctrinate or proselytize their audience; 6) which are not specifically designed to accommodate the free religious exercise of a particular group of citizens; and 7) which, as of this date, are deeply rooted in the nation's history and traditions." Epstein, *Rethinking the Constitutionality,* 2095.

[20] Ibid., 2091-2098. Epstein does not distinguish between American public religion and American civil religion. Ibid., 2096-2098.

[21] John F. Wilson, *Public Religion in America* (Philadelphia, PA: Temple University Press, 1979), 143-175.

Associated Pantheist Groups, the Atheist Law Center, Focus on the Family, and the Council for Secular Humanism as well as others.[22]

Another anticipated difficulty with analyzing American public religion in the religion clause opinions of Frankfurter and Scalia was that Scalia's jurisprudence is not philosophically predictable or mechanical, lending credence to his argument that his originalist methodology is not a vehicle for instituting conservative political values.[23] He has a definite originalist interpretive methodology of textualism, which he defends in his book *A Matter of Interpretation*, and he has authored opinions that support the claim that he is a "fairly principled jurist," as one scholar has put it.[24] Some exceptions to philosophical predictability in his jurisprudence include the following cases: *Board of Education of Kiryas Joel v. Grumet*, 512 U.S. 687 (1994)(dissenting from Justice Souter's Establishment Clause opinion striking down establishment of an orthodox Jewish school district in New York), *Church of Lukumi Babalu Aye v. City of Hialeah*, 508 U.S. 520 (1993)(concurring in part in Justice Kennedy's majority opinion in a free exercise case which one can construe as an exception to Scalia's *Employment Division v. Smith* opinion), *Texas v. Johnson*, 491 U.S. 397 (1989)(finding flag burning a protected free speech right), and *Crawford v. Washington*, 541 U.S. 36 (2004)(holding that the Sixth Amendment Confrontation Clause guarantees a criminal defendant's right to confront adverse witnesses face to face.) All of these cases present contradictory evidence from Scalia's tenure on the Court,

---

[22] See *Landmark Briefs and Arguments of the Supreme Court of the United States: Constitutional Law*, 2003 Term Supplement, vols. 335-336, eds. Gerhard Casper and Kathleen M. Sullivan- *Elk Grove United School District v. Newdow* (2004) (Bethesda, MD: LexisNexus Academic & Library Solutions, 2004).

[23] Antonin Scalia, "Foreword," in Steven G. Calabresi, ed., *Originalism: A Quarter Century of Debate* (Washington, DC: Regenery Publishers, 2007), 44.

[24] Antonin Scalia, *A Matter of Interpretation: Federal Courts and the Law* (Princeton, NJ: Princeton University Press, 1997); James B. Staab, *The Political Thought of Justice Antonin Scalia: A Hamiltonian on the Court* (Lanham, MA: Rowman & Littlefield Publishers, Inc., 2006), 293.

which warrant against facile conclusions as to how his methodology may work out with regard to interpretation of the religion clauses, and his conclusions on the constitutionality of different forms of American public religion or ceremonial deism. Therefore, careful scrutiny of his religion clause jurisprudence has to wrestle with the unpredictable aspects of his jurisprudence and consider whether or not his approach in fact presupposes a given view of the religion clauses or simply seeks to determine the intended meaning of the text of the religion clauses, and then apply it in a concrete case.

ANALYSIS OF SCHOLARSHIP RELEVANT TO AMERICAN PUBLIC RELIGION AND THE OPINIONS OF FRANKFURTER AND SCALIA

The work of several scholars has been important in the author's engagement with the issues related to Frankfurter and Scalia's treatment of American public religion in their religion clause opinions. Several sources by constitutional law Professor Sanford Levinson began to form the rudimentary ideas I have developed and attracted me to the potential relationship between the religion clause jurisprudences of Frankfurter and Scalia and American public religion. These include his book *Constitutional Faith* published by Princeton University Press in 1988 and several critical articles, which include observations about American public religion and the jurisprudence of Frankfurter and Scalia. The articles are: "The Democratic Faith of Felix Frankfurter," published in the Stanford University Law review in 1973, and "The Confrontation of Religious Faith and Civil Religion: Catholics Becoming Justices," published in the DePaul Law Review's 1990 edition. Professor Levinson has also written at least one piece concerning judicial supremacy, which relates to issues concerning the Court's power to influence American religion, and attendant debates about interpretation of the religion clauses. [25] In addition to the scholarship of Levinson, Robert Bellah's work on American civil religion, John F. Wilson's book on American public religion, and

---

[25] Sanford Levinson, "Our Populist Supreme Court: Is Reformation Thinkable (or possible)?" in *Law and the Sacred*, eds. Austin Sarat, Lawrence Douglas, and Martha Merrill Umphrey (Stanford, CA: Stanford University Press, 2007), 109-134.

Steven Epstein's law review article on ceremonial deism have served as background sources for my thinking about American public religion and ceremonial deism in regard to the religion clause jurisprudences of Frankfurter and Scalia.[26] Chapter Two will review the scholarship of Bellah, Wilson, and Epstein more completely, but it is relatively difficult to find an abundance of recent scholarship on American civil religion as compared to the response in the 1970s to Robert Bellah's initial article on the subject published in 1967. There is evidence, nonetheless, that critical thought on American civil religion has not been eclipsed as shown by John E. Semonche's *Keeping the Faith: A Cultural History of the U.S. Supreme Court*, and articles such as Michael M. Maddigan's "The Establishment Clause, Civil Religion, and the Public Church," Yehudah Mirsky's "Civil Religion and the Establishment Clause," and Richard V. Pierard's chapter in the *Oxford Handbook of Church and State in the United States* entitled, "The Role of Civil Religion in American Society."[27] Moreover, Charles H. Lippy has a chapter about American civil religion in a recent book about the current state of religion in American life, which raises questions as to the continuing viability, and relevance of American civil religion.[28]

---

[26] Robert Bellah, "Civil Religion in America," *Daedalus: Journal of the American Academy of Arts and Sciences* (Winter 1967): 1-21; Steven B. Epstein, "Rethinking the Constitutionality of Ceremonial Deism," *96 Columbia L. Rev. 2083* (1996); John F. Wilson, *Public Religion in American Culture* (Philadelphia, PA: Temple University Press, 1979).

[27] John E. Semonche, *Keeping the faith: A Cultural History of the U.S. Supreme Court* (Lanham, MD: Rowman & Littlefield, 1998); Michael M. Maddigan, "'The Establishment Clause, Civil Religion, and the Public Church," *81 Cal L. Rev. 293* (1993); Yehudah Mirsky, "Civil Religion and the Establishment Clause," *95 Yale L. J. 1237* (1986); and Richard V. Pierard, "The Role of Civil Religion in American Society," in *The Oxford Handbook of Church and State in the United States*, ed. Derek H. Davis (New York: Oxford University Press, 2010), 479-496.

[28] Charles H. Lippy, "American Civil Religion: Myth, Reality, and Challenges," in *faith in America: Changes, Challenges, New Directions, vol. 2, Religious Issues Today*, ed. Charles H. Lippy (Westport, CT: Praeger Publishers, 2006), 19-36.

Of importance to the argument developed herein are also the Supreme Court opinions of Frankfurter and Scalia, especially with reference to the Free Exercise Clause and the Establishment Clause, ass well as primary sources they have produced. Scalia's book *A Matter of Interpretation: Federal Courts and the Law* published in 1997 contains an explanation of his interpretive methodology along with responses, including those by historian Gordon S. Wood and legal scholar and theorist Ronald Dworkin.[29] Also, Scalia has recently defended originalist methodology in the United State's Senate in a public discussion with his peer on the Court, Justice Stephen Breyer, as well as in print.[30] Moreover, there are a growing number of law review articles about both Frankfurter and Scalia, which the author has engaged in seeking to explore the argument articulated herein about American public religion in the opinion clause opinions of Frankfurter and Scalia.[31]

---

[29] Antonin Scalia, *A Matter of Interpretation: federal Courts and the Law* (Princeton, NJ: Princeton University Press, 1997).

[30] Mike Sacks, "Justices Breyer and Scalia Take Their Constitutional Show to the Senate," available from http://www.huffingtonpost.com/2011/10/05 /supreme-court-stephen-breyer-antonin-scalia-senate- hearing_n_997156.html; Internet; accessed 18 October 2011; and Antonin Scalia, "Foreword," in Stephen G. Calabresi, ed., *Originalism: A Quarter Century of Debate* (Washington, DC: Regenery Publishers, 2007).

[31] Donald L. Beschle, "Catechism or Imagination: Is Justice Scalia's Style Typically Catholic?" *37 Villanova L. Rev. 1329* (1992); Richard A. Brisbin, "The Conservatism of Antonin Scalia," *105 Political Science Quarterly* (1990):2-22; Erwin Chemerinsky, "The Jurisprudence of Justice Scalia: A Critical Appraisal," *22 Haw. L. Rev. 385* (2000); Thomas B. Colby, "A Constitutional Hierarchy of Religions? Justice Scalia, the Ten Commandments, and the Future of the Establishment Clause," *100 Nw. U. L. Rev. 1097* (2006); Richard Danzig, "How Questions Begot Answers in Felix Frankfurter's First Flag Salute Opinion," *1977 The Supreme Court Rev. 257* (1977); Peter B. Edelman, "Justice Scalia's Jurisprudence and the Good Society: Shades of Felix Frankfurter and the Harvard Hit Parade of the 1950s," *12 Cardozo L. Rev. 1799* (1991); Sanford Levinson, "The Democratic Faith of Felix Frankfurter," *25 Stanford L. Rev. 430* (1973).

With regard to Frankfurter, the argument developed herein has also been influenced by various extrajudicial writings, interviews, and other primary sources which were published before he died in 1965. The most important of these sources are *Of Law and Men: Papers and Addresses of Felix Frankfurter, 1939-1956*, edited by Philip Elman, and several compilations edited by Philip B. Kurland including, *Felix Frankfurter on the Supreme Court: Extrajudicial Essays on the Court and the Constitution, Mr. Justice Frankfurter and the Constitution*, and *Of Law and Life & Other Things That Matter: Papers and Addresses of Felix Frankfurter, 1956-1963*.[32] Also, Joseph p. Lash edited a series of excerpts from Frankfurter's diaries, which was published in 1975, but there are warnings in the secondary literature on Frankfurter that he wrote these diaries with a view to their eventual publication so that their probative value is perhaps questionable. The books most relevant to analysis of Frankfurter's methodology for interpreting the Bill of Rights are Helen Shirley Thomas's *Felix Frankfurter: Scholar on the Bench* published by Johns Hopkins Press in 1960, H.N. Hirsch's *The Enigma of Felix Frankfurter*, Melvin I. Urofsky's *Judicial Restraint and Individual Liberties*, and Richard B. Stevens' *Frankfurter and Due Process*.[33]

Three recent books about Scalia have formed the nucleus of the author's engagement with his jurisprudence, interpretive methodology, and expressed views about American public religion and ceremonial deism in religion clause cases. *The Jurisprudential Vision of Justice Antonin Scalia* by David A. Schultz and Christopher E. Smith is a

---

[32] Philip Elman, ed., *Of Law and Men: Papers and Addresses of Felix Frankfurter, 1939-1956* (New York: Harcourt, Brace and Company, 1956); Philip B. Kurland, ed., *Felix Frankfurter on the Supreme Court: Extrajudicial Essays on the Court and the Constitution* (Cambridge, MA: Harvard University Press, Belknap Press, 1970); and Philip B. Kurland, *Mr. Justice Frankfurter and the Constitution* (Chicago: The University of Chicago Press, 1971).

[33] H.N. Hirsch, *The Enigma of Felix Frankfurter* (New York: Basic Books, Inc., 1981); Richard B. Stevens, *Frankfurter and Due Process* (Lanham, MD: University Press of America, Inc., 1987); Helen Shirley Thomas, *Felix Frankfurter: Scholar on the Bench* (Baltimore, MD: The Johns Hopkins Press, 1960).

critical and mainly negative evaluation of Scalia's jurisprudence, and contains an early examination of Scalia's religion clause perspectives.[34] Similarly, political scientist Richard Brisbin has critiqued Scalia for having a jurisprudence which is majoritarian because Scalia defers to legislatures that are more responsive to majority will than how legislation may affect the rights of political minorities. Brisbin has also argued that Scalia merely feigns objectivity and a principled methodology.[35]

The books about Scalia by James B. Staab and Ralph A. Rossum represent a more moderate approach to his jurisprudence. Staab argues that Scalia has a peculiar variant of conservative political philosophy influenced by Alexander Hamilton and the Federalism of the early Republic, but with some Madisonian tendencies in the area of federalism. Staab is critical of Scalia for violating his own methodology and for being disingenuous about his own objectivity, and his critique of Scalia is arguably more balanced than that of Schultz and Smith. Also, Staab's treatment contains a helpful overview of conservative political ideology, and makes an argument for placing Scalia the camp of a Hamiltonian conservative positivism which favors strong executive power, distrusts popular sovereignty, and includes biases in favor of expanding executive and congressional power but not the scope of individual rights.[36]

Ralph A. Rossum, on the other hand, evaluates Scalia's jurisprudence more positively. He defends Scalia's general methodological approach, which is a variant of originalism, but acknowledges that at times Scalia breaches his own interpretive

---

[34] Christopher E. Smith and David A. Schulz, *The Jurisprudential Vision of Justice Antonin Scalia* (Lanham, MD: Rowman & Littlefield Publishers, Inc., 1996).

[35] Richard A. Brisbin, Jr., *Justice Antonin Scalia and the Conservative Revival* (Baltimore, MD: Johns Hopkins Press, 1997); and Richard A. Brisbin, Jr., "The Conservatism of Antonin Scalia," *105 Political Science Quarterly* (1990): 2-22.

[36] James B. Staab, *The Political Thought of Justice Antonin Scalia: A Hamiltonian on the Supreme Court* (Lanham, MD: Rowman & Littlefield Publishers, Inc., 2006), xxx.

methodology though, in Rossum's opinion, without jeopardizing the value of originalist constitutional interpretation. Rossum's critical engagement with what he perceives to be Scalia's methodology, which looks to the text and tradition of a given portion of the Constitution for its meaning, is possibly the most valuable part of the book. The section of the book about Scalia's religion clause interpretation is helpful.[37] A similarly positive review of Scalia's Establishment Clause opinions is available in a recent Master's thesis by Gregory O. Nies entitled "Religious Liberty through the Lens of Textualism and a Living Constitution: The First Amendment Establishment Clause Interpretations of Justices William Brennan, Jr., and Antonin Scalia."[38]

The scholarly literature about the original meaning of the religion clauses is unsurprisingly voluminous and contentious, as is that related to the debate over interpretive methodology between originalism and the living Constitution approach. Good introductions to the historical and methodological debates are available in John Witte, Jr.'s *Religion and the American Constitutional Experiment, Freedom and the Court: Civil Rights and Liberties in the United States* by Henry Abraham and Barbara A. Perry; *A Nation Dedicated to Religious Liberty: The Constitutional Heritage od the Religion Clauses* by retired judge Arlin M. Adams and Charles Emmerich; and *Church and State in American History: Key Documents, Decisions, and Commentary from the Past Three Centuries* edited by John F. Wilson and Donald L. Drakeman.[39]

---

[37] Ralph A. Rossum, *Antonin Scalia's Jurisprudence: Text and Tradition* (Lawrence, KS: University of Kansas, 2006).

[38] Gregory O. Nies, *Religious Liberty Through the Lens of Textualism and a Living Constitution: The First Amendment Establishment Clause Interpretations of Justices William Brennan, Jr., and Antonin Scalia* (Waco, TX: Baylor University Press-Master's thesis, 2006).

[39] John Witte, Jr., *Religion and the American Constitutional Experiment*, 2d ed. (Boulder, CO: Westview Press, 2005); Henry J. Abraham and Barbara A. Perry, *Freedom and the Court: Civil Rights and Liberties in the United States*, 8th ed. (Lawrence, KS: University Press of Kansas, 2003); Arlin M. Adams and Charles Emmerich, *A Nation Dedicated to Religious Liberty: The Constitutional Heritage of the Religion Clauses* (Philadelphia, PA: University of Pennsylvania Press, 1990); and John F. Wilson and Donald L. Drakeman, eds. *Church and State in American History: Key Documents,*

Similarly, the debates over the Establishment Clause are enlightened and sharpened by the scholarship of Thomas J. Curry, Leonard L. Levy, and Philip A. Hamburger.[40] Judge Michael McConnell's article about the original meaning of the Free Exercise Clause provides depth and counter weight to scholarly concerns with the history behind the Establishment Clause while urging that the history of free exercise needs more attention.[41]

The author's understanding about the original meaning of the religion clauses has been shaped most by Donald L. Drakeman's treatment of the Establishment Clause in *Church-State Constitutional Issues: Making Sense of the Establishment Clause.*[42] In essence, Drakeman creates doubt about any bold and overly confident assertions as to the meaning of the religion clauses, and how they are to be applied by the Supreme Court today.[43] Rather, Drakeman stresses the

---

Decisions, and Commentary from the Past Three Centuries, 3d ed. (Boulder, CO: Westview Press, 2003). There are also two recent books about the meaning of the religion clauses relevant to the historical sources relied upon and analyzed by Frankfurter and Scalia—Donald L. Drakeman, *Church, State, and Original Intent* (New York: Cambridge University Press, 2010); and John Ragosta, *Religious Freedom: Jefferson's Legacy, America's Creed* (Charlottesville, VA: University of Virginia Press, 2013).

[40] Thomas J. Curry, *The First Freedoms: Church and State in America to the Passage of the First Amendment* (New York: Oxford University Press, 1986); Leonard J. Levy, *The Establishment Clause: Religion and the First Amendment* 2d ed. rev. (Chapel Hill, NC: University of North Carolina Press, 1994); and Philip A. Hamburger, *Separation of Church and State* (Cambridge, MA: Harvard University Press, 2002).

[41] Michael W. McConnell, "The Origins and Historical Understanding of the Free Exercise of Religion," *103 Harvard L. Rev. 1409* (1990).

[42] (New York: Greenwood Press, 1991).

[43] Donald L. Drakeman, "Religion and the Republic: James Madison and the First Amendment," *Journal of Church and State* 25 (Autumn 1983): 427-445. In this article Drakeman argues that theories about Madison's role in formation of the religion clauses are historically indecisive and unclear, though he concedes that Madison had a significant role. It is simply that the historical records are unreliable and indecisive in his view. Drakeman also

vague and ambiguous nature of the language of the religion clauses in the First Amendment, and of the historical context, which produced the First Amendment.   In his recent book *Church, State, and Original Intent* Drakeman alters his views on the meaning of the Establishment Clause to the extent that he submits the historical records warrant the conclusion the First Amendment was intended to prohibit the establishment of a "single national religion." Beyond this, however, he once again claims that the historical evidence is ambiguous as to the original intent of the Establishment Clause.[44] Supreme Court Justice Byron White further implies in one of his opinions that this leaves judges a lot of discretion as to how to interpret the clauses in any given concrete case.[45]

---

cites John F. Wilson's book on American public religion to posit the theory that Madison's inconsistencies with regard to the religion question commonly emphasized by "accommodationists" such as Gerald Bradley make sense as Madison's pragmatic concessions to the power of public religion in America at the time. In other words, Madison's inconsistent practices from a Church-State separation perspective are attributable to pragmatic political considerations for Drakeman. However, Drakeman has changed his view on the meaning of the Establishment Clause to a degree in his recent book on original intent, wherein he argues that the Establishment Clause was intended to prevent a "single" national religion, but that beyond this the historical records are ambiguous as to its meaning. Drakeman, *Church, State, and Original Intent*, 2010, ix.

[44] Drakeman, Ibid.

[45] *Committee for Public Education and Religious Liberty v. Nyquist*, 413 U.S. 756, 820 (1973) (WHITE, J., dissenting). J. Woodford Howard makes a similar point in his article, "The Robe and the Cloth: The Supreme Court and Religion in the United States," 7 *Journal of Law and Politics* 481 (1991). Other sources critiquing originalist methodology include: Michael Perry, "The Authority of Text, Tradition, and Reason: A Theory of Constitutional Interpretation," *58 S. Cal. L. Rev. 551* (1985); Larry Simon, "The Authority of the Framers of the Constitution: Can Originalist Interpretation Be Justified?" *73 Cal. L. Rev. 1482* (1985); and Paul Brest, "The Misconceived Quest for the Original Understanding," *60 Boston U. L. Rev. 204* (1980).

Historian John M. Murrin adds credence to these sentiments in his work on the founding era wherein he stresses the complexity and diversity of views present at the founding era with regard to the public role of religion in the early American republic. His treatment of these issues is published as "Fundamental Values, the Founding Fathers, and the Constitution," in *To Form a More Perfect Union* published by the University Press of Virginia, and in "Religion and Politics in America from the First Settlements to the Civil War," in *Religion and American Politics: From the Colonial Period to the Present*.[46] Additionally, Murrin submits that almost none of the key players in the formation of the religion clauses were evangelical Christians, but were more deistic in their convictions and adhered to a form of the Jefferson-Madison view on the religion question as to how church and state ought to relate to one another in the new nation. This scholarship has to account, however, for evidence regarding the influence of evangelical Christians in the founding era as submitted in the scholarship of John Witte, Jr., and Nicholas P. Miller. Moreover, if Witte is correct one has to account for the strong communitarian strains present at the time via the standing order in New England and the fading Anglican establishment in Virginia. Arguably, this only makes the task of negotiating the meaning of the religion clauses more difficult. In addition, this analysis leaves unanswered the question of how the First Amendment's religion clauses can apply to a context in 2014 that is radically more pluralistic than in the 1780s.[47]

---

[46] John M. Murrin, "Fundamental Values, the Founding Fathers, and the Constitution," in *To Form a More Perfect Union: The Critical Ideas of the Constitution*, eds. Herman Belz, Ronald Hoffman, and Peter J. Albert (Charlottesville, VA: The University Press of Virginia, 1992); and Murrin, "Religion and Politics in America from the First Settlements to the Civil War," in *Religion and American Politics: From the Colonial Period to the 1980s*, ed. Mark A. Noll (New York: Oxford University Press, 1990).

[47] John Witte, Jr., *Religion and the American Constitutional Experiment*, 2d ed. (Boulder, CO: Westview Press, 2005): 23-36; and Nicholas P. Miller, *The Religious Roots of the First Amendment: Dissenting Protestants and the Separation of Church and State* (New York: Oxford University Press, 2012).

APPROACH TO AMERICAN PUBLIC RELIGION AND THE RELIGION CLAUSE
INTERPRETATIONS OF FRANKFURTER AND SCALIA

This book will establish its thesis regarding the religion clause jurisprudences of Frankfurter and Scalia by first engaging scholarly literature on American public religion and ceremonial deism to demonstrate the ongoing validity of these concepts. This will include comparing the various treatments of American public religion and ceremonial deism by scholars Robert N. Bellah, Steven B. Epstein, and John F. Wilson.[48]

Next, the book will critically analyze the religion clause jurisprudences of Frankfurter and Scalia to show how they develop their respective methodologies for the clauses. This will involve a brief narrative engagement with their careers as judges, and with the United States Supreme Court's religion clause jurisprudence with special emphasis on the Court's jurisprudence after the clauses were applied to state and local governments beginning in 1940 with *Cantwell v. Connecticut*, 310 U.S. 296 (1940). This will frame the views of Frankfurter and Scalia against the backdrop of debates over the role of the Court, which emerged out of the controversies over substantive due process in the early twentieth century, and the New Deal Court's response.[49]

Then the book will analyze their respective opinions in Free Exercise Clause and Establishment Clause cases with particular

---

[48] Robert N. Bellah, "Civil Religion in America," *Daedalus: Journal of the American Academy of Arts and Sciences* (Winter 1967): 1-21; Bellah, *The Broken Covenant: American Civil Religion in Time of Trial* (Chicago, IL: University of Chicago Press, 1992); Steven B. Epstein, "Rethinking the Constitutionality of Ceremonial Deism," *96 Columbia L. Rev.* 2083 ((1996); and John F. Wilson, *Public Religion in American Culture* (Philadelphia, PA: Temple University Press, 1979).

[49] Many of the secondary sources on Frankfurter examine the reaction of the New Deal Court to the substantive due process jurisprudence of the late nineteenth and early twentieth centuries. Michael E. Parrish provides a narrative account in his biography of the early scholarly phase of Frankfurter's career in *Felix Frankfurter and His Times: The Reform Years* (New York: The Free Press, 1988), 252-272.

attention to their unique reliance on the history of the founding era. The author's approach at this point will also focus on the Supreme Court opinions of the two justices in religion clause cases in particular seeking explicit and implicit evidence of how the judges handle American public religion and ceremonial deism. Also, the author will consider other primary sources from the two justices that are relevant to their treatment of American public religion and ceremonial deism in official Supreme Court opinions and that can help further explain the originalist interpretive methodology of both judges, their common commitment to judicial restraint, and any general tendencies towards American public religion in their jurisprudence. Extrajudicial writings of the two judges as well as he commentary of close associates will also be considered in the analysis their treatments of American public religion and ceremonial deism within their official religion clause opinions. Critical scholarship directed to the religion clause jurisprudence of both judges will supplement the analysis, particularly law review articles.

The book applies a working definition of American public religion as a type of lowest common denominator form of public faith, which is intended to bind disparate groups together in a democracy. American public religion, as used herein, may include belief in a deity, but not necessarily. The scholarship of Steven B. Epstein, Robert N. Bellah, and John F. Wilson has helped to form this working definition, and it is assumed herein. Moreover, the definition of ceremonial deism adopted herein is from Epstein who has defined the term as follows:

> all practices involving: 1) actual, symbolic, or ritualistic; 2) prayer, invocation, benediction, supplication, appeal, reverent reference to, or embrace of, a general or particular deity; 3) created, delivered, sponsored, or encouraged by government officials; 4) during governmental functions or ceremonies, in the form of patriotic expressions, or associated with holiday observances; 5) which, in and of themselves, are unlikely to indoctrinate or proselytize their audience; 6) which are not specifically designed to accommodate the free exercise of a particular group of citizens; and 7) which, as of this date, are deeply rooted in the nation's history and traditions.[50]

---

[50] Epstein, *Rethinking the Constitutionality of Ceremonial Deism*, 2095.

Additionally, the author acknowledges at this point that I am analyzing the religion clause jurisprudence of these two judges from my own Protestant viewpoint or worldview which denies that America has any unique status in the eyes of God, but which also assumes that Christians should take part in the political sphere. Moreover, my working presuppositions include the belief that the United States is not and cannot be a Christian nation, and that it was not intended to be one historically, though I concede that this is a contested issue. My own general approach to this debate has been formed by the writings of Mark Noll, Nathan Hatch, George Marsden, Martin Marty, and John Courtney Murray, but my own view is not static in that the questions involved are extremely complex.[51]

The basic question the author is trying to answer in analysis of the religion clause jurisprudences of both judges is this: what is distinct about the way Frankfurter and Scalia treat American public religion in their religion clause jurisprudences? By seeking to answer this question with specific reference to their religion clause jurisprudences I hope to further the scholarly dialogue and debate about originalist methodology, American public religion and ceremonial deism, and the Supreme Court's role in determining the constitutionality of American public religion.

OUTLINE OF THE BOOK

The first chapter has stated the argument that Felix Frankfurter and Antonin Scalia find different forms of American public religion constitutional even though both judges apply originalist methodology to interpret the clauses, and the American public religion deemed

---

[51] Mark A. Noll, *One Nation Under God? Christian Faith and Political Action in America* (San Francisco, CA: Harper & Row, 1988); Mark A. Noll, Nathan O. Hatch, George M. Marsden, *The Search for Christian America* (Colorado Springs, CO: Helmers and Howard, 1989); Martin E. Marty, *Politics, Religion, and the Common Good: Advancing a Distinctly American Conversation about Religion's Role in Our Shared Life* (San Francisco, CA: Jossey-Bass Publishers, 2000); and John Courtney Murray, *We Hold These Truths : Catholic Reflections on the American Proposition* (Kansas City, KS: Sheed and Ward, 1988).

constitutional by Frankfurter is more secular than that in Scalia's opinions, which is more specifically theistic. This chapter has also partially reviewed the literature applicable to the book's argument about originalist methodology and American public religion in the opinions of Frankfurter and Scalia.

The second chapter will begin with a brief restatement of the book's argument. Then, chapter two will engage relevant scholarship on American public religion and ceremonial deism, beginning with its origins in the thought of Rousseau, and demonstrate how American public religion, civil religion, and ceremonial deism are both similar and distinct by definition. This chapter will also review relevant cases and literature regarding the Supreme Court's reliance on the American founders in religion clause cases following application of the religion clauses to state and local governments in the 1940s. By examining this scholarly literature the book will also seek to demonstrate that American public religion and ceremonial deism are concepts which one should consider in analyzing the religion clause jurisprudences of Frankfurter and Scalia.

The third chapter's focus is the Free Exercise jurisprudence of Felix frankfurter. This chapter will provide an introduction to Felix Frankfurter's life and thought, and document how Frankfurter relied on the American founders in his Free Exercise Clause opinions to find flag salute ceremonies comparable to religious practices constitutional. Chapter three will also analyze Frankfurter's religion clause methodology in the context of the Supreme Court's jurisprudence in free exercise cases since the application of the First Amendment religion clause to state and local governments in the *Cantwell* and *Everson* cases in the 1940s.[52]

Chapters four, five, and six will then provide further detailed analysis of the religion clause opinions of both justices. Chapter four will review the Establishment Clause jurisprudence of Frankfurter with emphasis on his reliance on American founders for authority, and in order to document Frankfurter's distinct treatment of the Establishment Clause and American public religion as compared to Scalia. Chapters five and six will then scrutinize the Free Exercise and Establishment

---

[52] *Cantwell v. Connecticut*, 310 U.S. 296 (1940), and *Everson v. Board of Education*, 330 U.S. 1 (1947).

Clause opinions of Scalia with specific attention to how Scalia has treated American public religion and ceremonial deism in these cases. Each of these chapters will incorporate discussion of the key Free Exercise and Establishment Clause cases Frankfurter and Scalia have participated in, especially those in which the judges played a key role.

Chapter seven will conclude the book by arguing that Frankfurter and Scalia have relied on American founders in their religion clause cases with distinct results, especially in Establishment Clause cases. In addition, the final chapter will submit that Frankfurter and Scalia have found different forms of American public religion constitutional even though both judges looked to the founders for guidance to interpret the religion clauses. This chapter will provide a brief review of the beliefs of the American founders regarding religious liberty that both Frankfurter and Scalia have referred to, albeit in different ways, as authority for their distinct findings about American public religion and ceremonial deism in religion clause cases. Finally, the book will end with a concise set of conclusions about the implications of the book's argument for originalist methodology, and its value as a way of discovering the meaning of the First Amendment's religion clauses.

CHAPTER 2
American Public Religion and Ceremonial Deism

The First Amendment religion clause jurisprudences of Felix Frankfurter and Antonin Scalia find distinct forms of American public religion constitutional. Felix Frankfurter's religion clause jurisprudence applied the Free Exercise Clause weakly, but the Establishment Clause strictly, as exemplified in the cases of *Minersville School District v. Gobitis*, 310 U.S. 586 (1940) and *McCollum v. Board of Education*, 333 U.S. 203 (1948). Scalia, on the other hand, has interpreted the religion clauses differently from Frankfurter by applying both the Free Exercise Clause and the Establishment Clause weakly in most cases, and this is evident in *Employment Division v. Smith*, 494 U.S. 872 (1990) and *McCreary County v. ACLU*, 545 U.S. 844 (2005).

The American public religion deemed constitutional in Frankfurter's religion clause opinions is more secular in nature in that it does not include belief in God. Rather, American public religion therein has elements similar to religious faith such as veneration of the American flag, and an appeal to the need for unifying beliefs in society.[1] Nonetheless, the mandatory flag salute Frankfurter's majority

---

[1] *Minersville School District v. Gobitis*, 310 U.S. 586, 591-600 (1940); and *West Virginia State Board of Education v. Barnette*, 319 U.S. 624, 646-672 (1943).

opinion held constitutional in *Gobitis* did not contain the words "under God," or require affirmation of belief in God.[2]

Scalia's religion clause jurisprudence, however, finds some forms of American public religion constitutional that do include belief in God such as public prayer at a middle school graduation ceremony, and display of the Ten Commandments.[3] This difference between the religion clause jurisprudences of Frankfurter and Scalia emerges in their different voting records with regard to the Establishment Clause, which Frankfurter has applied a strict form of judicial scrutiny to whereas Scalia has not found a violation of the clause.[4] For example, Frankfurter either authored an opinion that found an Establishment Clause violation or voted to find an infringement of the clause in nearly every case he participated in.[5] *McGowan v. Maryland*, 366 U.S. 420, 470-480 (1961) is the only disestablishment case in which Frankfurter did not find a violation of the clause, and this is because he reasoned that the Sunday closing law in question was secular in purpose.

Secondarily, the interpretive methodologies applied by both judges to the religion clauses rely in part upon references to America's founding history. Yet, the two judges do not appeal to the founding era in the same manner in free exercise cases even though their approach to the Free Exercise Clause is similar, nor do they emphasize the same founders in Establishment Clause opinions. Frankfurter emphasized the "historic" nature of the Supreme Court's task in religious liberty cases,[6] and cited Thomas Jefferson and James Madison primarily in his

---

[2] Steven B. Epstein, "Rethinking the Constitutionality of Ceremonial Deism," *96 Columbia L. Rev. 2083, 2118* (1996).

[3] *Lee v. Weisman*, 505 U.S. 577, 631-646 ((1992); and *McCreary County v. ACLU*, 545 U.S. 844, 886-898 (2005).

[4] Kathleen M. Sullivan, "Justice Scalia and the Religion Clauses," *22 U. Haw. L. Rev. 449, 449* (2000).

[5] *Everson v. Board of Education*, 330 U.S. 1 (1947); *McCollum v. Board of Education*, 333 U.S. 203 (1948); *Zorach v. Clauson*, 343 U.S. 307 (1952); *Kedroff v. Saint Nicholas Cathedral*, 344 U.S. 94 (1952); and *McGowan v. Maryland*, 366 U.S. 420 (1961).

[6] *Gobitis*, 310 U.S. at 594 where the justice stated: "In the judicial enforcement of religious freedom we are concerned with a historic concept . . . The

religion clause opinions in *Gobitis, Barnette, McCollum, Zorach,* and *McGowan.* To the contrary, Scalia has not emphasized historical tradition to the same extent in free exercise opinions, but he has referred to George Washington, John Adams, Thomas Jefferson, James Madison, and John Marshall as the basis for his opinions in Establishment Clause cases.[7] Additionally, Scalia explicitly stated in his dissenting opinion in *Lee* that judges should refer back to the founding era's history in order to properly interpret the Establishment Clause.[8]

Frankfurter relied primarily upon Jefferson and Madison in his religion clause opinions because he reasoned that they were the main influences on the clauses, and because the founding history was an important source of the meaning of the religion clauses for him.[9] Scalia, however, has written in *City of Boerne v. Flores,* 521 U.S. 507, 537-544 (1997) that the founders' views are compatible with his free exercise analysis, whereas in Establishment Clause cases he asserts that historical review of the founders' viewpoints is critical to effective interpretation of its language.[10]

The book will seek to establish its argument by examining the religion clause jurisprudences of Frankfurter and Scalia and other relevant sources related to their religion clause jurisprudences. However, before examining their religion clause jurisprudences in subsequent chapters, this chapter will review relevant literature

---

religious liberty which the Constitution protects has never excluded legislation of general scope not directed against doctrinal loyalties of particular sects. Judicial nullification of legislation cannot be justified by attributing to the framers of the Bill of Rights views for which there is no historic warrant."

[7] *Lee v. Weisman,* 505 U.S. 577, 631-646 (1992); and *McCreary County v. ACLU,* 545 U.S. 844, 886-889, 893-898 (2005).

[8] *Lee,* 505 U.S. at 631.

[9] *Gobitis,* 310 U.S. at 591-600; *McGowan,* 366 U.S. at 463-465; and *Everson v. Board of Education,* 330 U.S. 1, 28-63 (1947) (RUTLEDGE, J., dissenting). Frankfurter specifically joined the Rutledge dissent in *Everson.*

[10] *Lee,* 505 U.S. at 631.

regarding American public religion and ceremonial deism, as well as relevant literature and Supreme Court cases regarding the Supreme Court's interpretation of the religious clauses with specific attention to how the Court has appealed to America's founding era since the incorporation of the Free Exercise and Establishment Clauses in the 1940s.

RELEVANT SCHOLARSHIP REGARDING AMERICAN PUBLIC RELIGION AND CEREMONIAL DEISM

John F. Wilson authored *Public Religion in American Culture* in the 1970s.[11] This book examined the peculiar nature of public religion in the American context until that time, and concluded that scholarship emerging at the time about American civil religion was an effort to "revitalize" American culture. [12] He argued that Robert Bellah's writings on American public religion, beginning with Bellah's article in the journal *Daedalus*, represented an attempt to revive American culture in the face of significant change.[13] More specifically, Wilson argued that the idea of an American civil religion as articulated by Bellah was an effort to "cope" with "threats" to the then declining, but still dominant, Protestant cast of American public religion.[14] In other words, Wilson deemed the scholarship on American civil religion as a sign of insecurity about the prevailing status of public religion in America in the 1960s and 1970s.

Wilson did not specifically define American public religion in his book, however, but he did refer tot the thought of the American founder Benjamin Franklin for the idea that American society needed the public "influence of religion."[15] More specifically, Wilson cited Franklin's

---

[11] John F. Wilson, *Public Religion in American Culture* (Philadelphia, PA: Temple University Press, 1979).

[12] Ibid., 170-171.

[13] Ibid., refer to Robert N. Bellah, "Civil Religion in America," *Daedalus* 96 (Winter 1967): 1-21.

[14] Ibid., 171.

[15] Ibid., 7.

assertion about the importance of *"Publick Religion"* with reference to teaching history in a document related to an effort to establish a school in Philadelphia in 1749. Therein Franklin submitted that the positive merits of public education included development character in citizens, the exposure of "the Mischiefs of Superstition, &c. and the Excellency of the CHRISTIAN RELIGION above all others ancient or modern."[16] Wilson then traced the rising influence of Protestant public religion in America to what he perceived as its decline into religious pluralism in the 1960s.[17]

Robert Bellah's famously influential article on American civil religion was published in 1967. In it Bellah developed his proposal that "there actually exists alongside of and rather clearly differentiated from the churches an elaborate and well-institutionalized civil religion in America."[18] In order to establish this thesis Bellahv looked to the historical sources and events such as President John F. Kennedy's inaugural speech in 1961, the writings and speeches of certain American founders such as Benjamin Franklin and George Washington, and the American Civil War.[19]

Bellah submitted that the Civil War "was the second great event that involved the national self-understanding so deeply as to require expression in the civil religion."[20] Until the Civil War, he argued, the American founding and its leaders framed the American civil religion, but the events of the Civil War in the 1860s threatened the survival of this civil religion thereby creating substantial cultural anxiety with reference to national meaning. Bellah drew specific attention at this point to the legacy of President Abraham Lincoln, and the Memorial Day holiday that emerged from the Civil War.[21]

Then, in the concluding pages of Bellah's article, he argued that the American civil religion was "still very much alive," and grounded

---

[16] Ibid., emphasis in original.

[17] Ibid., 17-18.

[18] Bellah, *Civil Religion in America*, 1.

[19] Ibid., 1, 5-6, 9f.

[20] Ibid., 9.

[21] Ibid., 11.

this assertion in the responses to the assassination of President Kennedy in 1963, as well as themes he found in the New Frontier and Great Society political efforts of President John F. Kennedy and Lyndon Johnson. [22] For Bellah, the American civil religion provided a transcendent point of reference for the American people, and he defended it against critics who saw in it a corrupting influence on American church life."[23]

Bellah's proposal received a significant amount of critical evaluation after its publication in addition to John F. Wilson's book on American public religion. In a recent chapter regarding civil religion in America Richard V. Pierard lists some of the early critical responses to Bellah's civil religion thesis in his bibliography, including the chapters in *American Civil Religion* edited by Russell E. Richey and Donald G. Jones, and *Civil Religion and the Presidency* by Pierard and Robert D. Linder. [24] Moreover, Pierard's chapter in *The Oxford handbook of Church and State in the United States* documents at least five different ways that commentators have defined American civil religion since Bellah's initial article was published, and Pierard seems to concede that American civil religion is a "vague and elusive" concept with little scholarly consensus regarding it.[25] Pierard also provides a brief history

---

[22] Ibid., 12-13.

[23] Ibid., 12.

[24] Richard V. Pierard, "The Role of Civil Religion in American Society," in Derek H. Davis, ed. *The Oxford Handbook of Church and State in the United States* (New York: Oxford University Press, 2010), 493-496 citing Russell E. Richey and Donald G. Jones, eds. *American Civil Religion* (New York: Harper & Row, 1974); and Richard V. Pierard and Robert D. Linder, *Civil Religion and the Presidency* (Grand Rapids, MI: Zondervan, 1988).

[25] Pierard, *The Role of Civil Religion in American Society*, 480-482. Pierard's chapter defines civil religion as "essentially an alliance between politics and religion at the national level," and states that it "rests on a politicized ideological base consisting of four principles (1) there is a God; (2) the deity's will can be known and fulfilled through democratic procedures; (3) America has been his primary agent in modern history; and (4) the nation is the chief source of identity for Americans in both a political and religious sense." Ibid., 483.

of the term "civil religion" that was coined by Jean-Jacques Rousseau in *The Social Contract* in 1772.[26]

Several law review articles have also considered the topic of American civil religion and public religion, but with different conclusions about its relevance, constitutionality, and importance in American life. Yehudah Mirsky and Michael M. Maddigan have authored articles more positive about the value of public religion for American culture and society even though Mirsky does raise concerns about its constitutionality when the religious elements of civil religion are too prominent. Mirsky wrote that civil religion could pose an Establishment Clause problem if too much substantive religious content formed the basis of the civil religion.[27] Yet, Mirsky also concluded that courts should not find civil religion unconstitutional in many cases where it is distinguishable from "traditional, sacral religion."[28]

Maddigan, in contrast, develops an argument that American society has three primary aspects, namely, the state, the market, and civil society.[29] Then, he combines a critique of the Supreme Court's Establishment Clause jurisprudence for its ambiguity, with a proposal that there is a remedy available in the field of the "sociology of religion."[30] Maddigan asserts that the founders' belief that religion

---

[26] Ibid., 484. Pierard summarizes Rousseau's attempt to "harmonize j=individual freedom with membership in a social group ruled by law through a generic civic faith." Ibid. According to Rousseau the sovereign needed to shape this civil religion, and its elements should consist of "existence of a mighty, intelligent, and beneficent Divinity, possessed of foresight and providence; the life to come, the happiness of the just, the punishment of the wicked; the sanctity of the social contract and these laws: these are its positive dogmas." Ibid., 484-485, quoting Jean-Jacques Rousseau, *The Social Contract and Discourses*, ed. G.D.H. Cole (New York: Dutton, 1959), 139.

[27] Yehudah Mirsky, "Civil Religion and the Establishment Clause," *95 Yale L. Journal 1237, 1239-1241* (1986).

[28] Ibid., 1256-1257.

[29] Michael M. Maddigan, "The Establishment Clause, Civil Religion, and the Public Church," *81 California L. Rev. 293, 297* (1993).

[30] Ibid.

plays an important public role in society is still valid presently, and further that an understanding of this point can enable the Court to handle Establishment Clause cases more persuasively.[31]   Yet, he concedes that the Court has not reached consensus on the appropriate methodology for interpreting the religion clauses in his argument that the Court needs to at least consider his sociological model as a potential remedy for the confusion he finds in Establishment Clause cases.[32]

Steven B. Epstein also authored a law review article that was published in 1996 by Columbia University's law school on the constitutionality of a concept similar to American civil religion, ceremonial deism. In this law review article Epstein not only evaluates the constitutionality of ceremonial deism, however, but also provides the definition of ceremonial deism used herein, and compares ceremonial deism to American civil religion which Epstein does not differentiate between.[33]   In other words, Epstein does not discern a substantive difference between American civil religion and American public religion as he uses the terms in his article, but he does provide a distinctive definition of ceremonial deism that includes belief in a deity.

The Epstein law review article also makes a distinction between different types of American public religion by making specific reference to the scholarship of Robert N. Bellah and Sanford Levinson. In this regard, Epstein submits that the American public religion Bellah has written about is theistic or deistic in nature and thus closer to more traditional concepts of "true sacral religion, though in a watered-down sense," whereas Levinson's scholarship presents a form of American public religion that is characteristically secular in nature meaning that it "involves religion metaphorically, not actually."[34]   This distinction

---

[31] Ibid., 303-309.

[32] Ibid., 308-309.

[33] Steven B. Epstein, "Rethinking the Constitutionality of Ceremonial Deism," *96 Columbia L. Rev. 2083, 2091-2098* (1996).

[34] Ibid., 2096-2097 wherein Epstein distinguishes between the "radically different" civil religions of Bellah and Levinson as elaborated in Robert N. Bellah, *Beyond Belief: Essays on Religion in a Post-Traditional World* (New York: Harper & Row, 1970), 171-176; and Sanford Levinson in

between a theistic as opposed to a more secular and metaphorical form of public religion in the scholarship of Bellah and Levinson is helpful when comparing the religion clause jurisprudences of Frankfurter and Scalia because the kinds of public religion that they find constitutional are similarly distinct.

THE SUPREME COURT'S APPEALS TO AMERICA'S FOUNDING ERA IN RELIGION CLAUSE CASES

In his majority opinion in the *Minersville School District v. Gobitis* free exercise case Frankfurter appealed in part to the history of the founding era in America to make his argument that Jehovah's Witness children were not exempt from a mandatory flag salute.[35] He wrote that the interpretation of the First Amendment's guarantees of religious freedom "are concerned with a historic concept," and he cited Thomas Jefferson, James Madison, and Roger Williams in support of this notion.[36] Then, in his dissenting opinion in the *Barnette* case a few years later that overruled *Gobitis*, Frankfurter made a similar appeal, and relied upon Jefferson, Madison, John Adams, and Benjamin Franklin from the founding era.[37]

Subsequently, after both the Free Exercise and Establishment Clauses had been "incorporated" or applied to state and local

---

Constitutional Faith (Princeton, NJ: Princeton University Press, 1988), 10-12.

[35] *Minersville School District v. Gobitis,* 310 U.S. 586, 594-595 (1940).

[36] Ibid.

[37] *West Virginia State Board of Education v. Barnette,* 319 U.S. 624, 653 (1943). See Donald L. Drakeman's critique of the "law-office" history he finds in the Court's early interpretations of the Establishment Clause, especially with regard to the founders from Virginia—Jefferson and Madison—in *Church, State, and Original Intent* (New York: Cambridge University Press, 2010), 74-148. Drakeman is particularly critical of Justice Wiley B. Rutledge's historical approach to the Establishment Clause that Frankfurter and other members of the Court relied upon in the 1940s. He asserts that anti-Catholic sentiment and fear may lie behind Rutledge's "law-office" history. Ibid.

governments in the *Cantwell* and *Everson* cases,[38] the Court began to appeal to history from the founding era in order to interpret the religion clauses, especially in Establishment Clause cases.[39] This is particularly evident in the dissenting opinion of Wiley B. Rutledge in *Everson* wherein Rutledge looks to the struggle over disestablishment of the Church of England in Virginia in order to interpret the Establishment Clause.[40] Frankfurter joined Rutledge's opinion in the *Everson* case, and the author of the majority opinion Hugo Black agreed with Rutledge's historical account as well, even though Black came to different conclusions as to the facts and therefore did not find a violation of the Establishment Clause in the case.[41]

Subsequently, the Court has sometimes relied on the history of the founding era to interpret the religion clauses, especially the Establishment Clause, but the Court has not reached a consensus about the meaning of the religion clauses.[42] In addition, some members of the Court have challenged the viewpoint articulated in *Everson* by Rutledge that relied so heavily upon the thought of Jefferson and Madison. For example, former Chief Justice William Rehnquist also looked to history to interpret the Establishment Clause in his dissenting opinion in a school prayer case *Wallace v. Jaffree*, 472 U.S. 38 (1985), but Rehnquist concluded that the first Amendment allowed nonpreferential support for religion by the government. Similarly, another Chief Justice, Warren Burger, looked to the history of the First

---

[38] *Cantwell v. Connecticut*, 310 U.S. 296 (1940); *Everson v. Board of Education*, 330 U.S. 1 (1947).

[39] Michael W. McConnell, "The Origins and Historical Understanding of the Free Exercise of Religion," *103 Harvard L. Rev. 1409* (1990).

[40] *Everson*, 330 U.S. at 34-38. In this lengthy dissenting opinion in *Everson* Rutledge relies on the views of Thomas Jefferson and James Madison with reference to religious liberty, and he made Madison's *Memorial and Remonstrance* an appendix to his opinion. Ibid., 28-74.

[41] Ibid., 11-12 (BLACK, J., majority opinion). The Court "incorporated" the Establishment Clause in *Everson*, 330 U.S. at 14-15.

[42] Steven K. Green, ""Bad History": The Lure of History in Establishment Clause Adjudication," *81 Notre Dame L. Rev. 1717* (2005-2006).

Amendment to interpret it in a case involving an Establishment Clause challenge to legislative prayers, the case of *Marsh v. Chambers*, but Burger also interpreted and applied the historical evidence differently from Rutledge.[43] Lastly, as the book will demonstrate below in chapters four and five, Antonin Scalia has also looked to the history of the founding era in order to interpret both religion clauses, especially in Establishment Clause cases, though he has found different forms of American public religion constitutional as compared to Frankfurter.[44]

Some commentators have criticized the Court for how it handles history in cases both generally and in religion clause cases. An article by Alfred H. Kelly in *The Supreme Court Review* criticizes the Court for mishandling history, and asserts at one point that the Court has used a technique he labels "law-office" history in some cases.[45] In a similar manner, Steven K. Green has analyzed the use of history by the Court in Establishment Clause cases. Green argues that "since 1947 lawyers and judges have used history with abandon to justify their arguments and decisions about the proper relationship between church and state." [46] Also, he provides a footnote that lists examples in Establishment Clause opinions that includes the opinions of William Rehnquist in *Wallace v. Jaffree*, Warren Burger in *Marsh v. Chambers*, Felix Frankfurter in *McCollum v. Board of Education*, and Stanley Reed in *McCollum v. Board of Education*.[47]

---

[43] *Marsh v. Chambers*, 463 U.S. 783, 790 (1983).

[44] *Lee v. Weisman*, 505 U.S. 577, 631 f (1992); and *McCreary County v. ACLU*, 545 U.S. 844, 886-888 (2005).

[45] Alfred H. Kelly, "Clio and the Court: An Illicit Love Affair," *1965 The Supreme Court Review 119, 122* (1965). Kelly defines the law-office technique as "the selection of data favorable to the position being advanced without regard to or concern for contradictory data or proper evaluation of the relevance of the data proffered." Ibid., 122 n. 13.

[46] Steven K. Green, ""Bad History": The Lure of History in Establishment Clause Adjudication," *81 Notre Dame L. Rev. 1717, 1717-1718* (2005-2006).

[47] Ibid., 1718 n. 5.

THE RELEVANCE OF FRANKFURTER AND SCALIA'S APPROACHES TO AMERICAN PUBLIC RELIGION

The author chose to study these two judges because the deferential approach to the Free Exercise Clause employed by Frankfurter in *Gobitis* and *Barnette* is similar to the one applied in the jurisprudence of Scalia with his majority opinion in *Employment Division, Department of Human Services v. Smith*, 494 U.S. 872 (1990). In addition, Frankfurter's contribution to strict separationism with respect to the Establishment Clause that appeals to the history of the founding era as authority for its conclusions continues to appear in Supreme Court opinions today.[48] Though Scalia does not have the same voting record as Frankfurter in Establishment Clause cases he does make repeated reference to the founders in order to substantiate his view that government can preference generic monotheism in public religious practices, ceremonies, and displays. Yet, Scalia has also articulated a particular view of originalism that emphasizes the intent of the founders as expressed in the text of the Constitution, as well as the history that helps to interpret the text in no establishment cases.[49] Thus, Frankfurter and Scalia's religion clause jurisprudence deserves critical analysis in light of Scalia's ongoing contribution to the debates about original intent, public activities and speeches, and legacy of dissent.[50]

Study of the two justices is therefore important because they have played roles in the debates on the Supreme Court about interpretation of the religion clauses following the incorporation of the clauses in the

---

[48] Green, *The Lure of History*, Ibid.

[49] Antonin Scalia, *A Matter of Interpretation: Federal Courts and the Law* (Princeton, NJ: Princeton University Press, 1997), 37-47.

[50] Scalia has already received a considerable amount of scholarly attention for a sitting Supreme Court justice as documented by Ralph A. Rossum, *Antonin Scalia's Jurisprudence: Text and Tradition* (Lawrence, KS: The University Press of Kansas, 2006), 198-205. On page 205 of his book Rossum states that "he writes with the verve and panache he does in part to ensure his opinions are included in constitutional law casebooks, where they will influence the next generation of lawyers and legal scholars."

1940s in *Cantwell v. Connecticut*, 310 U.S. 296 (1940) and *Everson v. Board of Education*, 330 U.S. 1 (1947). Their appeals to the founders of the republic in their official opinions for the Court reveal a reliance on founders such as George Washington, John Adams, James Madison, Thomas Jefferson, and John Marshall. References to these American founders are evidence for the early American public religion that Frankfurter and Scalia cite in their religion clause opinions, and chapter seven will examine how Frankfurter and Scalia have relied on these founders as authority in their religion clause opinions with different results.

Lastly, the author chose to study Frankfurter and Scalia because both judges helped frame for me an ongoing attempt to define and better understand the appropriate boundary between a healthy form of patriotism and unhealthy American public religion and nationalism that is perhaps a form of idolatry forbidden by the Christian faith. The author serves as Pastor of a Baptist church that wrestles from time to time with questions related to this boundary between devotion to church and devotion to country, and the proper relationship between church and state remains a matter of disagreement. This tension is most acute on July 4 and other national holidays when patriotism becomes a potential theme for worship in the church, and the church experiences anxiety about giving due respect to the service rendered by church members who have fought and sacrificed in the military while not simultaneously contributing to a potentially idolatrous nationalism that subverts the highest loyalty due to God.

CHAPTER 3

Felix Frankfurter and American Public Religion

THE DEVELOPMENT OF FRANKFURTER'S MORE SECULAR APPROACH TO AMERICAN PUBLIC RELIGION

Felix Frankfurter was born in Vienna, Austria, on February 22, 1882, and bears the distinction of being the last immigrant to serve on the United States Supreme Court.[1] His family's faith was Judaism, and they immigrated to the United States to live in New York in 1894.[2] It was during his childhood in New York City that Frankfurter attended public schools on the lower east side, and began to develop the devotion to American democratic ideals which would subsequently replace his waning faith in Judaism with a secular faith in the American system of government.[3]

---

[1] Joseph P. Lash, "A Brahmin of the Law: A Biographical Essay: in *From the Diaries of Felix Frankfurter*, ed. Joseph P. Lash (New York: W.W. Norton & Company, 1975), 18.

[2] Melvin I. Urofsky, *Felix Frankfurter: Judicial Restraint and Individual Liberties* (Boston: Twayne Publishers, 1991), 181-185, (Chronology of Frankfurter's life).

[3] Jeffrey D. Hockett, *New Deal Justice: The Constitutional Jurisprudence of Hugo Black, Felix Frankfurter, and Robert Jackson* (Lanham, MD: Rowman & Littlefield Publishers, Inc., 1996), 207.

In his oral history given to Harlan B. Philips Frankfurter begins by noting that his earliest memories do not include Austria, but rather being able to buy and have his own newspaper in New York. In his words, "Certainly, I have no recollection comparable to the recollection of very soon after we came here, when I could for a penny or two cents—certainly not more than two cents—but a paper. I bought a paper. It was my paper. That opened up the world, or projected one into it."[4] Soon he met an Irish teacher named Miss Hogan at Public School 25 on Fifth Street in the city and she saw to it that the young immigrant learned English. In fact, as Frankfurter remembered, she threatened physical punishment to anyone whom she caught speaking German with him. He was thankful for her insistence that he learn English and abandon German even though most people in the neighborhood he moved into spoke German.[5] He deemed her "one of my greatest benefactors in life because she was a lady of the old school," and felt that learning English helped him to overcome the barriers to intellectual development and success as a young immigrant child in America.[6]

He could not remember much about his childhood other than developing an early interest in "the world of affairs."[7] One of his earliest heroes was the populist William Jennings Bryan though his family did not appreciate this very much because they preferred Bryan's rival William McKinley. Yet, young Felix Frankfurter admired Bryan for his advocacy for the farmers in the Midwestern United States near the end of the nineteenth century. Moreover, Frankfurter stressed:

> Here was a fellow who could entrance people by the quality of his voice, the beauty of his speech. It was all so fresh and romantic and the voice of hope.[8]

---

[4] Harlan B. Philips, *Felix Frankfurter Reminisces* (New York: Reynal & Company, Inc., 1960), 3.

[5] Ibid., 5.

[6] Ibid., 4.

[7] Ibid., 5.

[8] Ibid., 6.

When asked about the greatest debt he owed to his parents with regard to his education he replied that they allowed him to think for himself, "almost completely."[9] At one point during his secondary education he had the opportunity to attend the Horace Mann School and perhaps gain a better education, but he did not do well enough on the competitive examination to earn a scholarship. His parents offered, he remembered, to pay his way, but he argued that they should not have to and so they did not. That was the end of that. But, more importantly, Frankfurter connected this early experience of dashed hopes to his philosophy of life. He stated:

> I have such a deep feeling about the importance of contingency in life. These people who plan their careers—I have so little respect for them. You know what Holmes says? Somebody boasted of being a self-made man and Holmes said, "Well, a self-made man usually hasn't made much.[10]

At an ill-defined point early in his life Felix Frankfurter lost his personal faith in Judaism, the faith of his family. In his oral history he remembers that he was an observant member of his faith during his childhood, but eventually ascribed to the influence and reasoning of the "Victorian agnostics" which included John Morley, the author of *On Compromise*. He also notes in his oral history that his parents were "observant," but not orthodox, and their devotion served as a family tradition rather than a foundation for living. For Felix, the Jewish rituals had . . . the warmth of the familiar, the warmth of the past and of the association of family festivals."[11]

Yet, as a young man he stopped going to the Synagogue regularly, and gradually felt more and more of a distance from the faith of his family heritage. He described having a moving emotional experience in college when he went to a Yom Kippur service where he felt pangs of guilt for being in the midst of those worshipping. He described his feeling at the time as follows:

---

[9] Ibid., 9.

[10] Ibid., 11.

[11] Ibid., 289.

thinking that it was unfair to me, a kind of desecration for me to be in the room with these people to whom these things had the meaning they had for them when for me they had no other meaning than adhering to a creed that meant something to my parents but had ceased to have meaning for me. I no longer had roots in that kind of relation to the mysteries of the universe, and I remember leaving the synagogue in the middle of the service saying to myself, 'It's a wrong thing for me to be present in a room in a holy service, to share these ceremonies, these prayers, these chants, with people for whom they have inner meaning as against me for whom they have ceased to have inner meaning.'[12]

Though Felix Frankfurter maintained a lifelong passion for Zionism as documented by his biographers[13] he would never again go to a Yom Kippur service, and from then on he preferred to call himself a "reverent agnostic."[14] He rejected belief in the God of his ancestors, but soon he began a period in his life, which inculcated a devotion to American democracy.[15]

Upon graduation from high school Frankfurter attended City College of New York where he struggled at first, but soon he began to excel academically demonstrating the intellectual abilities that would characterize the rest of his life as a scholar and judge. He developed a broad range of interests during his college years as well as a passion for learning. Yet, it was not the City College of New York, which would

---

[12] Ibid., 289-290.

[13] See Leonard Baker, *Brandeis and Frankfurter: A Dual Biography* (New York: Harper and Row Publishers, 1984), 41-42, 76-79, 338-339; Harlan B. Phillips, *Felix Frankfurter Reminisces* (New York: Reynal & Co., 1960), 178f; as well as Bruce Allen Murphy, *The Brandeis/Frankfurter Connection: The Secret Political Activities of Two Supreme Court Justices* (New York: Oxford University Press, 1982), 46-72.

[14] Phillips, *Frankfurter Reminisces*, 291.

[15] His "democratic faith" was acknowledged, articulated, and analyzed by Sanford Levinson while he was a law student in "The Democratic Faith of Felix Frankfurter," *25 Stanford L. Rev. 430, 430-448* (1973).

serve as the institutional foci for the young Frankfurter's "quasi-religious" feelings, but rather Harvard Law School.[16]

In 1901 he graduated from City College, and then he was admitted to Harvard Law in the fall of 1902 where his tuition was a mere $150. For Frankfurter the transition from college to law school proved intimidating. He described his feelings of inferiority early on during his tenure as a law student by comparing himself to "a little minnow" in a very large pond.[17] Nonetheless, it did not take Frankfurter long to find his comfort zone at Harvard Law School because he loved the challenge of the stiff academic competition and the democratic environment present there. He discovered that it did not matter what one's background was so long as one excelled in the curriculum, and this placed everyone on the same level playing field, irrespective of background.

Moreover, those in leadership at Harvard Law, such as Dean James Barr Ames, were principally committed to the search for truth, and not to "making disciples."[18] This leadership, according to Frankfurter, led to the development of an institutional aura, which encouraged "disinterestedness", and the pursuit of success based purely on performance, not social status.

It was also at Harvard Law School that Felix Frankfurter first encountered one of his two primary mentors as a lawyer and judge: Louis D. Brandeis. On May 4, 1905, Brandeis gave a speech at Harvard Law School and Frankfurter was a student in the audience. Brandeis, an attorney at the time, admonished the students to achieve "a great work" as lawyers, and to strive towards becoming a "people's attorney" in lieu of merely seeking personal gain.[19] The speech

---

[16] Phillips, *Frankfurter Reminisces*, 19.

[17] Ibid., 18.

[18] Ibid., 22-24.

[19] Leonard Baker, *Brandeis and Frankfurter: A Dual Biography* (New York: Harper & Row, 1984), 45 and Urofsky, *Judicial Restraint and Individual Liberties*, 181-185. At the time Brandeis was an attorney developing a reputation as a formidable advocate, especially on behalf of American labor against business interests. He was nominated as an associate justice on the Supreme Court by President Woodrow Wilson on January 28, 1916, and then

inspired the young immigrant law student to think deeply about his future as an attorney in America and served as a starting point for his relationship with Brandeis, who also would eventually develop a close relationship on the Supreme Court with Frankfurter's other mentor, Oliver Wendell Holmes, Jr.[20]

One does not have to read very far into Frankfurter's primary source materials to find evidence of his admiration for Holmes.[21] He frequently referred to Holmes in his diaries, authored a book about Holmes' tenure on the Supreme Court, sometimes infuriated other Supreme Court justices by lecturing them with references to Holmes, and cited Holmes as the inspiration and authority for his eventual rejection of the concept of "preferred freedoms" in the Bill of Rights.[22]

---

confirmed by a close and controversial vote of 47-22 on June 1, 1916. *The Oxford Companion to the Supreme Court of the United States*, 2d ed., Kermit L. Hall ed. (New York: Oxford University Press, 2005), 1132. For a comparison between Justices Brandeis and Frankfurter see Robert A. Burt, *Two Jewish Justices: Outcasts in the Promised Land* (Berkeley: University of California Press, 1988).

[20] Frankfurter's relation to both Brandeis and Holmes has been well documented, and several scholars have argued that Holmes was the defining influence on Frankfurter with regard to his Supreme Court jurisprudence, in accord with H.N. Hirsch and Sanford V. Levinson. See Urofsky, *Judicial Restraint and Individual Liberties*, 5; H.N. Hirsch, *The Enigma of Felix Frankfurter* (New York: Basic Books, Inc., 1981), 129-130; and Sanford V. Levinson, "Skepticism, Democracy, and Judicial Restraint: An Essay on the Thought of Oliver Wendell Holmes and Felix Frankfurter," (Ph.D. diss., Harvard University, 1969), 9.

[21] Felix Frankfurter, "Federalism and the Supreme Court," in *Of Law and Life and Other Things that Matter: Papers & Addresses of Felix Frankfurter, 1956-1963* ed. Philip B. Kurland (Cambridge, MA: The Belknap Press of Harvard University Press, 1965), 130 where Frankfurter indicated that Holmes was the "greatest intellect who ever sat on this Court" in his opinion.

[22] See Harlan B. Phillips, *Felix Frankfurter Reminisces* (New York: Reynal & Co., 1960), 24, 58f, 247; Felix Frankfurter, *Mr. Justice Holmes and the Supreme Court* (Cambridge, MA: Harvard University Press, 1938), 61-63; Urofsky, *Judicial Restraint and Individual Liberties*, 47 (regarding

More importantly according to one commentator, however, Felix Frankfurter would eventually incorporate a form of Holmesian skepticism into his jurisprudence with potentially significant implications in Frankfurter's jurisprudence.[23]

Yet, his early career included many important experiences as a professor and public servant before he was nominated to serve on the Supreme Court in 1939. After graduating from Harvard Law School in 1905 he accepted a position with the New York law firm Hornblower, Byrne, Miller and Potter. Subsequent to this Frankfurter worked for Henry Stimson in the United States Attorney's office in 1906 before following Stimson, another important influence on his life, into private practice from 1909 to 1910. During this period of his early professional career Frankfurter also worked in Stimson's unsuccessful gubernatorial campaign in New York. He matriculated to the United States War Department in 1911 and then served a stint as counsel for the Bureau of Insular Affairs. All of this was prelude, however, for the first truly significant phase of Felix Frankfurter's adult life: his tenure as a law Professor at Harvard University, which began in the summer of 1914.[24]

From 1914 until his nomination to serve as the seventy-eighth justice of the United States Supreme Court on January 5, 1939, Felix Frankfurter developed a reputation as an influential and even dangerous

---

Frankfurter's habit of lecturing his peers with references to Holmes at Saturday conference meetings and how this perturbed other justices such as Brennan); and Arthur E. Sutherland, "All Sides of the Question: Felix Frankfurter and Personal Freedom," in *Felix Frankfurter: The Judge* (New York: Reynal & Company, 1964), 122.

[23] Levinson, *Skepticism, Democracy, and Judicial Restraint*, 40, 103, 126; and James Bradley Thayer, Oliver Wendell Holmes, and Felix Frankfurter, *On John Marshall* (Chicago: The University of Chicago Press, Phoenix Books, 1967), 159, 172-173 where Frankfurter argues against the application of "sonorous abstractions" in a system of liberal government and law. He calls for a "sturdy doubt" as to whether one has found standards with exact meaning for a complex society: "sonorous abstractions do not solve problems with intractable variables." Ibid., 159.

[24] Urofsky, *Judicial Restraint and Individual Liberties*, 181-185.

liberal and progressive intellectual.[25] Joseph P. Lash's "Biographical Essay" in *From the Diaries of Felix Frankfurter* provides a narrative which describes his various activities during this period, including: service as a mentor to numerous Harvard law students who ended up in government service, editorial writer for the New Republic magazine, founding member of the American Civil Liberties Union, vigorous critic of the Supreme Court's activism, and commentator regarding the trial and execution of Nicola Sacco and Bartolomeo Vanzetti in the 1920s.[26] His other significant activities during this period included involvement in the American Zionist movement with Louis Brandeis, advocacy before the bar of the Supreme Court on behalf of progressive causes such as in the Oregon minimum wage case in 1917, and government service as a mediator and commentator on labor problems including the Mooney Report to President Wilson in 1918, and an incident involving "deportations" of some 1,100 copper miners in Bisbee, Arizona.[27]

The presence of anti-Semitism at Harvard Law School also marked this epoch of his life. Though his diaries from the time period around 1919-1920 do not mention anti-Semitism specifically, they do contain evidence of conflict involving Professor Frankfurter, Law School Dean Roscoe Pound, and the university's "Brahmin" President, A. Lawrence Lowell.[28] At issue in part were quotas for Jewish students at the university as well as faculty appointments in the law school which were

---

[25] Leonard Baker, *Brandeis and Frankfurter: A Dual Biography* (New York: Harper & Row Publishers, 1984), 369. Frankfurter was also the sixth person born outside the United States to serve as a justice on the Supreme Court. Ibid. See also, Peter Charles Hoffer, "Frankfurter, Felix," in *The Oxford Companion to the Supreme Court of the United States*, 2d ed., Kermit L. Hall, Ed. In Chief (New York: Oxford University Press, 2005), 364-367.

[26] Joseph P. Lash, "A Brahmin of the Law: A Biographical Essay," in *From the Diaries of Felix Frankfurter* (New York: W.W. Norton & Company, Inc., 1975), 15ff. Another account of this part of the judge's life is Michael E. Parrish, *Felix Frankfurter and His Times: The Reform Years* (New York: The Free Press, 1982).

[27] Baker, *A Dual Biography*, 148-149.

[28] Lash, *From the Diaries*, 124-140.

allegedly used by the university establishment, President Lowell in particular, as a wedge to drive the "dangerous" Jewish Professor away from Cambridge, Massachusetts, by making him so uncomfortable there that he would voluntarily take leave of the institution. His friend and mentor Oliver Wendell Holmes, Jr., is reported by biographer Leonard Baker to have stated:

> There is also a prejudice against Frankfurter: I think partly because he . . . is a Jew.[29]

Frankfurter remained very busy during this time, which has been characterized by some commentators as the most radical of his professional life, in spite of opposition and prejudice.[30] In articles in the 1920s and 1930s Frankfurter criticized the Supreme Court's judicial activism pursuant to the Fourteenth Amendment's Due Process Clause for stifling the progressive reform efforts of legislatures at both the national and the state levels. Many of these articles, some published as unsigned editorials, were subsequently edited, compiled and published in *Felix Frankfurter on the Supreme Court* by Professor Philip B. Kurland.[31] Herein Frankfurter takes the Supreme Court to task for interposing by judicial fiat the personal economic philosophies of the individual justices in order to block progressive economic regulatory legislation formed in the executive and legislative branches. At one point he considered the idea of commending the removal of the Due Process Clause of the Fourteenth Amendment by means of

---

[29] Baker, *A Dual Biography*, 220-221.

[30] Lash, *From the Diaries*, 33-34.

[31] (Cambridge, MA: The Belknap Press of Harvard University Press, 1970). Of special interest with reference to judicial restraint are the following segments of this compilation of essays: "Can the Supreme Court Guarantee Toleration?", "The Supreme Court as Legislator," "Social Issues Before the Supreme Court," "The Orbit of Judicial Power," and "The Judicial Process and the Supreme Court." Ibid., 174-179, 181-186, 286-306, 338-358, and 496-509.

constitutional amendment in order to stop the judicial activism that he objected to.[32]

Frankfurter was nominated by President Franklin Delano Roosevelt to become an associate justice on the United States Supreme Court on January 5, 1939. He was sworn in on January 30, and delivered his first opinion in the case of *Hale v. Bimco Trading* on February 27, 1939. The holding in *Bimco Trading* was unanimous in keeping with the tradition on the Court for a new justice's first opinion. Yet, the unity among the members of the Supreme Court in this case's decision did not last long because the justices on the Court soon became divided in personal conflict according to Melvin Urofsky.[33] Frankfurter became a disappointment to some liberals and progressives during his tenure on the nation's highest Court because they wanted him to lead the Court both as a consensus builder and in the protection of individual rights and liberties found in the Bill of Rights, or the first ten amendments to the United States Constitution.[34]

Subsequently, though, after his appointment to the Supreme Court, Frankfurter surprised many of his contemporaries with his consistent emphasis on judicial restraint, and his general unwillingness to aggressively protect civil liberties from the bench.[35] Law Professor

---

[32] Kurland, *Felix Frankfurter on the Supreme Court*, 166-167, 254-255.

[33] Urofsky, *Judicial Restraint and Individual Liberties*, 181-185; Levinson, *Democratic Faith of Felix Frankfurter*, 433. As to conflict on the Supreme Court during the early part of Justice Frankfurter's career see M.I. Urofsky, *Division and Discord: The Supreme Court under Stone and Vinson, 1941-1953* (Columbia, SC: University of South Carolina Press, 1997).

[34] H.N. Hirsch, *The Enigma of Felix Frankfurter* (New York: Basic Books, Inc., 1981), 127f; Lash, *From the Diaries*, 67, 72-73.

[35] Bruce Allen Murphy, *The Brandeis/Frankfurter Connection: The Secret Political Activities of Two Supreme Court Justices* (New York: Oxford University Press, 1982), 250 where he notes: "The public had reason to expect from Frankfurter the same judicial performance it had had from Brandeis. For that matter, Brandeis himself must have had similar expectations about his former lieutenant. But everyone would be surprised, and perhaps even somewhat disappointed by Frankfurter's performance. For in reality there were more substantial differences than similarities between

Sanford Levinson has argued that Frankfurter deemed his teaching post at Harvard Law School an excellent "forum" within which to shape the future leaders of American democracy, and other scholars have emphasized how he later sought to place his former students in powerful positions while on the Court.[36] Frankfurter's tenure as a professor at Harvard was thus marked by extensive political activities and helped him earn a reputation as a liberal, progressive activist. Some even considered him subversive of the state at the time, as noted above.[37] A book Frankfurter published in 1930 entitled *The Public and Its Government* provides primary source evidence, as well, that the future judge deemed his role as shaper of future leaders in America as an important one.[38] In this book he expresses confidence in the ability of American democracy to achieve progress so long as it has capable, expert administrative guidance. Subsequently, however, after his appointment to the Supreme Court, Frankfurter surprised many of his contemporaries with his consistent emphasis on judicial restraint, and his general unwillingness to aggressively protect civil liberties from the bench.[39]

Frankfurter and his old patron." In accord, see Lash, *From the Diaries*, 36-37 and 68-70. Lash also describes how Frankfurter's peer at Harvard University, the writer Archibald MacLeish, wrote of his appointment to the Supreme Court in terms to the effect that Frankfurter would fervently defend the Bill of Rights against legislative encroachments. Ibid., 36-37.

[36] Ibid. Bruce Allen Murphy, *The Brandeis/Frankfurter Connection: The Secret Political Activities of Two Supreme Court Justices* (New York: Oxford University Press, 1982), 313f.

[37] Lash, *From the Diaries*, 29.

[38] Felix Frankfurter, *The Public and Its Government* (New Haven, CT: Yale University Press, 1930).

[39] Murphy, *Brandeis/Frankfurter Connection*, 250 where he notes: "The public had reason to expect from Frankfurter the same judicial performance it had had from Brandeis. For that matter, Brandeis himself must have had similar expectations about his former lieutenant. But everyone would be surprised, and perhaps even somewhat disappointed, by Frankfurter's performance. For in reality there were more substantial differences than similarities between Frankfurter and his old patron." In accord, see Lash, *From The*

This was because Frankfurter's reputation as a liberal progressive while at Harvard as a professor in the 1920s and 1930s was well founded. He was educated as a legal thinker during this time of industrial transformation in American life.[40] According to Jeffrey D. Hockett progressives during this era, including Felix Frankfurter, were divided into two camps with reference to the question whether the federal or the local government was the right place from which to seek the transformation of society.[41] Nevertheless, they were united in their criticism of the Supreme Court's activism at the time in striking down progressive legislation, which initiated social and economic reform. The "Lochner" Court of the time, progressives claimed, used the concept of substantive due process found implicitly in the Fourteenth Amendment's Due Process clause as a vehicle to read laissez faire economics into the Constitution,[42] and thereby to strike down as unconstitutional legislation which progressives desired.[43]

Diaries, 36-37 and 68-70. Lash also describes how Frankfurter's peer at Harvard University, the writer Archibald MacLeish, wrote of his appointment to the Supreme Court in terms to the effect that Frankfurter would fervently defend the Bill of Rights against legislative encroachments. Ibid., 36-37.

[40] Hockett, *New Deal Justice*, 54-55.

[41] Ibid. In the camp committed to transformation through the federal government Hockett places Herbert Croly (another important influence on Frankfurter) and Teddy Roosevelt, while he includes Justice Louis Brandeis and President Woodrow Wilson among those who believed state governments should serve as the proper "agents of reform."

[42] Ibid., 55-56.

[43] Examples of legislation desired by the Progressives at the time, but which the Supreme Court struck down via the due process clause, include legislation related to maximum working hours, mandatory minimum wages, and "wage settlements in labor disputes." David A. Schultz and Christopher E. Smith, *The Jurisprudential Vision of Justice Antonin Scalia* (Lanham, MD: Rowman & Littlefield Publishers, Inc., 1996), 20. Herbert Hovencamp, "The Political Economy of Substantive Due Process," *40 Stanford L. Rev. 379, 379-447* (1988) provides an overview of Supreme Court jurisprudence on substantive due process from the Civil War to the New Deal in the 1930s.

In this context of conflict between the economic substantive due process jurisprudence of the Supreme Court and progressive legislative efforts Felix Frankfurter helped establish *The New Republic* in 1914, a journal committed to progressive causes whose editor-in-chief was Herbert Croly.[44] Croly was the author of the book *The Promise of American Life*, which combined patriotism with "domestic reform," and advocated a strong national government combined with development of bureaucratic and administrative technical prowess.[45]

Frankfurter scholars also have documented his other activities which occurred during the early decades of the twentieth century including: the Zionist movement, the labor movement, opposition to the Red Scare of the 1920s, the founding of the American Civil Liberties Union, and activity in the Presidential election of 1924.[46] In addition, as noted above, scholars have submitted that he used his position as a teacher and mentor of many of the best and brightest young, legal minds at the time to place students in positions such as that of law clerk for Supreme Court Justices Louis Brandeis and Oliver Wendell Holmes, Jr.[47]

Therefore, based upon this established record of commitment to liberal and progressive causes, much was expected of newly appointed associated justice when he became a member of the "New Deal" Court upon appointment by the man he possibly admired more than anyone in

---

See also, Henry J. Abraham and Barbara A. Perry, *Freedom and the Court: Civil Rights and Liberties in the United States*, 6th ed. (New York: Oxford University Press, 1994), 9-14 for a brief summary of the Court's jurisprudence from the Court of Chief Justice John Marshall through the New Deal Court.

[44] Hockett, *New Deal Justice*, 147.

[45] Ibid., 144-146.

[46] Lash, *From the Diaries*, 31-35.

[47] Former students of Frankfurter who clerked for the Supreme Court included Dean Acheson who clerked for Louis Brandeis, and Mark DeWolfe Howe who clerked for Holmes. Ibid., 30.

American life, President Roosevelt. [48]   Yet, as scholarship on Frankfurter has demonstrated, those who expected predictable and formulaic progressivism or libertarianism from Frankfurter were bound for disappointment.   In addition to his well-documented progressive credentials, Frankfurter had consistently advocated judicial restraint as a law professor, and he disfavored the notion of absolutes or what he considered simplistic abstract formulas that he argued paraded as panaceas for judicial and political controversies. [49]   Additionally, Frankfurter's philosophical skepticism has been analyzed further by Sanford Levinson with specific reference to Frankfurter's majority opinion in *Minersville School District v. Gobitis*, 310 U.S. 586, 591-600 (1940) which denied First Amendment relief to Jehovah's Witness children who were expelled from public school for refusing to salute the American flag in defiance of a Pennsylvania law which compelled the salute irrespective of religious beliefs.[50]

---

[48] Ibid., 40-49.   Lash questions whether Frankfurter admired President Roosevelt too uncritically.

[49] Ibid., 49 where Lash notes that Frankfurter often said of political controversies that there are no absolutes-just a question of where to draw the line. See also, Hockett, *New Deal Justice*, 194 where he argues Frankfurter's consistent commitment to judicial restraint on the Supreme Court represented opposition to "judicial efforts to impose a system of justice on the country . . . a pernicious form of judicial abstraction; application of the provisions of the Bill of Rights against the states fails to account for the particular circumstances of distinctive communities." It is not inaccurate to find Frankfurter's reaction to the substantive due process jurisprudence of the Lochner era behind his advocacy of judicial restraint, too.   His extrajudicial writings later published by Professor Kurland and mentioned supra in footnote 29, document his conviction well.

[50] Sanford Levinson, *Skepticism, Democracy, and Judicial Restraint: An Essay on the Thought of Oliver Wendell Holmes and Felix Frankfurter* (Ph.D. diss., Harvard University, 1969), 3-6, 226-227 wherein Levinson establishes Frankfurter's skepticism as to the basis of all values, and not just religious principles, but then argues that Frankfurter applied a type of formulaic judicial restraint in both of the flag salute cases.

Some commentators thus remember Frankfurter as a significant disappointment for libertarians and progressives because of his preeminent role as an advocate of judicial restraint while he served on the Supreme Court from 1939 until his retirement in 1962.[51] Our discussion of the secular nature of American public religion in Frankfurter's religion clause jurisprudence will now turn to the early Free Exercise Clause cases during Frankfurter's tenure on the Court which helped cause the disappointment of progressives and liberals, and then to the Establishment Clause cases which provide further evidence for his interpretive methodology that appealed to the viewpoints of Thomas Jefferson and James Madison with regard to American public religion.

The reasons Frankfurter expressed for his passive jurisprudence included: reaction to the economic substantive due process of the "Lochner" Court era, belief that the legislative and executive branches are the proper vehicles for social progress, confidence in the abilities of President Roosevelt and in the New Deal, and the influence of Harvard Law Professor James B. Thayer.[52] Also, in the free exercise opinions analyzed below Frankfurter's passive jurisprudence contributed to his rationale for denial of First Amendment relief to members of a minority faith, the Jehovah's Witnesses. Moreover the free exercise opinion of Antonin Scalia in *Employment Division v. Smith*, 494 U.S. 872 (1990) has similarly denied free exercise protection to members of a minority faith, two members of a native American church, but the *Smith* case did not involve a compulsory pledge and salute to the American flag.

---

[51] Lash, *From the Diaries*, 72-73 and Melvin I. Urofsky, *Felix Frankfurter: Judicial Restraint and Individual Liberties* (Boston: Twayne Publishers, 1991), x where Urofsky claims his legacy on the Court is "all but ignored by the courts" and by legal academics some 25 years after his death.

[52] Philip B. Kurland, ed. *Felix Frankfurter on the Supreme Court* (Cambridge, MA: The Belknap Press of Harvard University Press, 1970), 286-306, 496-509; Michael E. Parrish, *Felix Frankfurter and His Times: The Reform Years* (New York: The Free Press, 1982); Levinson, *Skepticism, Democracy, and Judicial Restraint*, 3-6 and 226-227.

SECULAR AMERICAN PUBLIC RELIGION IN THE RELIGION CLAUSE
JURISPRUDENCE OF FELIX FRANKFURTER: FREE EXERCISE CASES

When Roosevelt appointed Frankfurter to the United States Supreme
Court there were expectations that Frankfurter would serve as a leader
on the Court. As one biographer has argued, "His familiarity with its
history and judgments, with its personnel and their habits, and its
problems and needs, was unmatched."[53]
    It was not long, however, before the new justice encountered a
case related to the Free Exercise Clause of the First Amendment, which
would influence his legacy significantly. The facts of the case, which
developed within the contextual backdrop of World War II's early
political machinations in 1930s Europe, concerned two Jehovah's
Witness children in the public schools of Minersville School District,
Schuylkill County, Pennsylvania.[54] Lillian and William Gobitis aged
twelve and ten respectively, were expelled from Minersville's public
schools on November 6, 1935 when they would not salute the
American flag "as part of a daily school exercise."[55]
    Their refusal was based upon the belief of Jehovah's Witnesses
that the Bible is authoritatively the Word of God, and as such is due
obedience as their ultimate source of authority. More specifically,
these petitioners to the Supreme Court held that Exodus Chapter 20 in
the Old Testament forbids idolatry by means of its command to have no
other gods before Yahweh, and its command not to bow down to or to
serve other gods. Furthermore, no one in the case disputed the
Jehovah's Witnesses sincerity with regard to their conviction that the
Bible is authoritatively the Word of God. Finally, there was no

---

[53] Philip B. Kurland, "Felix Frankfurter," in *The Supreme Court Justices:
Illustrated Biographies, 1789-1995*, ed.   Clare Cushman, 2nd ed.
(Washington, D.C.: Congressional Quarterly, 1995), 389.

[54] *Minersville School District v. Gobitis*, 310 U.S. 586, 591-593 (1940)

[55] *Gobitis*, 310 U.S. at 591. See also, *Landmark Briefs and Arguments of the
Supreme Court of the United States: Constitutional Law- Minersville School
District v. Gobitis* (1940), vol. 37, eds. Philip B. Kurland and Gerhard
Casper (Arlington, VA: University Publications of America, Inc., 1975),
335.

disagreement as to the fact that Lillian and William Gobitis had been raised by their parents to "conscientiously believe" that saluting the flag was condemned by this authoritative text of Scripture.[56] The pledge to the flag at that time did not include the theistic language "under God," however. This phrase was added in June 1954.[57]

The children were young enough when their expulsion from the Minersville public schools occurred to come within Pennsylvania's mandatory school attendance law, and as the majority opinion by Frankfurter noted their expulsion prevented them from obtaining a free education in public schools thereby forcing their parents to pay the cost of sending them to private schools.[58] The flag salute ceremony in the case was as follows. Teachers and children were required to put their right hands over their hearts and then to say the following pledge of allegiance together: "I pledge allegiance to my flag, and to the Republic for which it stands; one nation indivisible, with liberty and justice for all."[59] Also, during the ceremony teachers and students would extend their right hands in order to salute the flag in a manner similar to the salute Nazis made in Germany at the time.[60]

The Pennsylvania School Code in 1935 contained several provisions, which the Minersville School Board relied upon in order to expel the Gobitis children for insubordination. One provision gave the board in each school district in Pennsylvania authority to "adopt and enforce such reasonable rules and regulations as it may deem necessary and proper . . . regarding the conduct and deportment of all pupils

---

[56] Ibid., 591-592.

[57] Steven B. Epstein, "Rethinking the Constitutionality of Ceremonial Deism," *96 Columbia L. Rev. 2083, 2118* (1996).

[58] Ibid., 592.

[59] Ibid., 591.

[60] Ibid. See also, Shawn Francis Peters, *Judging Jehovah's Witnesses: Religious Persecution and the Dawn of the Rights Revolution* (Lawrence, KS: University Press of Kansas, 2000) for an extended treatment of the factual background of the *Gobitis* case and the mistreatment of Jehovah's Witnesses in the context of World War II.

attending the public schools in the district."[61] School administrators and authorities were also given authorization to temporarily suspend or expel students "on account of disobedience or misconduct" in the school codes. Additionally, the codes prescribed teaching of "the history of the United States and Pennsylvania, [and] civics, including loyalty to the State and National Government" throughout the Commonwealth of Pennsylvania.[62] Pursuant to these codes the Minersville School Board in 1935 passed a resolution requiring salute of the national flag, "and provided that a refusal to salute the flag should be regarded as an act of insubordination."[63]

Subsequent to the expulsion of the children from Minersville public schools for insubordination their father Walter Gobitis sued the defendants Minersville School District, Board of Education of Minersville School District (including David I. Jones, Dr. E.A. Valibus, Claude L. Price, Dr. T.J. McGurl, Thomas B. Evans and William Zapf), and the Superintendent of the Minersville Public Schools, Charles E. Roudabush, on May 3, 1937 seeking an injunction preventing the defendants from requiring the flag salute as a precondition for attendance at the public schools.[64] The lawsuit was filed in the federal district court for the Eastern District of Pennsylvania, a federal trial court, and claimed that the mandatory flag salute violated the Gobitis children's constitutional right to the free exercise of religion. Subsequent to a trial in this Court the Gobitis's were granted a final decree in their favor on June 18, 1938 by the Honorable Albert B.

---

[61] Kurland and Casper, *Landmark Briefs-Gobitis*, 340. The public school system in Pennsylvania had been established pursuant to the Commonwealth's Constitution as described in the "Brief for Petitioner," Ibid., 338-339.

[62] Ibid. The specific School Code statutes cited were Act of May 18, 1911, P.L. 309, art. XVI, Section 1607, as amended by Act of May 20, 1937, P.L. 732, Section 1 (24 P.S. Section 1551).

[63] Ibid., 340-341.

[64] Kurland and Casper, *Landmark Briefs-Gobitis*, 335.

Maris, which ruled that the children should be allowed to return to school without having to participate in the flag salute.[65]

The school district, however, refused to accept the trial court's decree and appealed to the Third Circuit Court of Appeals. At this level of the legal proceedings the Jehovah's Witness children once again prevailed when the appellate court ruled in their favor that the mandatory flag salute violated the First and Fourteenth Amendments. In an opinion by Circuit Judge Clark for the Third Circuit Court of Appeals the court upheld the district court's decree, which enjoined the school district from extending the expulsion of the children and requiring the flag salute.[66] Judge Clark concluded his opinion by quoting George Washington's letter of 1789 to some Quakers wherein Washington wrote:

> I assure you very explicitly, that in my opinion the conscientious scruples of all men should be treated with great delicacy and tenderness; and it is my wish and desire, that the laws may always be as extensively accommodated to them, as a due regard to the protection and essential interests of the nation may justify and permit.[67]

Once again, the school district decided to appeal, and the United States Supreme Court granted their Petition for Writ of Certiorari on March 4, 1940, because the third circuit's holding was contrary to four previous *per curiam*[68] decisions of the Supreme Court which all ruled the mandatory flag salute constitutional.[69]

---

[65] Ibid., 335-336. The opinion is reported in *Gobitis v. Minersville School Dist.*, 24 F. Supp. 271 (E.D. Penn. 1938).

[66] *Minersville School District v. Gobitis*, 108 F. 2d 683, 693 (1939). For a discussion of the lower court cases see Shawn F. Peters, *Judging Jehovah's Witnesses: Religious Persecution and the Dawn of the Rights Revolution* (Lawrence, KS: University Press of Kansas, 2000), 46-71.

[67] *Minersville School District*, 108 F. 2d at 693.

[68] A *per curiam* decision is an opinion given by an appellate Court without identifying the author of the opinion, and thus serves as the opinion for the

The Supreme Court allowed two *amicus curiae* briefs to be filed by the Committee on the Bill of Rights of the American Bar Association and the American Civil Liberties Union which both argued for affirmance of the lower federal courts in favor of the Gobitis children. The American Bar Association brief noted that 18 states had compulsory flag salute statutes, and 120 students had refused to make the mandatory salute. Yet, the Bar Association claimed that the "practical importance" of the case was that it infringed "upon the integrity of American liberties," and also the basic right of "freedom of conscience" by endorsing the government's power to "force people to express themselves in a certain way" which is tantamount to coercing a religious ritual.[70] Moreover, the amicus brief argued that courts should deem the flag salute ceremony a "religious ritual" for the Jehovah's Witnesses even though no court had been willing to make this determination so far.[71] Otherwise, the ABA committee concluded, the government would be able to "strike at the heart of religious liberty" and "thus [deny] the right of private judgment."[72]

The petition on behalf of the school district, on the other hand, submitted that the passage of the resolution requiring the flag salute was within the school board's power, was supported by Supreme Court precedent as well as state court precedent, and did not violate the provisions of either the United States' or Pennsylvania Constitutions. In addition the school district disputed the Gobitis's claim that refusal to salute the flag was grounded in religious belief. To the contrary, the

---

entire Court. *Black's Law Dictionary*, 9th ed. Ed-in-Chief, Bryan A. Garner (St. Paul, MN: West's Publishing, Inc., 2009), 1201.

[69] *Leoles v. Landers*, 302 U.S. 656; *Hering v. State Board of Education*, 303 U.S. 624; *Gabrielli v. Knickerbocker*, 306 U.S. 621; *Johnson v. Deerfield*, 306 U.S. 621 cited by Frankfurter in his majority opinion in *Gobitis*, 310 U.S. at 592, n. 2.

[70] Kurland and Casper, *Landmark Briefs-Gobitis*, 461.

[71] Ibid., 454-455, 467.

[72] Ibid., 464. The ABA committee did concede that the legislature could restrict religious freedom, but only when this was "essential" to protect the "public interest." Ibid., 465.

district argued that the flag salute did not involve religious "beliefs" of students at all, but was "a ceremony clearly designed to inculcate patriotism," and "[t]here is nothing in the salute or the pledge of allegiance which constitutes an act of idolatry, or which approaches to any religious observance."[73] Additionally, the school district's Petition claimed that the flag salute actually strengthened religious liberty by symbolically representing the "principle that people may worship as they please or need not worship at all."[74]

According to Frankfurter biographer Joseph P. Lash Chief Justice Charles Evan Hughes assigned the opinion for the majority in *Gobitis* to Frankfurter after Frankfurter made an impassioned statement during conference deliberations about the influence of American public schools in his life.[75] Additionally, other commentators have written that those familiar with Frankfurter's fervent patriotism and strong faith in American democracy should not have been surprised by his eventual conclusions in the case.[76] During his Senate confirmation hearings only a few years before the *Gobitis* case Senator Pat McCarran engaged in an aggressive line of questions that challenged Frankfurter's loyalty to the Constitution, and in reply Frankfurter stated:

> Senator, I do not believe you have ever taken an oath to support the Constitution of the United States with fewer reservations than I have or would now, nor do I believe you are more attached to the theories and practices of Americanism than I am.[77]

---

[73] Ibid., 324 (quoting *Nicholls v. Mayor and School Committee of Lynn*, 7 N.E. 2d 577, 579 (Mass. 1937).

[74] Ibid., 325 (quoting *People v. Sandstrom*, 279 N.Y. 523, 529, 18 N.E. 2d 840, 842 (1939).

[75] Lash, *From the Diaries*, 68-69.

[76] His patriotism and "ideals of citizenship" as a naturalized citizen caused him to depreciate the conscience of the Jehovah's Witnesses as well as the scruples of conscientious objectors in the context of World War I, according to Melvin I. Urofsky, *Felix Frankfurter: Judicial Restraint and Individual Liberties* (Boston: Twayne Publishers, 1991), 50.

[77] Lash, *From the Diaries*, 66.

Additionally, in April 1938 Frankfurter had previously said, "I can express with very limited adequacy the passionate devotion to this land that possesses millions of our people, born like myself under other skies, for the privilege this country has bestowed in allowing them to partake of its fellowship."[78] Subsequent to his death, in an article in tribute to Frankfurter the poet Archibald MacLeish commented regarding his patriotic devotion to America, "There may have been other justices of the Court who have held American democracy in as great respect as Mr. Frankfurter holds it: none has respected it more, or more earnestly resented its disrepute."[79]

Frankfurter's 8-1 opinion for the Court in *Gobitis* began with an appeal to the history of the struggle for religious liberty behind the First Amendment religion clauses enshrined in the Bill of Rights. He noted how the history of religious wars and conflict led to the religion clauses of the First Amendment, and how the clauses "sought to guard against repetition of those bitter religious struggles by prohibiting the establishment of a state religion and by securing to every sect the free exercise of its faith."[80]

But then to focus of the Frankfurter opinion turned toward the needs of society, which judges needed to balance against religious liberty. He wrote for the Court:

> So pervasive is the acceptance of this precious right that its scope is brought into question, as here, only when the conscience of individuals collides with the felt necessities of society.[81]

A reading of the majority opinion in *Gobitis* reveals, too, that Frankfurter's analysis of the relative weight of the Gobitis's religious liberty claim as compared to the "felt needs of society" warranted ruling in favor of the government's expressed interest in social

---

[78] Ibid., 68.

[79] Archibald MacLeish, "Law and Politics," in *Felix Frankfurter: A TRIBUTE*, ed. Wallace Mendelson (New York: Reynal & Company, 1964), 221.

[80] *Minersville School District v. Gobitis*, 310 U.S. 586, 593 (1940).

[81] Ibid.

cohesive sentiment. The decision reversed the lower federal courts and held for the Minersville School District ultimately requiring that students salute the flag irrespective of religious scruples, and minimized the harm done by the holding to the religious liberty of Lillian and William Gobitis.[82]

It is important to evaluate the rationale offered by Frankfurter in his *Gobitis* opinion with reference to its basis in his arguments for judicial restraint, and with regard to his reliance on the founders' views on religious liberty. When his opinion is compared with the arguments for judicial restraint made by James B. Thayer in an article in the *Harvard Law Review* in 1893 the influence of Thayer's views of Frankfurter becomes apparent. Thayer argued in his article that judges should only administer judicial review and strike down laws as unconstitutional when the legislature did not have any rational or reasonable basis consistent with the Constitution for the law in question.[83] Also, Thayer submitted that this standard of judicial review had an early and consistent basis in American law and history.[84] Then lastly, Thayer reasoned that this deferential type of judicial review best

---

[82] See Urofsky, *Judicial Restraint and Individual Liberties,* 52 and Peters, *Judging Jehovah's Witnesses,* 46-71 as to the attacks on Jehovah's Witnesses, which occurred as a result of the *Gobitis* case.

[83] James B. Thayer, "The Origin and Scope of the American Doctrine of Constitutional Law," *VII Harvard L. Rev. 129, 140* (1893). In the article Thayer further explains the rational basis test as best suited for a constitutional government where different legislators may interpret the Constitution differently with a reasonable basis for each interpretation though each basis may not seem reasonable to the other legislator or to a judge. Thus, the appropriate form of judicial review according to him is one that is deferential, and thereby respectful of the range of meanings, judgments, and choices available to legislators in the lawmaking process. In other words, for Thayer, in order to protect the legislature's range of choice as granted by the Constitution courts should defer to bases for legislation that are rational. Ibid., 144.

[84] Ibid., 140-142 wherein Thayer traces this standard of judicial review back to 1811. He also writes that the rational basis standard is not only early, but has had to "maintain itself against denial and dispute." Ibid., 145.

comports with vigorous protection of "private rights" and liberties precisely because it does not leave this protection to the courts. Rather, a policy of judicial restraint requires that the people and their elected representatives take primary responsibility for protecting rights and liberties under the Constitution.[85]

In the *Gobitis* opinion Frankfurter based his holding that the religious freedom of the Jehovah's Witnesses children had to yield to social priorities on several arguments. First of all, he submitted that no freedom, even religious freedom, in unlimited.[86] Moreover, he added, in seeking to balance the needs of society against claims of individuals one needs to "recall the truth that no single principle can answer all of life's complexities."[87] Therefore, religious liberty, as an abstract principle, should not necessarily take precedence over other competing rights or values of society. Otherwise, he concluded, religious liberty and freedom of conscience or private judgment would undermine the very same free society with a "plurality of principles" which protected religious freedom. He wrote:

> But to affirm that the freedom to follow conscience has itself
> no limits in the life of a society would deny that very plurality
> of principles which, as a matter of history, underlies protection
> of religious toleration.[88]

Here the influence of Frankfurter's aversion to formulaic abstractions, noted above, and perhaps even the influence of Holmesian skepticism have shaped his opinion, and yet the quoted language does not necessarily mean or imply this. Rather, Frankfurter more likely is asserting here that all freedoms, even freedom of conscience, have limits.

Second, he grounded the opinion on the general principle from Supreme Court precedent, later relied upon in *Employment Division v. Smith* by Scalia in 1990, that American constitutional law had never

---

[85] Ibid., 155-156.

[86] *Gobitis*, 310 U.S. at 594.

[87] Ibid.

[88] Ibid., 594.

required general laws of neutral applicability to yield to religious conscience.[89] According to his opinion this principle had consistently held throughout American constitutional history that:

> The religious liberty which the Constitution protects has never excluded legislation of general scope not directed against doctrinal loyalties or particular sects.[90]

Neither the history, the framers, nor the tradition of religious liberty in the United States, he claimed, warranted such a broad accommodation of religious beliefs.[91] To find otherwise, he stressed, would render the order, tranquility, and security of society precarious and subject to the dictates of a multitude of divergent consciences. This, he reasoned,

---

[89] Ibid., "Conscientious scruples have not, in the course of the long struggle for religious toleration, relieved the individual from obedience to a general law not aimed at the promotion or restriction or religious beliefs." Citing the writings of Thomas Jefferson, James Madison, Roger Williams, and W.K. Jordan, *The Development of Religious Toleration in England*, passim. Ibid., n. 3.

[90] Ibid. As precedent he cites the early Mormon cases and a few others which emerged from the context of relative Protestant homogeneity of the 19th and early 20th centuries when American Protestant civil religion was at its height- *Reynolds v. United States*, 98 U.S. 145; *Davis v. Beason*, 133 U.S. 333; *Selective Draft Law Cases*, 245 U.S. 366; and *Hamilton v. Regents*, 293 U.S. 245. Ibid., 595.

[91] It is interesting to compare the appeals of Frankfurter to the framers and to precedent in *Gobitis* and his other religion clause opinions to the methodology of Scalia. Both look to the framers, to precedent, and tradition as interpretive authority, but Frankfurter does not appeal to the text of the First Amendment nor its tradition with the same results. Liva Baker, *Felix Frankfurter* (New York: Coward-McCann, Inc., 1969), 223-231; Philip B. Kurland, *Felix Frankfurter on the Supreme Court: Extrajudicial Essays on the Court and the Constitution* (Cambridge, MA: Harvard University Press, Belknap Press, 1970), 176-178, 451-459; Antonin Scalia, *A Matter of Interpretation: Federal Courts and the Law* (Princeton: Princeton University Press, 1997), 47.

impermissibly weakens the national consensus and security, which are values "inferior to none in the hierarchy of legal values."[92]

Then, in the remainder of the opinion Frankfurter explicitly combined a rationale of judicial restraint in the context of constitutional challenges to legislation with the need for "the binding tie of cohesive sentiment" across America in order to reject the Gobitis's claim that their right to religious liberty had been violated.[93] He quoted Abraham Lincoln's expression of the "profoundest problem confronting a democracy" in order to frame this part of the opinion where he articulates his argument that social cohesiveness outweighs sectarian scruples in this instance:

> Must a government of necessity be too strong for the liberties
> of its people, or too weak to maintain its own existence?[94]

It is this section of the opinion which manifests evidence of his arguments in favor of the ideal of a procedurally open and free society where the best and brightest are able to succeed, yet wherein religious minorities like the Lillian and William Gobitis who will not assimilate to secular ceremonies like the flag salute and pledge are sometimes denied relief pursuant to the Free Exercise Clause because the government action at issue has a rational basis, namely, having a socially cohesive and free society.

He began the majority opinion by acknowledging the troubling policy dilemma for the Court because it was wrestling with an

---

[92] Ibid., 595. His appeal here to a "hierarchy of values" has been criticized as ironic in light of his criticisms against formulaic abstractions and judicial activism, and his professed methodological approach which stressed neutral, reasoned, detachment like that of Oliver Wendell Holmes. See Melvin I. Urofsky, *Felix Frankfurter: Judicial Restraint and Individual Liberties* (Boston: Twayne Publishers, 1991), 49 who quotes Frankfurter's counterpart on the Court William O. Douglas who said of Frankfurter, "no one poured his emotion more completely into his decision while professing just the opposite." Ibid., 50.

[93] Ibid., 596.

[94] Ibid.

extremely difficult question: how can a government achieve strength to maintain national security without injuring the rights of the people enshrined in the Constitution?[95] Then, he appealed directly to the societal need for consensus and community centered in "the binding tie of cohesive sentiment" which is "[t]he ultimate foundation of a free society."[96] Where does this cohesive sentiment come from? "Such sentiment," he submitted, "is fostered by all those agencies of mind and spirit which may serve to gather up the traditions of a people, transmit them from generation to generation, and thereby create that continuity of a treasured common life which constitutes a civilization."[97] The flag was, for Frankfurter, the symbol of all the foundational and ultimate values of a free American society without which it would not have freedom, the consent of the governed, rule of law, protection of the weak, security against "arbitrary power," and "absolute safety for free institutions against foreign aggression."[98]

His argument for judicial restraint in the case varied little from the same argument for judicial passivity in a democracy, which he made repeatedly during the course of his tenure on the Supreme Court.[99] The

---

[95] Ibid. In addition, he stated, "No mere textual reading or logical talisman can solve the dilemma. And when the issue demands judicial determination, it is not the personal notion of judges of what wise adjustment requires which must prevail."

[96] Ibid.

[97] Ibid.

[98] Ibid. The inclusion of "absolute safety for free institutions against foreign aggression" seems a direct reference to the Nazi threat looming across the Atlantic Ocean at the time.

[99] Sanford Levinson and Melvin I. Urofsky both criticize Frankfurter for hypocrisy because they assert that Frankfurter follows a formulaic approach to judicial restraint, but then objects to the formalism of others. Levinson, *Skepticism, Democracy, and Judicial Restraint*, 225-227 and Urofsky, *Judicial Restraint and Individual Liberties*, 57-59. Urofsky accuses Frankfurter of becoming the "prisoner of an idea," something which Frankfurter criticized Hugo Black for in their debates over Incorporation of the Bill of Rights.

courts have no unique wisdom, he submitted, with regard to how to achieve educational policy or any other policy, and thus should not serve either as a "school board for the country" or as a super legislature.[100] Moreover, as long as the democratic process was free and open so that all citizens could influence legislation, then courts ought to uphold the constitutionality of legislation unless "the transgression of personal liberty is too plain for argument."[101] Thus, Frankfurter and a majority of the Court, for the time being, adopted the view that legislation challenged pursuant to the Free Exercise Clause was constitutional so long as there was a rational basis for its constitutionality. The application of this standard of judicial review in *Gobitis* adopted the position that legislatures should have very broad constitutional discretion to draft laws so long as there was some reasonable basis for their constitutionality, and this standard of judicial review was adapted from James B. Thayer's Harvard Law Review article that was influential for Frankfurter.[102]

Another reason for his adoption of this stance on judicial review, according to the *Gobitis* opinion, was the value of citizen involvement in the democratic process of legislation. He expressed this aspect of his rationale as follows, "Where all the effective means of inducing political changes are left free from interference, education in the abandonment of foolish legislation is itself training in liberty. To fight out the wise use of legislative authority in the forum of public opinion and before legislative assemblies rather than to transfer such a contest to the judicial arena, serves to vindicate the self-confidence of a free people."[103]

---

[100] Ibid., 598.

[101] Ibid., 599-600.

[102] James B. Thayer, "The Origin and Scope of the American Doctrine of Constitutional Law," *VII Harv. L. Rev. 129* (1893).

[103] Ibid., 600. The influence of James B. Thayer's view of judicial restraint in the *Gobitis* opinion is evident at this point where Frankfurter argues, like Thayer, that the primary responsibility for protecting rights belongs to the people and their elected representatives. James B. Thayer, "The Origin and Scope of the American Doctrine of Constitutional Law," *VII Harv. L. Rev. 129, 155-156* (1893).

Several aspects of Frankfurter's free exercise jurisprudence were exhibited in the *Gobitis* opinion. His commitment to judicial restraint is evident in the decision, along with his confidence in the American legislative process's ability to cultivate progress as long as the process was free and open to everyone. Also, he avoided any mention of problems with the doctrine of incorporation, and he acknowledged that the Court had the responsibility for judicial review. But, also notable, was the opinion's confidence in the American democratic process, and its deference via judicial restraint to the mandatory flag salute's secular rationale of "cohesive sentiment" among the American people, which outweighs sectarian scruples such as those exhibited by the Jehovah's Witnesses. This deference in *Gobitis* is toward a governmentally sponsored and secular form of common sentiment.

The *Gobitis* holding was criticized for exhibiting indifference to the rights of religious minorities, and scholars have documented the persecution of Jehovah's Witnesses subsequent to the decision.[104] This opinion was also a surprise to some commentators because Frankfurter's reputation led some of them to expect him to side with the Jehovah's Witnesses. In a letter to Chief Justice Harlan Fiske Stone intended to sway Stone against dissenting in the case Frankfurter acknowledged his sympathies, "After all, the vulgar intrusion of law in the domain of conscience is for me a very sensitive area."[105]

The 8-1 opinion for the Court in *Gobitis* was the opposite of what some expected from a judge who wrote:

> a good part of my mature life has thrown whatever weight it
> has had against foolish and harsh manifestations of coercion
> and for the amplest expression of dissident views, however

---

[104] Shawn Peters, *Judging Jehovah's Witnesses: Religious Persecution and the Dawn of the Rights Revolution* (Lawrence, KS: University Press of Kansas, 2000), 46-71.

[105] Alpheus Thomas Mason, *Security Through Freedom: American Political Thought and Practice* (Ithaca, NY: Cornell University Press, 1955), 217, "Appendix," reproducing a letter dated May 27, 1940 from the Chambers of Justice Felix Frankfurter to Stone about case No. 690, the *Gobitis* case. The letter begins, "Dear Stone: Were No. 690 an ordinary case, I should let the opinion speak for itself."

absurd or offensive these may have been to my own notions of rationality and decency.[106]

Yet, Frankfurter both articulated and adhered to a judicial policy of restraint that shaped his majority opinion in the case so that the result did not favor his own libertarian ideals, but rather expressed deference to the government's rationale for the flag salute. How does one explain this result?[107]

According to the rationale stated in the *Gobitis* case and subsequently defended in his dissent in *West Virginia State Board of Education v. Barnette*, 319 U.S. 624 (1943) Frankfurter was striving to serve as a dispassionate, passive, and disinterested jurist who respected the legislature's ability to enact laws rationally consistent with the Constitution.[108] Frankfurter restated his arguments for judicial restraint in a letter to Harlan Fiske Stone that attempted to dissuade the Chief Justice from dissenting in the case.[109] He submitted to Stone:

---

[106] Ibid.

[107] In the diary of Harold L. Ickes, a friend of Frankfurter's at the time of FDR's administration, he wrote of the case: "To my utter astonishment and chagrin, he rendered an opinion in the Supreme Court on Monday which, sad to relate, was concurred in by every member of the Court except Justice Stone; it held that a state, in this case Pennsylvania, had the right to exclude from school two little children, members of the crazy Jehovah's Witnesses sect, who had refused to salute the flag at the behest of their fanatical parents who believe that to salute the flag is idolatrous. As if the country can be saved, or our institutions preserved, by forced salutes of our flag by these fanatics or even by conscientious objectors!" *The Secret Diary of Harold L. Ickes, Vol. III: The Lowering Clouds, 1939-1941* (New York: Simon And Schuster, 1954), 199.

[108] Much of his letter to Chief Justice Stone trying to dissuade him from dissenting in *Gobitis* is dedicated to a recapitulation of his emphasis on judicial restraint that he adopted from James B. Thayer. Mason, *Security Through Freedom*, 218-219.

[109] Ibid., 217.

this case would have a tail of implications as to legislative power that is certainly debatable and might easily be invoked far beyond the size of the immediate kite, were it to deny the very minimum exaction, however foolish as to the Gobitis children, of an expression of faith in the heritage and purposes of our country.[110]

Also, for Frankfurter the case served his purpose to "use this opinion as a vehicle for preaching the true democratic faith of not relying on the Court for the impossible task of assuring a vigorous, mature, self-protecting and tolerant democracy by bringing the responsibility for a combination of firmness and toleration directly home where it lies-to the people and their representatives themselves."[111] If the religious liberty of the Jehovah's Witness children was diminished in this instance, then according to Frankfurter the proper remedy was recourse to the legislative process. One scholar has argued that Frankfurter's assimilation to the "true democratic faith" he had learned in the public schools of New York City and at Harvard Law School has influenced the judge's jurisprudence at this point.[112]

Sanford Levinson and other scholars [113] have written about Frankfurter's democratic faith in some detail, and stressed the important place for public schools within the formative influences for Frankfurter, as exemplified in *Gobitis*. Their scholarship explains that his line of reasoning in both *Gobitis* and in his dissent in the case, which overruled it three years later, *West Virginia State Board of Education v. Barnette,*[114] was consistent with his commitment to

---

[110] Ibid., 219.

[111] Ibid., 220.

[112] Richard Danzig, "Justice Frankfurter's Opinions in the Flag Salute Cases: Blending Logic and Psychologic in Constitutional Decision-making," *36 Stan. L. Rev. 675, 690-692f* (1983-1984).

[113] Ibid. and Helen Shirley Thomas, *Felix Frankfurter: Scholar on the Bench* (Baltimore: The Johns Hopkins Press, 1960), 45-68 discussing the *Gobitis* case in the context of World War II, and arguing that the case established Frankfurter's view that public education helps form social unity.

[114] 319 U.S. 624, 646-671 (1943).

American democracy. First of all, Levinson submitted that Frankfurter, much like his mentor Louis Brandeis, emphasized "the Aristotelian notion of the polity as characterized by consensus on a common good."[115] In this sense, then, Frankfurter was not an ordinary "liberal" in that "liberalism rejects the idea of a preexisting community and focuses instead on atomistic individuals coming together in uneasy compromise for their own interests."[116]

Thus, his confidence in American democracy and his patriotism as a naturalized immigrant who had succeeded on his own merits and ability to reason may have influenced the opinions Frankfurter authored in *Gobitis* and *Barnette* according to some commentators. Helen Shirley Thomas explained the importance of American public schools for Frankfurter in her book about him:

> Those sections of the opinion [*Gobitis*] that deal with the flag salute as an objective means for transmitting national values and with the role of the public school are extremely important for an understanding of Justice Frankfurter's philosophy . . . A product of public schools and a city college, he knew through his own experience how much these "agencies of mind" had helped an immigrant boy adjust to a new pattern of living. In instilling the cohesive sentiment that directs a nation's destiny, schools have to utilize various techniques. The flag salute was one of these and as such was legitimate for Jehovah's Witnesses as well as anybody else. The religious freedom issue dealt with in the opinion was preliminary, if not peripheral, to this central point.[117]

The case of *West Virginia State Board of Education v. Barnette*, 319 U.S. 624 (1943) was similar to *Gobitis* on its facts. In response to the decision of the Court in *Gobitis* in 1940 the West Virginia legislature passed an amended law which required all "schools therein to conduct courses in history, civics, and in the Constitutions of the

---

[115] Levinson, *Democratic Faith of Felix Frankfurter*, 435.

[116] Ibid.

[117] Thomas, *Scholar on the Bench*, 50.

United States and of the State" for the stated "purpose of teaching, fostering, and perpetuating the ideals, principles and spirit of Americanism, and increasing the knowledge of the organization and machinery of government."[118] The law also made these requirements mandatory for all schools including private and parochial schools. The state Board of Education also passed a resolution on January 9, 1942, based on the *Gobitis* decision mandating a flag salute for all students and teachers, and stipulating that refusal to participate "be regarded as an act of insubordination."[119] Regulations were also passed which contained penalties for parents and students if they refused to make the salute.

After some students, the Parent and Teachers Association, and the Boy Scouts complained that the salute was "too much like Hitler's" the law was modified, but when Jehovah's Witnesses offered to make a pledge in lieu of the flag salute ceremony state authorities refused to cooperate.[120] The actual language of the pledge required by West

---

[118] *West Virginia State Board of Education v. Barnette*, 319 U.S. 624, 625 (1943). The third paragraph of the revised law came directly from *Gobitis*: "WHEREAS, The West Virginia State Board of Education recognizes that the manifold character of man's relations may bring his conception of religious duty into conflict with the secular interests of his fellowman; that conscientious scruples have not in the course of the long struggle for religious toleration relieved the individual from obedience to the general law not aimed at the promotion or restriction of the religious beliefs; that the mere possession of convictions which contradict the relevant concerns of political society does not relieve the citizen from the discharge of political responsibility." Ibid., n. 2.

[119] *Barnette*, 319 U.S. at 626.

[120] According to the majority opinion by Justice Jackson Jehovah's Witnesses offered to make a pledge instead of the flag salute. The pledge said, "I have pledged my unqualified allegiance and devotion to Jehovah, the Almighty God, and to His Kingdom, for which Jesus commands all Christians to pray. I respect the flag of the United States and acknowledge it as a symbol of freedom and justice for all. I pledge allegiance and obedience to all the laws of the United States that are consistent with God's laws, as set forth in the Bible." *Barnette*, 319 U.S. at 628, n. 4.

Virginia at the time was as follows: "I pledge allegiance to the Flag of the United States of America and to the Republic for which it stands; one Nation, indivisible, with Liberty and justice for all."[121] If a child refused to participate then he or she was expelled and deemed "unlawfully absent" then subsequently prosecuted "as a delinquent."[122] The student's parents were then also subject to being prosecuted with potential penalties of a fine up to $50 along with a jail term as of many as 30 days.

Walter Barnette, Paul Stull, and Lucy McClure filed a lawsuit in the United States District Court in Charleston, West Virginia, seeking an injunction that would prevent enforcement of these laws and regulations against them. They claimed that the flag salute laws violated their constitutional rights under the Federal Constitution.[123] More specifically, the Jehovah's Witnesses argued that the West Virginia laws violated their First and Fourteenth Amendment rights of "freedom of speech, freedom of conscience, freedom to worship Almighty God, freedom of the children to attend the public schools, and freedom to direct the moral and spiritual education of the children."[124] The trial court, in spite of the Supreme Court's 8-1 decision in *Gobitis*, ruled in favor of the Jehovah's Witnesses and granted them an injunction, then the case was appealed directly to the United States Supreme Court under the jurisdictional provisions of 28 U.S.C. Sections 266 and 345 which permit appeals directly to the Supreme Court "from a final decree rendered by a district court granting an injunction and restraining enforcement of a state statute or regulation."[125] In his statement of the facts in the majority opinion in *Barnette* Justice Robert Jackson also noted that Jehovah's Witness

---

[121] Ibid., 628-629.

[122] Ibid., 629.

[123] Philip B. Kurland and Gerhard Casper, eds., *Landmark Briefs and Arguments of the Supreme Court of the United States: Constitutional Law- West Virginia State Board of Education v. Barnette*, (Arlington, VA: University Publications of America, Inc., 1975), 40:51, 57.

[124] Ibid., 62.

[125] Ibid., 52.

children had been expelled from school based on these laws alone, "threatened with exclusion" and that some state officials had warned that they would "send them to reformatories maintained for criminally inclined juveniles."[126] Also, some parents had been prosecuted or warned of criminal proceedings for the delinquency of their kids from school.

Much had changed in the climate on the Supreme Court since the 8-1 decision in *Gobitis* in 1940 when Frankfurter authored the majority opinion. In *Barnette* Justices Hugo Black, Frank Murphy, and William O. Douglas all switched their votes to join the 6-3 majority opinion, which ruled this time in favor of the Jehovah's Witnesses, though the decision was based primarily on the Free Speech Clause of the First Amendment.[127] Some commentators attribute these switched votes to personal characteristics of Frankfurter, which annoyed his peers and others to the persecution of Jehovah's Witnesses after *Gobitis*, which shocked the conscience of liberals both on and off of the Supreme Court.[128]

In spite of all the clamor and reactionary criticism of the *Gobitis* majority opinion in the press and scholarly legal circles, Frankfurter nonetheless held his ground.[129] He issued a personal dissent in the *Barnette* case which Richard Danzig called his *"cri de Coeur."*[130] Its

---

[126] *Barnette*, 319 U.S. at 630.

[127] Urofsky, *Judicial Restraint and Individual Liberties*, 56f and Danzig, *Blending Logic and Psychologic*, 711.

[128] Urofsky, *Judicial Restraint and Individual Liberties*, 50, 52; Harold L. Ickes, *The Secret Diaries of Harold L. Ickes* (New York: Simon & Schuster, 1954), 3:199, 211; Danzig, *Blending Logic and Psychologic*, 711, 722.

[129] *West Virginia State Board of Education v. Barnette*, 319 U.S. 624, 646 (1943)(FRANKFURTER, J., dissenting.)

[130] Danzig, *Logic and Psychologic*, 711. Danzig and Urofsky both provide documentation for the seriousness with which Frankfurter approached the *Barnette* dissent. Ibid. Urofsky, *Judicial Restraint and Individual Liberties*, 57 where he points out that Frankfurter sent copies of the dissenting opinion to former Chief Justice Charles Evans Hughes and President Franklin D. Roosevelt as well as friends in the press at the New Republic and the Boston

first paragraph is a combination of personal appeal, and a repetition of his reasoning in favor of judicial passivity and restraint. He begins by writing:

> One who belongs to the most vilified and persecuted minority in history is not likely to be insensible to the freedoms guaranteed by our Constitution. Were my purely personal attitude relevant I should wholeheartedly associated myself with the general libertarian views in the Court's opinion, representing as they do the thought and action of a lifetime.[131]

Yet, he continued, justices on the Supreme Court who are ostensibly committed to impartiality cannot allow their religious biases, whether Jewish, Gentile, Catholic, or agnostic to affect their jurisprudence. Rather, they are to achieve a form of detached, rational objectivity, which cabins the influence of personal presuppositions as if they were priests in a monastery immune to the pressures of the world. "As a member of this Court," he emphasized, "I am not justified in writing my private notions of policy into the Constitution, no matter how deeply I may cherish them or how mischievous I may deem their disregard. The duty of a judge who must decide which of two claims before the Court shall prevail, that of a State to enact and enforce laws within its general competence or that of an individual to refuse obedience because of the demands of his conscience, is not that of the ordinary person."[132]

The remainder of the opinion is a sustained, lengthy argument in favor of judicial restraint when the Court is reviewing the constitutionality of legislation and the legislation is question indirectly affects civil rights. He repeatedly quoted James Thayer's views on judicial restraint in support of the notion that the framers of the Constitution would not have favored a higher level of judicial review for laws which impacted civil rights only indirectly, such as the flag

---

Herald emphasizing that judicial dignitaries including retired Justice Louis Brandeis and Judge Learned Hand agreed with him on the *Gobitis* case.

[131] *Barnette*, 319 U.S. at 646-647.

[132] Ibid., 647.

salute laws and regulations.[133]   To do otherwise, he contended, would both endanger the Court's power of judicial review by creating animosity in the other branches of government, and entangle Courts in decisions better made in an open and free democracy by legislatures. Moreover, he reiterated in the opinion his strong belief that courts need to grant legislatures broad parameters within which to experiment and make mistakes, even if these mistakes infringe indirectly on civil liberties, because this is the healthiest form of democracy. Otherwise, he stressed, citizens will become complacent and lazy, and legislatures will abdicate their proper roles as the appropriate arbitrators of the values and wisdom of legislation.[134]

Moreover, the opinion stressed, if courts apply a high degree of scrutiny to all legislation, which somehow impacts private judgment, or "conscientious scruples" this will lead to bad consequences. Courts might then second guess all kinds of necessary legislation, such as tax laws, and usurp the legislature's role by creating accommodations for sects which may or may not be reasonable depending on one's opinion, and the opinions of judges regarding the validity of any given religion are no more or less valuable in a democracy than those of legislators. Too, he maintained, courts would then be in the business of evaluating the sincerity of a multitude of variant faiths in America and this would undermine the very same values of religious liberty, which the First Amendment sought to protect.[135]   Plus, judicial accommodation of conscientious scruples would lead to various kinds of exemptions from laws which "may disrupt society," in violation of what the founders of the United States intended.[136]   At this point in the opinion he referred to the writings of the "great exponents of religious freedom" Thomas Jefferson, James Madison, John Adams, and Benjamin Franklin and then stipulated their authority for the general principle that:

> So far as the state was concerned, there was to be neither orthodoxy nor heterodoxy. And so Jefferson and those who

---

[133] Ibid., 653, 667-668, 670-671.

[134] Ibid., 651-652.

[135] Ibid., 658-659.

[136] Ibid., 653f.

followed him wrote guaranties of religious freedom into our constitutions. Religious minorities as well as religious majorities were to be equal in the eyes of the political state. But Jefferson and the others also knew that minorities might disrupt society. It never would have occurred to them to write into the Constitution the subordination of the general civil authority of the state to sectarian scruples.[137]

The core of Frankfurter's opinion, just as in *Gobitis*, came from his view that the American democratic process was open and free to all citizens, including representatives of minority faiths such as the Jehovah's Witnesses. Therefore, the proper remedy for infringement of their consciences by laws of a state such as the flag salute laws in Pennsylvania and West Virginia would be to seek and achieve legislative change. The Jehovah's Witnesses could achieve recognition of their religious freedom in the legislative process, according to Frankfurter, if their merited protection and success there.[138] There was, for Felix Frankfurter, a free market for ideas in America. This belief was central to his conclusions in the case, and central to his view of judicial restraint, which serves as an important aspect of his reasoning in both flag salute cases.

The treatment of Jehovah's Witnesses in the context of World War II and the *Gobitis* and *Barnette* cases, however, raises questions for some commentators about the faith in American democracy, which Felix Frankfurter had. If the Jehovah's Witnesses had not been able to seek judicial remedies at the time for denial of their free exercise rights would they have really been able to find sympathy or a legal remedy in the legislatures of Pennsylvania, West Virginia, or another state such as Mississippi?[139]

---

[137] Ibid.

[138] Danzig, *Logic and Psychologic*, 691-693.

[139] Shawn F. Peters, *Judging Jehovah's Witnesses: Religious Persecution and the Dawn of the Rights Revolution* (Lawrence, KS: The University Press of Kansas, 2000), 187-202 documents the legally sanctioned persecution of Jehovah's Witnesses in Mississippi via a state law intended to maintain "peace and safety" during the 1940s. Jehovah's Witnesses in that state tried unsuccessfully to gain relief for their religious liberty interests in the state

Frankfurter, however, stressed in *Gobitis* and *Barnette* that courts alone cannot cultivate and protect the "liberal spirit" "by judicial invalidation of illiberal education," and refused to concede that his commitment to judicial restraint equated to judicial abdication of protection for the rights of religious minorities.[140] While Frankfurter maintained in *Gobitis* and *Barnette* that the Supreme Court should not serve as a "super-legislature" or a school board for the nation, he did not always act passively when reviewing laws challenged pursuant to the First Amendment.[141] This is demonstrated when one examines the lack of deference he gave to legislatures in Establishment Clause cases which this book will now consider.

---

executive, legislative, and judicial branches of government. According to the account, their only remedy was in federal court.

[140] Ibid., 670.

[141] Ibid., 648.

Chapter 4

American Public Religion: Frankfurter's No Establishment Cases

A review of Establishment Clause cases, which Frankfurter participated in, reveals a consistent "separationist" position therein.[1] In these cases he rejected laws of legislative branches, which diminished the strict separation of church and state. His explanations for these exceptions to his general insistence on judicial passivity include his expressed opposition to absolutism or formulaic abstractions,[2] even an unqualified

---

[1] Helen Thomas and other commentators have noticed that Frankfurter's adherence to judicial restraint toward legislatures was absent in Establishment Clause cases. Thomas, *Scholar on the Bench*, 62-64; Urofsky, *Judicial Restraint and Individual Liberties*, 165f; Hockett, *New Deal Justice*, 202-204; and Silverstein, *Constitutional Faiths*, 148-149.

[2] Aleaxander Bickel, "Applied Politics and the Science of Law: Writings of the Harvard Period," in *Felix Frankfurter: A Tribute*, ed. Wallace Mendelson (New York: Reynal & Company, 1964), 187 stresses that Frankfurter consistently expressed an "abhorrence of absolutes," especially in civil rights cases. He quotes Frankfurter as saying, "absolute is the most false and the most odious of words. Ibid. Also, Bickel points out yet again the influence of Holmes's skepticism in the conviction that Frankfurter attributed to Holmes: "that our constitutional system rests on tolerance and that its greatest enemy is the Absolute." Ibid. Frankfurter's hypocrisy and

commitment to judicial restraint; the meaning of the Establishment Clause's text and history; and that these Establishment Clause cases involved legislation which did not have a rational basis for its constitutionality. [3] For these reasons Frankfurter voted to find Establishment Clause violations or authored opinions finding that the clause had been violated in all the Establishment Clause cases he participated in except for *McGowan v. Maryland*, 366 U.S. 420 (1961). Thus, he developed an overall approach to the religion clauses from which some scholars inferred that he opposed alternatives to the national "cohesive sentiment" expressed by the mandatory flag salute ceremony in *Gobitis*.[4]

The first Establishment Clause case that came before the Supreme Court during his tenure was the case of *Everson v. Board of Education*, 330 U.S. 1 (1947). In *Everson* a New Jersey taxpayer named Arch R. Everson challenged the constitutionality of an Ewing Township resolution and a New Jersey statute, which combined to authorize reimbursement payments to parents for the cost of transport to parochial schools. Approximately $357.74 was paid to parents of pupils transported to these Roman Catholic schools in Trenton, New Jersey, and religious courses were taught at the schools. Additionally, a Roman Catholic priest served as Superintendent of the schools. Generally, Everson believed that the laws violated the Establishment Clause of the First Amendment, the Due Process Clause of the Fourteenth Amendment, and the New Jersey Constitution.[5]

---

inconsistency here is unmistakable in light of the contradiction between the flag salute cases and his Establishment clause views.

[3] In an interesting article by one of Frankfurter's former law clerk's Joseph L. Rauh, Jr., "Felix Frankfurter: Civil Libertarian," *11 Harv. Civ. Rts.-Civ. Liberties L. Rev. 496, 504* (1976) Rauh dismisses Frankfurter's adherence to judicial restraint as merely one tool in his toolbox for jurisprudence, which he used when it suited him. Too, Rauh makes the case that Frankfurter's opinion in *Gobitis* was driven by his personal dislike for the Jehovah's Witnesses.

[4] Bickel, *Applied Politics*, 187.

[5] Philip B. Kurland and Gerhard Casper, eds., *Landmark Briefs and Arguments of the Supreme Court of the United States: Constitutional Law-Everson v.*

In the New Jersey Supreme Court Everson prevailed, but the New Jersey Court of Errors and Appeals reversed this ruling and found in favor of the Board of Education. Everson then appealed directly to the United States Supreme Court since the New Jersey Court of Errors and Appeals was the highest state court in New Jersey. Significantly, amicus curiae briefs were filed in *Everson* by: the American Civil Liberties Union, the Commonwealth of Massachusetts, the General Conference of Seventh-Day Adventists, the National Councils of Catholic Men and Women, and the state of New York. A comparison of the briefs submitted on appeal by the American Civil Liberties Union and by counsel for appellant Everson reveals that Everson's attorneys did not emphasize the history of the Establishment Clause whereas the ACLU amicus curiae brief did. As will be shown herein below eight members of the Supreme Court would essentially adopt the historical "separationist" interpretation of the ACLU in the *Everson* case, especially the version articulated at length in Rutledge's dissent, even though they divided 5-4 over how to apply this history to the specific facts of the case.[6] This historical account in Rutledge's opinion looked almost exclusively to the thought of Thomas Jefferson and James Madison for its account of the founders' views on the separation of church and state.[7]

Frankfurter did not write an opinion in *Everson* but he did specifically join the dissenting opinions of Justices Robert Jackson and Wiley Rutledge. Both dissents interpreted the Establishment Clause in favor of Everson's claim that tax subsidies to parochial schools violated the strict separation of church and state. Rutledge's opinion, as noted above, has a lengthy articulation of the "separationist" history behind the Establishment Clause which emphasizes the Virginia struggle to disestablish the Anglican Church and James Madison's *Memorial and Remonstrance*, whereas Jackson's opinion criticizes the majority

---

Board of Education, (Arlington, VA: University Publications of America, Inc., 1975), 44:692-693.

[6] Compare "Brief of American Civil Liberties Union as Amicus Curiae," in *Landmark Briefs-Everson*, eds. Kurland and Gasper, 849-862 and the Rutledge dissent in *Everson*, 330 U.S. at 28-74.

[7] *Everson*, 330 U.S. at 34-38.

opinion of Hugo Black in memorable fashion for stating the strict separationist position in principle, but then immediately violating it in the Court's decision. Black's majority opinion contained language stating in expansive and strong terms that church and state should remain strictly separate at the levels of federal and state government. He wrote for the Court's majority that:

> Neither a state nor the Federal Government can set up a church. Neither can pass laws which aid one religion, aid all religions, or prefer one religion over another.[8]

Both dissenting opinions Rutledge and Jackson also formulated versions of the "separationist" view, which are grounded in the history of the founding era, and Frankfurter joined both.

Jackson's dissenting opinion comes first in the official Supreme Court reports. In it he notes that the actual cost to the taxpayers of New Jersey was minimal in the case. Yet, he adds that the principles involved are substantial.[9] Even though he concedes that American public education was essentially a product of Protestantism, and that claims to strict and lofty neutrality with regard to religion in public education are dubious, Jackson joins in Rutledge's historical and principled conclusions that church and state shall remain strictly separate.[10] He further adds that church and state separation as required by the Establishment Clause forbids the government from spending money to "secure religion against skepticism."[11]

Next, Jackson articulated the viewpoint, also evident in the *Barnette* majority opinion, which he authored, that the freedoms protected by the provisions of the First Amendment including religion are "preferred" and therefore deserve special protection from the courts.[12] Not only did he stress the importance of the First

---

[8] Ibid., 15.

[9] Ibid., at 19-20.

[10] Ibid., 24-26.

[11] Ibid., 25.

[12] Ibid., 26.

Amendment, but he also emphasized the primary importance of religion. "This freedom was the first in the Bill of Rights," he wrote, "because it was first in the forefathers' minds; it was set forth in absolute terms, and its strength is its rigidity."[13] At this point it is notable that Frankfurter did not follow a preferred freedom approach to the First Amendment Free Exercise Clause in *Gobitis* or *Barnette*, and yet he did not object to this portion of Jackson's opinion, which he joined. Moreover, Frankfurter did not dissent from the majority opinion's "incorporation" of the Establishment Clause as to the states in *Everson* even though he carried on a sustained and sometimes bitter debate with Hugo Black about the issue of incorporation of the Bill of Rights via the Due Process Clause of the Fourteenth Amendment.[14]

In the remainder of his dissenting opinion Jackson spelled out in fairly systematic fashion what he considered to be the intent of the separation of church and state as the principle is found in the sixteen words of the First Amendment, "Congress shall make no law respecting an establishment of religion, or prohibiting the free exercise thereof . . . ."[15] First, according to Jackson, these words were intended to prevent conflict and controversy in public life over religion. Secondly, the Establishment Clause had the purpose of preventing the state from interfering with religious liberty by means of onerous regulation of schools or religious institutions. He put it this way:

---

[13] Ibid.

[14] Ibid., 15 where Justice Black's opinion for the majority in *Everson* incorporates the Establishment Clause. For two different accounts of the debate between Frankfurter and Black over incorporation see Wallace Mendelson, *Justices Black and Frankfurter: Conflict in the Court* (Chicago: University of Chicago Press, 1961) and Mark Silverstein, *Constitutional Faiths: Felix Frankfurter, Hugo Black, and the Process of Judicial Decision-Making* (Ithaca, NY: Cornell University Press, 1984). Both justices wrote opinions in the case of *Adamson v. California*, 332 U.S. 46 (1947) on the issue and Frankfurter published an article on the debate entitled, "Memorandum on the 'Incorporation' of the Bill of Rights into the Due Process Clause of the Fourteenth Amendment," *78 Harv. L. Rev. 746, 746-783* (1965).

[15] United States Constitution, Amendment I.

> If the state may aid these religious schools, it may therefore
> regulate them.[16]

Furthermore, he pointed out, once the state provides funding for religious activities or practices it is not then a violation of due process for the state to regulate what it has subsidized.[17]

In the conclusion of his opinion Jackson then turned his attention to the majority opinion of Black, which had relied on the same history for the intent of the Establishment Clause that is found in Rutledge's dissent, but then voted to allow the aid to parochial school parents.[18] He implicitly chastised Black and the majority for giving in to public opinion in favor of parochial schools when he wrote, "[the] great purposes of the Constitution do not depend on the approval or the convenience of those they restrain."[19] Instead of clearly setting down the constitutional principle of strict separation and then applying it straightforwardly, the Court had taken several steps back and possibly forever damaged the effort in American life "to separate political from ecclesiastical affairs."[20] As he observed earlier in the opinion:

> In fact, the undertones of the [majority] opinion, advocating
> complete and uncompromising separation of Church from
> State, seem utterly discordant with its conclusion yielding
> support to their commingling in educational matters. The case
> which irresistibly comes to mind as the most fitting precedent
> is that of Julia who, according to Byron's reports, "whispering
> 'I will ne'er consent,'—consented.[21]

---

[16] Ibid., 27.

[17] Ibid., 28.

[18] The portion of Black's majority opinion which is dedicated to examining the history and tradition behind the Establishment Clause is found at *Everson*, 330 U.S. at 11-14.

[19] Ibid., 28.

[20] Ibid.

[21] Ibid., 19.

Rutledge's dissent, also joined by Frankfurter in *Everson*, was much longer and contains a prolonged account of the historical struggle for religious liberty in the colonies that eventually became the United States. The opinion pays special attention to the efforts of James Madison and Thomas Jefferson to disestablish the Anglican Church in Virginia.[22] Rutledge argued that the facts of the case demanded that the Court determine the meaning of the Establishment Clause. He found the meaning of the broad and general language in the clause perspicuous. It meant simply that the First Amendment prescribed the strict separation of church and state.[23] Moreover, Rutledge asserted that Madison was the author of the clause and the key figure in the development of the clause's substantive meaning, therefore interpreters of the Establishment Clause needed to consult Madison's writings to discern its meaning. He found its requirement of separation "complete and permanent" writing, "The prohibition broadly forbids state support, financial or other, of religion in any guise, form or degree. It outlaws all use of public funds for religious purposes."[24]

Next, Rutledge shifted the focus of his opinion to a historical investigation of the Establishment Clause, arguing that no constitutional provision is more closely tied to "its governing history" than the Establishment Clause of the First Amendment. In the Virginia struggle against the Anglican establishment of the eighteenth century led by Jefferson and Madison he discerned "irrefutable confirmation of the Amendment's sweeping content."[25] He found that the Virginia Declaration of Rights of 1776 and James Madison's *Memorial and Remonstrance Against Religious Assessments* contained Madison's definitive views on disestablishment, and thus the formative meaning of the religion clauses.[26]

---

[22] *Everson,* 330 U.S. at 28-74, especially 34-38 regarding the Virginia struggle.

[23] Ibid., 29.

[24] Ibid., 33.

[25] Ibid., 34.

[26] Ibid., 37.

In addition, Madison opposed "every form and degree of official relation between religion and civil authority."[27] This then led to his articulation of the general notion that religion's influence on the "general welfare" of the nation or the virtue of the people was to come purely and solely from the private sphere. Therefore, the judiciary and the legislatures had no competence to handle or decide religious issues or to prescribe religious truth or virtue. Moreover, Rutledge agreed with Jackson's assertion, which Frankfurter would emphasize again in his *McCollum*, 333 U.S. 203 (1948) and *Zorach v. Clauson*, 343 U.S. 307 (1952) opinions that the public policy behind the religion clauses was to prevent social conflict, and thus implicitly to promote tolerance in the public square. This final element of the Rutledge-Jackson view of strict separation is consistent with Frankfurter's commitment to civil tolerance, and criticism of absolutes or rigid principles.[28]

Rutledge finished his opinion in *Everson* by appealing to the concept of "neutrality" toward religion implied in the religion clauses. He interpreted neutrality in the religion clauses to neither connote nor imply that government must subsidize private education at parochial schools. He conceded that this placed those who sent their children to private schools at a relative disadvantage economically, but he insisted that strict separation demanded the refusal to provide funding as the only mechanism to insure the state's neutral position with regard to sectarian requests for public funds.[29] His last paragraph appealed to church and state separation in principle, warned against commingling church and state in public schools, and alluded one more time to the influence of James Madison by restating his admonition that citizens should raise the alarm upon the "first experiment upon our liberties."[30] He cautioned his peers on the Court that they needed to "keep the question from becoming entangled in corrosive precedents."[31]

---

[27] Ibid., 39.

[28] Ibid., 54.

[29] Ibid., 59.

[30] Ibid., 63.

[31] Ibid.

All of the Supreme Court opinions in *Everson v. Board of Education* are written from the "separationist" perspective. Justices Black, Jackson, and Rutledge all refer to the history of the religion clauses as important to understanding the intent behind the broad and general language of the two clauses. In addition, all three grant a special place to the influence of the Virginia struggle to disestablish Anglicanism, and especially to the Madisonian view of establishments as found in his *Memorial and Remonstrance*. Yet, Black wrote in the official majority opinion for the Court that it was not unconstitutional to uphold the de minimis payment of public funds to parochial schools under the facts of *Everson*. Jackson and Rutledge, on the other hand, agreed with Black in principle, but disagreed with how Black failed to adhere to the very principle of strict separation of church and state he had just explicated. Both warned that Black opened Pandora's box by qualifying the principle with a "corrosive precedent," and Frankfurter agreed with them both by joining their dissenting opinions. In three subsequent Establishment Clause cases Frankfurter further clarified his agreement with the view that the religion clauses demanded strict separation.

McCollum v. Board of Education, 333 U.S. 203 (1948) involved a released time program in the public schools of Champaign County, Illinois. The Illinois compulsory education law required children aged 7 to 16 to go to public schools at the times when the schools were in regular session. Children of parents who signed "request cards" were authorized to go to religion classes during the regular school day at public schools. The Superintendent of Schools provided oversight and "approval" for the selection of teachers, which a council of religious advisers proffered to schools for consideration. The teachers in the program came from a range of different religious perspectives.[32] Violations of the law were legal misdemeanors, and the punishment included potential fines with the exception that children could comply with the law by attending private or parochial schools in compliance

---

[32] *McCollum v. Board of Education*, 333 U.S. 203, 92 L. Ed. 649, 649 (1948), some of the information regarding the facts of *McCollum* in this paragraph come from the case "SUMMARY" in the Lawyer's Edition publication of the case.

with state guidelines. Illinois law in force at the time gave supervisory authority to district boards of education for each school district.[33]

Vashti McCollum, a taxpayer residing in Champaign who sent her child to Champaign public schools filed a lawsuit based upon her status as a taxpayer seeking a mandamus order from a state court, which would force the termination of all religious teaching in "all public schools in Champaign School District Number 71."[34] The released time program in question allowed the selected religious teachers to be paid by "private religious groups." The classes were during school hours, and the outside religious teachers provided instruction about religion for 30 minutes instead of the material normally scheduled according to the mandatory public school curriculum. McCollum complained in her suit that the program violated both the First and Fourteenth Amendments to the Constitution, and therefore she asked the courts to grant a writ of mandamus ordering that the school district discontinue the program and forbid any type of religious indoctrination "in all public school houses and buildings in said district when occupied by public schools."[35]

Both Illinois state courts, including the Illinois Supreme Court, which considered the case ruled against McCollum, and she appealed to the United States Supreme Court. Amicus Briefs were filed on appeal by the Synagogue Council of America, the American Civil Liberties Union, the American Ethical Union, the Joint Conference Committee Public Relations of several Baptist conventions, the American Unitarian Association, the General Conference of Seventh Day Adventists, the Attorney General of Illinois, and the Protestant Council of New York City. The Illinois Attorney General's brief was the only amicus brief in support of the released time program. The Supreme Court's majority opinion by Hugo Black found in favor of McCollum and decided that the Illinois released time program was unconstitutional pursuant to the Due Process Clause of the Fourteenth Amendment and the Establishment Clause of the First Amendment. The Court's vote in the *McCollum* case was 8-1, and Justice Reed issued a strongly dissent

---

[33] *McCollum*, 333 U.S. at 205 (1948).

[34] Ibid.

[35] Ibid.

writing that the Court was moving too far in the direction of mandating hostility to religion in the public square. Frankfurter voted with Black and the majority against the permissibility of the released time program, except in this case he decided to write a concurring opinion.

The concurring opinion of Frankfurter in *McCollum v. Board of Education* was his first Establishment Clause opinion wherein his usual deference to the legislative branch of government is not evident. He expressed concern that social conflict could result from the released time program, and this qualified his commitment to judicial review in this instance. The majority applied a "separationist" interpretation of the Establishment Clause in *McCollum* and Frankfurter agreed with this interpretation, but he wrote separately to reemphasize his view of the important role of public schools with regard to American public values.

His concurrence restated his conviction that the Constitution absolutely "forbids" the mixing of religious and secular teaching in public schools.[36] Next, he argued that a proper judicial analysis of the Illinois released time program should begin with careful review of the "historic setting of religious education in America."[37] He traced the evolution of education in America from its roots in religious education in Massachusetts in the 1640s to the modern secular public schools of the 1940s that had a philosophy derived from the First Amendment's view of freedom.[38] James Madison's *Memorial and Remonstrance* emerged from the struggle over religious freedom, he noted, and he referred to the history of common schools in New York and Massachusetts as proof for a trajectory toward purely secular public education in America. According to Frankfurter's account of the common schools, persons such as Horace Mann worked diligently in Massachusetts to remove "sectarian teachings" from the "common school to save it from being rent by denominational conflict."[39] The result of this trajectory, Frankfurter submitted, was the American people eventually chose the separation of religious and secular

---

[36] *McCollum*, 333 U.S. at 212.

[37] Ibid., 213.

[38] Ibid., 214.

[39] Ibid., 214-215.

instruction as their "guiding principle, in law and feeling."[40] Moreover, Frankfurter concluded that this principle of separation was grounded in "the whole experience of our people."[41]

He also claimed that the principle of separation in public schools was grounded in America's religious heterogeneity, and contrasted this diversity with the homogeneity of England. Yet, in his references to the influences of James Madison and Horace Mann in the development of the trajectory toward separation in public education Frankfurter did not point out that these public schools were also grounded in a world view which was essentially Protestant.[42]

Nonetheless, Frankfurter's concurring opinion held that the Establishment Clause's formative history and its development afterwards demanded exclusion of sectarian teaching from public schools as the remedy for conflict over religion in the schools, just as Jackson and Rutledge had in their *Everson* dissents.[43] He argued against Reed's notion that "secular" public schools implied hostility or indifference toward religion, or a secularist agenda. To the contrary, he saw the public school as "perhaps the most powerful agency for promoting cohesion among a heterogeneous democratic people," and pled the "the public school must be kept scrupulously free from entanglement in the life of sects."[44] The insistence on separation in this manner would prevent conflict which threatened unity in the political community leading Frankfurter also to conclude that religious instruction is a matter best left to the private spheres of the individual citizen both at church and at home.[45]

---

[40] Ibid., 215.

[41] Ibid.

[42] James Davison Hunter, "Religious Freedom and the Challenge of Modern Pluralism," in *Articles of Faith, Articles of Peace: The Religious Liberty Clauses and the American Public Philosophy*, eds. James Davison Hunter and Os Guinness (Washington, D.C.: Brookings Institution Press, 1990), 55f.

[43] Ibid., 216.

[44] Ibid., 216-217.

[45] Ibid., 217.

The importance of public schools as the "symbol" of American unity and cohesion was so important to Frankfurter because he considered their "secular unity" a profound achievement which only occurred after a long tortuous struggle.[46] Also, it is not impossible to see Frankfurter's personal experience of success in the public schools of New York City behind his strong belief expressed in the opinion that these same public schools serve as guarantors of the rights minority groups. If the secular unity of the schools is endangered by sectarian strife, he worried, then the rights of minorities would suffer as well. In *McCollum* he characterized minority religious interests as shifting and changing from time to time, but as also symbolizing the "common interest of the nation" in their "totality."[47] The means to protect these minority groups, he wrote, was to maintain the secular nature of public schools pursuant to the Establishment Clause.

Frankfurter also cited the history of state statutes known as Blaine Amendments with approval as additional evidence that by the end of the nineteenth century Americans desired school systems "free from sectarian control."[48] The history of religious released time programs, which he traced in the opinion originated in an Interfaith Conference on Federation in New York City in 1905.[49] He then reasoned that these early programs were not intended to change the secular functions of public schools, but rather to make up for time lost in religious training while religious students attended public schools. They did not occur on public school campuses and did not use public resources, but were privately funded. According to his historical account, these programs struggled financially at first, but eventually began to grow thus creating the increasingly felt need for religious instruction at public schools to facilitate proper education in religious values and virtue. The growing size and influence of the released time movement in turn led to the

---

[46] Ibid.

[47] Ibid.

[48] Ibid., 220, n. 9 where he stresses that all states admitted to the union after 1876 required secular public schools including, North and South Dakota, Montana, Washington, Utah, Oklahoma, New Mexico, Arizona, Wyoming, and Idaho.

[49] Ibid., 221f.

constitutional dilemma posed by the specific released time program in Champaign County, Illinois, where an "ominous breach in the wall of separation" was evident to Frankfurter.[50]

The reasons he gave for finding the Champaign program unconstitutional included, first of all, his finding that the school superintendent had too much control over the program. This led to unconstitutional and inherent government coercion in religious matters within the public school system. Secondly, there was pressure on students to attend the religious instruction provided, but not all sects could participate in the process. This amounted to an unfair, selective, and biased program whereby some children were unfairly excluded from the process without justification.[51] The unambiguous signal this sent to religious minorities or nonreligious students who did not participate was that their membership in the political community counted for less than those who did participate.

In addition, the program represented to him a step backwards toward religious favoritism and more divisive religious conflict. Public schools, for him, were intended to prevent this kind of religious conflict, and to serve the positive purpose of creating unity and common values amidst religious diversity. The released time program in Illinois corrupted the public schools as "training ground[s] for habits of community" important to Frankfurter under the Establishment Clause, and forced impressionable children to accept training in religious beliefs which their parents opposed.[52]

He did not insist that all released time programs were unconstitutionally divisive or coercive, and allowed that some may pass muster with different facts. Yet, he once again relied upon the views of the founder Thomas Jefferson by citing his metaphor of a "wall of separation" between church and state, and insisted that: "Separation means separation, not something less."[53] Moreover, he cautioned that this wall of separation should not amount to "a fine line easily

---

[50] Ibid., 225.

[51] Ibid., 227.

[52] Ibid., 228.

[53] Ibid., 231.

overstepped."[54] Reiterating the importance of public schools as centers for training in cohesive sentiment not weakened by sectarian divisiveness he wrote:

> The public school is at once the symbol of our democracy and the most pervasive means for promoting our common destiny. In no activity of the State is it more vital to keep out divisive forces than in its schools, to avoid confusing, not to say fusing, what the Constitution sought to keep strictly apart.[55]

In other words, for Frankfurter the public school served as an institutional guarantor of secular values and a form of secular unity, and the principle of the separation of church and state spelled out in his opinion accomplished this purpose in keeping with the Establishment Clause. He wrote at the end of the opinion, "It is the Court's duty to enforce this principle in its full integrity," and in the realm of church state relations, "good fences make good neighbors."[56]

Establishment Clause cases, then, required a different kind of judicial scrutiny according to Frankfurter to protect the public schools from religious divisiveness, and he reasoned in his *McCollum* opinion that the history behind the Establishment Clause supported this analysis. Whereas Frankfurter had demonstrated a lower level of scrutiny in reference to the claims of Jehovah's Witnesses in the *Gobitis* and *Barnette* free exercise cases, he shifted to a more aggressive form of scrutiny in the Establishment Clause cases *Everson* and *McCollum*.

This is established further in another case surrounding religious teaching and public schools in *Zorach v. Clauson*, 343 U.S. 307 (1952). In *Zorach* New York City had developed a released time program similar in some ways to the program challenged by Vashti McCollum in Illinois. It was in public schools and allowed students to attend religious classes during school if their parents provided written authorization. The classes, however, were given off of school premises

---

[54] Ibid.

[55] Ibid.

[56] Ibid., 231-232.

in this case, and all expenses for the religious classes were paid by the religious institutions involved. Those students who refused to participate in the program of religious education remained on campus and went to their regularly scheduled classes. Religious institutions also submitted required attendance reports that notified the school authorities about students who had been absent from the religion classes after release from school pursuant to the program.[57]

New York City drafted the New York Education Law so that parents and students were responsible for registering for the instruction, and for insuring that their school authorities had a copy of the registration documents. The weekly attendance reports had to be filed with the principal or a teacher, and the law also stipulated that "Only one hour a week is to be allowed for such training, at the end of a class session, and where more than one religious school is conducted, the hour of release shall be the same for all religious schools."[58] Additionally, the public schools in question could not announce the programs in any form, and teachers and administrators were prohibited from mentioning who participated in the program or what their attendance record was.

Taxpayers in the city with children in the public schools challenged the laws enabling the program for the same basic reasons Vashti McCollum had in Illinois. They submitted that these laws placed the institutional authority of the school as a government institution on the side of religious teaching. Also, they argued that the laws enmeshed public school teachers in the activities of private religious schools through monitoring of students participating in the religious instruction. Then, the opponents of the program asserted that it disrupted the public school's classes when the students in the program asserted that it disrupted the public school's classes when the students in the program got up to leave, and the churches had unconstitutionally used the public schools by making them a "crutch on which the churches are leaning for support in their religious training."[59] All of these elements combined together to make the released time

---

[57] *Zorach,* 343 U.S. at 308.

[58] Ibid., n. 1(b).

[59] Ibid., 309-310.

program unconstitutional pursuant to the religion clauses according to Tessim Zorach and Esta Gluck who had instigated the lawsuit against the New York City Board of Education. The sole issue the majority opinion by Justice William O. Douglas considered was:

> Whether New York by this system had either prohibited the "free exercise" of religion or has made a law "respecting an establishment of religion" within the meaning of the First Amendment.[60]

Douglas and a six member majority of Court ruled in favor of the New York program contrary to the precedent established in the *McCollum* case by distinguishing the cases on factual grounds. The majority could not find the same kind of coercion present in this case which was so determinative in *McCollum,* and the Douglas opinion referred to the doctrine of strict separation announced by the Court in *Everson* while denying that this meant separation "in every and all respects."[61] In addition, Douglas authored the following language in the case:

> We are a religious people whose institutions presuppose a Supreme Being. We guarantee the freedom to worship as one chooses. We make room for as wide a variety of beliefs and creeds as the spiritual needs of man deem necessary. We sponsor an attitude on the part of government that shows no partiality to any one group and that lets each flourish according to the zeal of its adherents and the appeal of its dogma. When the state encourages religious instruction or cooperates with religious authorities by adjusting the schedule of public events to sectarian needs, it follows the best of our traditions.[62]

Frankfurter, in dissent, found unconstitutional coercion and chastised the majority for failing to see the connections between this

---

[60] Ibid., 310.

[61] Ibid., 312.

[62] Ibid., 313-314.

case and *McCollum*.[63] He agreed with the dissenting opinion of his colleague Robert Jackson, and objected in his opinion that formal religious instruction replaced secular instruction in the New York City public schools. The schools and the school board, as agents of the government, effectively forced parents to place their children in these programs due to the pressure to conform or suffer the stigma of exclusion.[64] Therefore the New York program was as unconstitutional as the Illinois one, and the Supreme Court had in his view again failed in an Establishment Clause case to uphold separationist principles.

Frankfurter once again reasoned that use of public schools to offer sectarian education during school is "deeply divisive," and this divisiveness could be prevented if such instruction was given after school hours.[65] The insistence that public schools have religious training similar to Sunday school during school, moreover, amounted to an admission of insecurity on the part of those religious adherents who favored the released time programs, in his opinion. If the religion they believed in had merit then it did not need public schools to help it attract adherents and flourish.

Thus, in the *Zorach* case Frankfurter once again argued against the divisive presence of sectarian religious values in a public school setting. He objected to the divisiveness of released time programs, and the threat that they posed to secular school activity. Moreover, he criticized his colleagues for failing to stick to the separationist history and principles announced in *Everson* and *McCollum*.

In summary, then, Frankfurter applied judicial restraint in the free exercise cases *Gobitis* and *Barnette*, but strict judicial scrutiny in Establishment Clause cases including *Everson*, *McCollum*, and *Zorach*. In cases involving both religion clauses he referred to the American founders, especially Thomas Jefferson and James Madison and the Virginia struggle to disestablish the Anglican Church, in order to interpret the language of the First Amendment. He also examined the history behind the religious programs at issue in *McCollum* and

---

[63] *Zorach*, 343 U.S. at 320-323. Justices Black and Jackson also dissented in *Zorach*.

[64] Ibid., 321.

[65] Ibid., 323.

Zorach, and found in both cases that the programs involving religious instruction either during or after public school hours breached the Establishment Clause. His voting record in these religion clause cases supports the conclusion that he applied the Free Exercise Clause weakly, but the Establishment Clause strongly in every case he participated in except the case of *McGowan v. Maryland*, 366 U.S. 420 (1961) and in that case, discussed more fully in chapter seven below, he found a secular rationale for the challenged Sunday closing laws.

The mandatory flag salute ceremonies that Frankfurter found constitutional in *Gobitis* and *Barnette* were secular in nature as well. They did not include references to deity or require the children attending public schools to make theistic affirmations. On the other hand, the ceremonies were analogous to religion in that they promoted a form of cohesive sentiment that binds people together in society according to Frankfurter. Thus, the combination of his free exercise opinions in *Gobitis* and *Barnette* with Frankfurter's strong application of the Establishment Clause in *Everson*, *McCollum*, and *Zorach* distinguishes his religion clause jurisprudence from Scalia's. This is because Scalia has not interpreted the Establishment Clause in the same manner as Frankfurter, but has found some forms of theistic American public religion constitutional. The book will therefore transition to chapters that will examine Scalia's opinions in free exercise and establishment cases before contrasting the religion clause jurisprudences of Frankfurter and Scalia in the final chapter.

CHAPTER 5

American Public Religion and Antonin Scalia

INTRODUCTION

Frankfurter interpreted the First Amendment religion clauses with a methodology that applied the Free Exercise Clause weakly, but the Establishment Clause strongly.   He was, therefore, deferential to government action in free exercise cases, but not establishment cases. In addition, Frankfurter appealed primarily to American founders Thomas Jefferson and James Madison as authority for his interpretation of the religion clauses. Scalia has not interpreted the religion clauses in the same manner as Frankfurter even though he has also appealed to American founders as authority for his interpretation of the religion clauses. Moreover, Scalia has found some theistic forms of American public religion constitutional in religion clause cases whereas Frankfurter did not. The next two chapters will examine the religion clause jurisprudence of Scalia to demonstrate the differences between the religion clause interpretations of Frankfurter and Scalia and to show that they find different types of American public religion constitutional.

Antonin Scalia grew up in Queens, New York, and eventually attended Jesuit-run Saint Francis Xavier Military Academy in Manhattan.   He was valedictorian of his high school class, and continued to excel academically when he matriculated to Georgetown University in Washington, D.C., where he once again became valedictorian in 1957. Subsequent to this the future Supreme Court justice attended law school at Harvard where he proved his intellectual acumen once again graduating with an L.L.B. degree magna cum laude in 1960.[1]

Scholars who have studied Scalia disagree as to which influences from the formative period of his life shaped his jurisprudence the most. It is, of course, speculative to identify, which influences were most important.[2] Nonetheless, one scholar has argued that his jurisprudence was shaped by Roman Catholic influences from his childhood during the early years of the twentieth century before Vatican II.[3] George Kannar has also attributed Scalia's commitment to a textual and originalist interpretation of the Constitution to the lingering anti-Catholicism prevalent in mid-twentieth century America, to his strong education in classical Greek and Latin, and to the tutelage of his father, who was a Professor of Romance Literature at Brooklyn College of the City University of New York.[4] Yet, another commentator, biographer Richard Brisbin, rejected this thesis in favor of the argument that Scalia was more profoundly influenced by the *Legal Process School* which was influential at the Harvard Law School when he studied there in the late 1950s.[5]

---

[1] Richard A. Brisbin, *Justice Antonin Scalia and the Conservative Revival* (Baltimore: The Johns Hopkins University Press, 1997), 11-12.

[2] Gregory O. Nies, "Religious Liberty through the Lens of Textualism and a Living Constitution: The First Amendment Establishment Clause Interpretations of Justices William Brennan, Jr. and Antonin Scalia," (M.A. Thesis, Baylor University, 2006), 111-116.

[3] George Kannar, "The Constitutional Catechism of Antonin Scalia," *99 Yale L.J. 1297, 1308-1317* (1990); and Kannar, "Strenuous Virtues, Virtuous Lives: The Social Vision of Antonin Scalia," *12 Cardozo L. Rev. 1845, 1845-1867* (1991).

[4] Kannar, *Constitutional Catechism*, 1308, 1316 where Kannar wrote: "For him, the importance of literalism was-literally-brought home. Scalia's "deeply religious" immigrant father, Brooklyn College Professor of Romance Literature, S. Eugene Scalia, was a specialist in and strenuous critic of the art of literary translation. Like son, like father: Throughout his career Eugene Scalia believed strongly that, to avoid destroying "what is unique" in reading any text, "literalness . . . is essential.""

[5] Brisbin, *Conservative Revival*, 14.

Some of the legal scholars and prominent lawyers who represented this legal philosophy included Henry Hart, Jr., Albert Sacks, Paul Freund, a law clerk for Frankfurter, Lon Fuller, and Louis Jaffe, who expounded on the earlier scholarship of Frankfurter. Frankfurter produced his contributions to this legal philosophy while on the faculty of Harvard Law School.[6] All of these legal scholars were committed in one form or another to the *Legal Process School*, which reacted to *Legal Realism*. Adherents of *Legal Realism* generally hold "a version of the view that the law is whatever judges say it is, and that legal texts are mere sources of law."[7] Representatives of *Legal Realism* included Jerome Frank, Oliver Wendell Holmes, Jr., and K.N. Llewellyn who all emphasized the influence of a judge's personal predilections upon the outcome of cases.[8]

Representatives of the *Legal Process School*, on the other hand, argued in their scholarship and in their teaching that legal process and procedure deserved emphasis and that the judiciary should maintain a passive stance with regard to social policy, thus leaving the shaping of societal mores to the legislative branch of government.[9] A result of this emphasis on legal process, according to Richard Brisbin, was the judicial philosophy that judges should seek out and apply neutral principles of law in constitutional cases via objective reason and then apply "sustained, disinterested, merciless examination" of these neutral principles to the specific case in question.[10] A further "implication"

---

[6] Ibid., 15.

[7] *Philosophy of Law*, eds. Joel Feinberg and Jules Coleman, 8th ed. (Belmont, CA: Thomson Wadsworth, 2008), 6.

[8] Ibid., 117-133. See esp., Ibid., Oliver Wendell Holmes, Jr., "The Path of the Law," 120-126.

[9] Brisbin, *Conservative Revival*, 15. For a version of this approach to the Constitution which emphasizes process as opposed to normative values in the Constitution, see John Hart Ely, *Democracy and Distrust: A Theory of Judicial Review* (Cambridge, MA: Harvard University Press, 1980). There is an analysis of *Democracy and Distrust* in Abraham and Perry, *Freedom and the Court*, 24.

[10] Brisbin, *Conservative Revival*, 15.

was advocacy of a form of judicial positivism, which held that the law produced by legislatures and interpreted by courts, has no "necessary" connection to any specific ethical theory or substantive moral content, contra natural law theories.[11]

In 1967 Scalia moved to the University of Virginia Law School, where he served as professor of commercial and administrative law and published several articles about legal process, legal expertise, and access to the federal courts.[12] Then, from 1971 until 1976 he entered public service by working for President Richard Nixon and, subsequently, as Assistant Attorney General under President Ford in 1974. He was insulated from the Watergate scandal because he worked for the Administrative Conference of the United States in 1972 when the scandal led to the collapse of the Nixon Administration.[13] Brisbin documented Scalia's first foray into the public debate over Constitutional interpretation, which occurred when he argued against the constitutionality of the legislative veto of federal agency decisions in the 1970s. In this early example of Scalia's view as to proper methodology for interpretation of the Constitution, the future justice relied upon case precedent, James Madison's 1787 notes containing arguments against the legislative veto, the Constitution's text, and his

---

[11] Ibid., 15, 25-29. Brisbin makes an extensive argument at the beginning of his book that Scalia's jurisprudence was shaped more by this school than other influences because *Legal Process* thought was ascendant at Harvard Law School when Scalia attended in the late 1950s. In *Democracy and Distrust* Ely argued that sources of substantive values read into the Constitution by judges including their personal values, natural law, neutral principles, reason, tradition, consensus, or even "social progress" are all problematic. Ely, *Democracy and Distrust*, 43-72. He notes that the Supreme Court used natural law as a rationale for its rulings that women should not serve in the legal profession in the case of *Bradwell v. Illinois*, 16 Wall 130, 141 (1872)(Bradley, J., concurring); and that state segregation laws were constitutional in the case of *Plessy v. Ferguson*, 163 U.S. 537, 544 (1896). Ibid., 51 and 211, n. 43.

[12] Brisbin, *Conservative Revival*, 16-17.

[13] Ibid., 19-21.

view of the separation of powers.[14]   All these sources of authority would later reappear as aspects of Scalia's methodology for interpretation of the Constitution.

Scalia was nomination as an Associate Justice to the United States Supreme Court by President Ronald Reagan in 1986. He had served on the prestigious District of Columbia Circuit Court of Appeals beginning in 1982 before his nomination to the Supreme Court. The Senate confirmed his nomination to the Court in 1986 following confirmation hearings by a vote of 98-0. The groups that opposed the nomination included the National Organization for Women, the Americans with Disabilities Association, the Nation Institute, the National Abortion Rights Action League, and Americans United for the Separation of Church and State. Senator Edward Kennedy expressed reservations about the nomination during floor debate but voted for Scalia, stating that it was "difficult to maintain that Judge Scalia is outside the mainstream."[15]

Scalia also commented during his Senate confirmation hearings on his views regarding the originalism-living constitution debate and the state of the Supreme Court's religion clause jurisprudence. In these comments Scalia signaled his originalist leanings, but the tenor of his testimony related to this debate was somewhat vague and noncommittal.[16] He declared:

> In any case, I start from the original meaning, and I think there is room for dispute as to what extent some of those elements of meaning are evolvable, such as the cruel and unusual punishment clause. The starting point, in any case, is the text of the document and what it meant to the society that adopted it. I think it is part of my whole philosophy, which is essentially a democratic philosophy that even the Constitution is, at bottom, a democratic document.[17]

---

[14] Ibid., 21.

[15] Ibid., 21, 60-62.

[16] Ibid., 182-183, 202.

[17] Ibid., 202.

Senator Paul Simon asked Scalia for his opinion of the Supreme Court's religion clause jurisprudence to date. Scalia replied that he agreed with most commentators who considered the court's jurisprudence in this area muddled and confusing. He stated that there is a "natural conflict between the Establishment Clause and the Freedom-of–Religion Clause."[18] He indicated that he believed both clauses were important but noted that sometimes the creation of a religious accommodation or exception to an otherwise valid law based in the Free Exercise Clause leads to Establishment Clause problems. Senator Simon asked him about a hypothetical free exercise situation where a Jehovah's Witness requested unemployment benefits from the government because the individual would not work on Saturday, which is the Sabbath for Jehovah's Witnesses. The Senator wanted to know whether Scalia thought the Free Exercise Clause required payment of benefits to the Jehovah's Witness making the claim. Scalia responded:

> Well, yes, that does protect freedom of religion, but, on the other hand, doesn't that somehow amount to an establishment of religion to have the State make a special rule to accommodate the religious belief of this sabbatarian?[19]

Then, he concluded that if he were asked to name one area of constitutional law which "is in an unsettled state, I think that that's the one."[20]

Scalia's tenure on the Court has included Free Exercise and Establishment Clause opinions in the following cases: *Employment Division, v. Smith,* 494 U.S. 872 (1990); *Church of Lukumi Babalu Aye, Inc., v. Hialeah,* 508 U.S. 520 (1993); *City of Boerne v. Flores,* 521 U.S. 507 (1997); *Edwards v. Aguillard,* 482 U.S. 578 (1986); *Texas Monthly, Inc., v. Bullock,* 489 U.S. 1 (1989); *Lee v. Weisman,* 505 U.S.

---

[18] Ibid., 192.

[19] Ibid. The sabbatarian at issue in this hypothetical discussion was a Jehovah's Witness who wants to have Saturday off instead of Sunday, and therefore applies for unemployment benefits when forced to turn down a job requiring work on Saturday.

[20] Ibid.

577 (1992); *Lamb's Chapel v. Center Moriches Union Free School District*, 508 U.S. 384 (1993); *Board of Kiryas Joel v. Grumet*, 521 U.S. 687 (1994); and *McCreary County v. ACLU*, 545 U.S. 844 (2005). An examination of the free exercise cases below will show that Scalia has relied more on reasoning and precedent in these cases than upon the founding history. His Establishment Clause opinions, on the other hand, frequently refer to practices and statements from America's founding era in the late eighteenth century that emerged from the views on public religion held by what John Witte, Jr., has classified as Enlightenment views and Civic Republican views.[21] Witte has stated that four different views present during the founding era influenced the consensus behind the First Amendment religion clauses: Puritan, Evangelical, Enlightenment, and Civic Republican. Enlightenment thinkers included Thomas Jefferson and James Madison whereas George Washington and John Adams were Civic Republicans. Additionally, as Witte has shown in his research, Enlightenment thinkers generally demonstrated suspicion of organized religion and favored separation of church and state, but Civic Republicans favored public religion generally and their thought was also influenced by the Puritan viewpoint's support for a Christian Commonwealth.[22]

Scalia has combined references from both the Enlightenment and Civic Republican viewpoints in his Establishment Clause opinions.[23] Frankfurter, on the other hand, grounded his Free Exercise and Establishment Clause opinions almost exclusively in historical references to Enlightenment representatives, especially Thomas Jefferson.[24] Neither justice has cited as support for his opinions the

---

[21] John Witte, Jr. *Religion and the American Constitutional Experiment*, 2d ed. (Boulder, CO: Westview Press, 2005), 29-35.

[22] Ibid., 31, 33-35.

[23] *Lee v. Weisman*, 505 U.S. 577, 633-635 (1992); and *McCreary County v. ACLU*, 545 U.S. 844, 886-889 (2005).

[24] *Minersville School District v. Gobitis*, 310 U.S. 586, 594-595 (1940); *West Virginia State Board of Education v. Barnette*, 319 U.S. 624, 652-653 (1943); and *McGowan v. Maryland*, 366 U.S. 420, 463-464 (1961).

representatives of the Evangelical viewpoint, such as John Leland, who defended freedom of conscience from a religious perspective.[25]

ANTONIN SCALIA'S TEXTUALISM AND FREE EXERCISE JURISPRUDENCE

Even though these are important differences between the religion clause jurisprudences of Scalia and his predecessor Felix Frankfurter, both judges have applied a similar approach to the Free Exercise Clause. Both have interpreted the Free Exercise Clause with a milder form of judicial scrutiny so that some religious minorities were in effect subject to majority will, with one exception in the jurisprudence of Scalia.[26] This section of the book will demonstrate this with reference to Scalia's Free Exercise Clause jurisprudence and his originalist methodology for interpreting the Constitution.

In a speech given as the William Howard Taft Constitutional Law Lecture at the University of Cincinnati in 1988 Scalia explained his form of "faint-hearted" originalism.[27] He called himself a "faint-hearted" originalist because he conceded that there were problems with this manner of interpreting the Constitution.[28] He explained that he adopted originalism because it was a better form of constitutional interpretation than the one that claimed the Constitution was a "living" document open to progressive interpretive meanings as society changes. Also, Scalia rejected the claim made by proponents of the "living" Constitution approach that Supreme Court judges should try to use their power as judges in order to influence social mores.[29]

In one passage in the speech Scalia stated:

---

[25] Witte, *American Constitutional Experiment*, 27.

[26] *Church of Lukumi Babalu Aye, Inc., v. Hialeah*, 508 U.S. 520, 557-559 (1993)(SCALIA, J., Concurring).

[27] Antonin Scalia, "Originalism: The Lesser Evil," *57 U. Cincinnati L. Rev. 849* (1989).

[28] Scalia, *The Lesser Evil*, 864.

[29] Ibid., 863.

> The purpose of the constitutional guarantees-and in particular those constitutional guarantees of individual rights that are at the center of this controversy-is precisely to prevent the law from reflecting certain changes in original values that the society adopting the Constitution thinks fundamentally undesirable. Or, more precisely, to require the society to devote to the subject the long and hard consideration required for a constitutional amendment before those particular values can be set aside.[30]

He stated that the Constitution established as fundamental certain rights which society dare not abandon without the appropriate remedy of a constitutional amendment. Moreover, his rationale for this interpretive approach included the assertion that the nature of American democracy itself will change if certain fundamental rights were abandoned. This change, he argued, should not take place because of the temporary and fallible decision of five persons on the Court, but should only occur if a super majority of the people passes a constitutional amendment.

In addition, Scalia expressed doubt as to whether judges had the ability to determine the evolving meaning of the Constitution once the original meaning of the text of the Constitution, even with all of its interpretive challenges, was rejected. He submitted, "I also think that the central practical defect of nonoriginalism is fundamental and irreparable: the impossibility of achieving any consensus on what, precisely, is to replace the original meaning, once that is abandoned."[31] For Scalia, the admitted problems associated with originalism such as the task of historically determining exactly what the original intent was, as well as the task of accounting for changes in society between the time of the founding era and the modern welfare state, were outweighed by the problems with non-originalism or the "Living Constitution" methodology. Also, in an interview with Joan Biskupic years later, Scalia defended this methodology because he submitted that it better enabled judges to keep their religious beliefs from influencing their opinions in cases. He said:

---

[30] Ibid., 862.

[31] Ibid., 862-863.

> If I were an evolving constitutionalist, how could I keep my religion out of it? That is precisely one of the reasons I like textualism. It is an objective criterion that you can repair to, and if you find what that understanding [regarding a particular constitutional provision] was at the time, you don't have to inject your own biases and prejudices.[32]

Scalia has explained his methodology further in his book *A Matter of Interpretation: Federal Courts and the Law.*[33] He stated the following therein, to clarify what he meant by textualism:

> I am not a strict constructionist, and no one ought to be-though better that, I suppose, than a nontextualist. A text should not be construed strictly, and it should not be construed leniently; it should be construed reasonably, to contain all that it fairly means."[34] When the Court does not follow this methodology, he submitted, the basic principles of democracy are violated because, "It is simply not compatible with democratic theory that laws mean whatever they ought to mean, and that unelected judges decide what that is.[35]

To further explain what he understood textualism to mean, Scalia provided the following case example from a case that he had participated in as a judge. It involved a criminal law that authorized "an increased jail term" for crimes committed with a firearm. The defendant tried to obtain cocaine by trading his firearm for the drug, and the court, of which Scalia was a member, sentenced the defendant to an increased term pursuant to the statute. Scalia dissented and argued that the statute's language did not apply to crimes such as this because it "fairly connoted use of a gun for what guns are normally

---

[32] Joan Biskupic, *American Original: The Life and Constitution of Supreme Court Justice Antonin Scalia* (New York: Sarah Crichton Books, 2009), 209.

[33] Antonin Scalia, *A Matter of Interpretation: Federal Courts and the Law* (Princeton, NJ: Princeton University Press, 1997), 3-47.

[34] Scalia, *A Matter of Interpretation*, 23.

[35] Ibid., 22.

used for, that is, as a weapon."[36] In other words, Scalia submitted that textualism is neither rigid literalism nor acceptance of an unlimited range of meaning for words, but rather the application of reason to discern the "limited range of meaning" for words in the text of a law.[37]

Scalia noted that interpreting the Constitution would usually be a difficult procedure because of the general and sometimes vague nature of its language. He also acknowledged that the Constitution sometimes demands "an expansive rather than a narrow interpretation-though not an interpretation that the language will not bear."[38] In order to interpret the Constitution correctly, then, judges should conduct an examination of the original meaning of the text of the Constitution, not the original intent of the framers. He explained the difference between the textualism he preferred and seeking to find the original intent of the framers in this way:

> What I look for in the Constitution is precisely what I look for
> in a statute: the original meaning of the text, not what the
> original draftsmen intended.[39]

In the case of *Employment Division v. Smith*, 494 U.S. 872 (1990), Scalia authored his most important majority opinion in a religion clause case. It represented a change in Free Exercise Clause jurisprudence and created a backlash ultimately resulting in congressional passage of the Religious Freedom Restoration Act in 1993, which was intended to reverse the outcome of the case and nullify much of Scalia's opinion.[40] The case from Oregon involved two Native Americans named Alfred

---

[36] Ibid., 23-24.

[37] Ibid., 24.

[38] Ibid., 37.

[39] Ibid., 38.

[40] See Michael W. McConnell, "Free Exercise Revisionism and the *Smith* Decision," *57 U. Chicago L. Rev. 1109* (1990), and the discussion of the Religious Freedom Restoration Act in Edwin S. Gaustad's book *Proclaim Liberty Throughout all the Land: A History of the Religion Clauses* (New York: Oxford University Press, 2003), 133-134.

Smith and Galen Black, who were fired from their jobs as drug rehabilitation counselors because they both used peyote as part of a worship ceremony of the Native American Church.[41] Peyote use was illegal at the time according to Oregon law which prohibited "the knowing or intentional possession of a 'controlled substance' unless the substance has been prescribed by a medical practitioner."[42]

Peyote was considered a "controlled substance" under Oregon law because the State Board of Pharmacy included peyote as a "Schedule I" drug by virtue of legal authority it had been given in Oregon's statutory law. As noted in Scalia's opinion, peyote is a "hallucinogen derived from the plant *Laphophora williamsii Lemaire*," and Oregon's criminal law made use of the hallucinogen a Class B felony.[43]

After their dismissal Black and Smith applied to the Employment Division, Department of Human Resources of Oregon for unemployment benefits, but their claim was denied on the basis that they were deemed "ineligible" since "they had been discharged for work-related 'misconduct.'" [44] They subsequently appealed to the Oregon Court of Appeals that reversed the Employment Division's ruling by holding that the Employment Division's decision amounted to an unconstitutional restriction on their free exercise of religion.

This decision was then appealed to the Oregon Supreme Court by the Employment Division, which argued "the denial of benefits was permissible because respondents' consumption of peyote was a crime under Oregon law."[45] That court again ruled in favor of Black and Smith's free exercise claim, however. It rejected the Employment Division's arguments, holding instead that the purpose of Oregon's "misconduct" provision in its unemployment compensation statute was to "preserve the financial integrity of the compensation fund," and not

---

[41] *Smith*, 494 U.S. at 874. It was a stipulated fact in the case that Smith and Black members of the Native American church.

[42] Ibid., citing Ore. Rev. Stat. Section 475.992(4) (1987).

[43] Ibid.

[44] Ibid.

[45] Ibid., 875.

to "enforce the State's criminal laws."[46]   Moreover, the Oregon Supreme Court found that preservation of the financial integrity of the compensation fund was not a weighty enough reason to violate Black and Smith's religious liberty as protected by the First Amendment. The court based this decision on the United States Supreme Court's interpretation of the Free Exercise Clause set forth in cases including *Sherbert v. Verner*, 374 U.S. 398 (1963) and *Thomas v. Review Bd. of Indiana Employment Security Div.*, 450 U.S. 707 (1981). Thus, according to the Oregon Supreme Court, Black and Smith were entitled to unemployment benefits, and the Free Exercise Clause of the First Amendment prevented infringement of their religious liberty for the nominally important reason of "preservation of the financial integrity of the compensation fund."

The *Sherbert* case that the Oregon Supreme Court relied on to apply the Free Exercise Clause to Black and Smith's case contained a type of judicial test for free exercise cases called the compelling interest test. Courts sometimes applied the compelling interest test to laws challenged under the Free Exercise Clause, and upheld laws "only if" they satisfied both elements of the test.[47] The two parts were:

(1) does the government have a compelling interest for the law at issue, and

(2) is the law *"narrowly tailored* to achieve that interest, not intruding on the claimant's rights any more than is absolutely necessary."[48] Scholar John Witte, Jr., noted in his analysis of judicial tests applied in free exercise cases that the compelling interest test represents a high degree of judicial scrutiny, but he argued that courts do not apply the test predictably.[49]

The Supreme Court accepted the Employment Division's appeal of the Oregon Supreme Court's ruling. On the first appeal to the Supreme

---

[46] Ibid.

[47] John Witte, Jr. *Religion and the American Constitutional Experiment*, 2d ed. (Boulder, CO: Westview Press, 2005), 147.

[48] Ibid., 147 emphasis in the original.

[49] Ibid., 146-148.

Court the Court remanded the cases to Oregon for a determination of the question whether or not Black and Smith's use of peyote was proscribed by Oregon's controlled substance law.[50] On remand the Oregon Supreme Court determined that this was in fact the law in Oregon, but ruled again that the criminality of peyote use under Oregon's statutory law was insufficient reason to hinder Black and Smith's religious liberty in violation of the First Amendment.[51] Once again, the Employment Division appealed the Oregon Supreme Court's ruling to the Supreme Court and certiorari was granted.

Scalia's majority opinion ruled in favor of the Employment division of rehearing of the case and modified First Amendment free exercise law in the process. It distinguished the Supreme Court's prior unemployment benefit free exercise cases on the basis that those cases, *Sherbert v. Verner* and *Thomas v. Review Board,* did not involve conduct criminalized by law, as did *Employment Division v. Smith.*[52]

Then, the opinion, after noting the Court's prior dicta in its first treatment of *Smith* that states are free to deny unemployment benefits for illegal conduct notwithstanding its religious inspiration,[53] shifted to a general statement of free exercise law. Scalia noted that the Free Exercise Clause prevents government regulation of "religious beliefs as such"[54] and prohibits forced "affirmation of belief," punishment of "the expression of religious doctrines it believes to be false," "special disabilities on the basis of religious views or religious status," "or [the state's] lending its power to one or the other side in controversies over religious authority or dogma."[55]

Scalia's majority opinion then transitioned to the more problematic area of free exercise jurisprudence wherein the state regulates not only religious beliefs, but also actions. He stipulated that the state couldn't directly either forbid or require religious actions as such. Nonetheless,

---

[50] Ibid.

[51] Ibid., 876.

[52] Ibid., 876.

[53] Ibid.

[54] Ibid., 877.

[55] Ibid.

he went on to reason that the facts of this case did not amount to direct infringement of free exercise liberty because the Oregon statute in question did not target the religious conduct at issue. Rather, the statute did not mention religion at all; it only made the use of peyote a class B felony. Finding a Free Exercise Clause violation in cases such as this would stretch the words of the First Amendment beyond their meaning, according to Scalia's majority opinion. He wrote:

> As a textual matter, we do not think the words must be given that meaning.[56]

For example, he continued, the Free Exercise Clause's text does not prohibit a general tax law, which does not target religion merely because some members of society consider the law's requirement of "organized government to be sinful."[57] This is because the law in question only incidentally burdens religious scruples and does not infringe on religious liberty as "the object of the tax."[58]

Moreover, he added, the Court's precedents in this area supported his conclusions for the majority. He wrote, "We have never held that an individual's religious beliefs excuse him from compliance with an otherwise valid law prohibiting conduct that the State is free to regulate."[59] Then, he referred to Frankfurter's opinion in *Minersville School District v. Gobitis* to support his rationale, though he did not mention that the holding in this case was subsequently overruled in 1943 by *West Virginia State Board of Education v. Barnette*, 319 U.S. 624 (1943). He wrote that "the record of more than a century of our free exercise jurisprudence contradicts that proposition," and he cited Frankfurter's language from *Gobitis* wherein Frankfurter wrote, "Conscientious scruples have not, in the course of the long struggle for religious toleration, relieved the individual from obedience to a general law not aimed at the promotion or restriction of religious beliefs. The mere possession of religious convictions that contradict the relevant

---

[56] Ibid., 878.

[57] Ibid.

[58] Ibid.

[59] Ibid., 878-879.

concerns of a political society does not relieve the citizen from the discharge of political responsibilities."[60]

Moreover, Scalia relied in *Smith* upon the *Reynolds v. United States*, 98 U.S. 145 (1879) polygamy case as precedent in the same paragraph of the opinion, wherein he referred to *Gobitis*. *Reynolds* was cited as further precedent for his argument in *Smith* that religious beliefs cannot excuse citizens from compliance with general laws, because this would result in too many religious loopholes and thereby undermine the rule of law. Then Scalia reasoned further that judicial consideration of religious exemptions to neutral laws that indirectly infringe on religious liberty "would be to make the professed doctrines of religious belief superior to the law of the land, and in effect to permit every citizen to become a law unto himself."[61] This has never been required by the Court's free exercise precedent, he stated, nor is it required by the text of the Free Exercise Clause. Rather, neither the text nor the Court's precedents had required exemptions to laws that restrict actions within the government's authority to oversee.[62] In effect, Scalia's opinion rejected the *Sherbert* compelling interest test at this point, which resulted in passage of the Religious Freedom Restoration Act by Congress in 1993 with the intent of reversing the *Smith* ruling.

The *Smith* majority opinion's rationale is similar to Frankfurter's rationales in *Gobitis* and *Barnette* that deferred to government's interests for laws with neutral language regarding religion. As Frankfurter had in these previous free exercise cases, Scalia's *Smith* opinion warns against potential anarchy emanating from aggressive application of the Free Exercise Clause in cases where neutral laws indirectly infringe on religious liberty. He reasoned that the Free Exercise Clause does not warrant a "private right" to disregard these kinds of laws.[63] Subsequently, at a conference he defended a jurisprudence that restricts the influence of natural law scruples as the basis for conscientious exemptions to neutral laws with general

---

[60] Ibid., 879.

[61] *Employment Division v. Smith*, 494 U.S. 872, 879 (1990).

[62] *Smith*, 494 U.S. at 878-879.

[63] Ibid., 886.

applicability.[64] In an address to the Symposium on the Political Order and the Common Good in Rome, Italy, in 1996 Scalia reiterated his views on natural law in a democracy. He stated that in a democracy when a law is "bad" the proper way to challenge it is to convince the people that it is "bad" through legislative process thereby inculcating change. In addition, he maintained that the government in a democracy couldn't provide "for its people a society that is any better than the virtue of its people. And if the people do not have that virtue, the state cannot impose it."[65]

The free exercise approach Scalia articulated in *Smith* applied stricter judicial review, though, if a law explicitly and directly discriminated against the religious beliefs or practices of members of a religion. Scalia also argued that stricter scrutiny applied to a free exercise claim combined with an additional "constitutional protections" such as the Free Exercise Clause.[66] Scalia, moreover, admitted that the *Smith* holding worked to the detriment of minority faiths at the end of the majority opinion in the case, but he also argued that the diversity of religious beliefs in America requires the holding because courts should not decide the "centrality" of a given practice with reference to an individual's faith as this would impermissibly interject courts into the business of evaluating the merits of various religions.[67] His opinion also asserted that the pluralism of American religion supported the result in the case, because the diversity of religion in America could lead to presumptive invalidation of multiple laws that indirectly infringe on religious actions.[68] The *Smith* majority opinion authored by

---

[64] Scalia defended his views in this regard in a lecture followed by a question and answer session at the Vatican's Gregorian University in Rome in 1996. Justice Antonin Scalia, "Of Democracy, Morality and the Majority," *Origins: CNS Documentary Service* Vol. 26, No. 6, (June 27, 1996), 81-90.

[65] Ibid., 81.

[66] *Smith*, 494 U.S. at 881-882 wherein Scalia's opinion delineates "hybrid situation[s]" where a free exercise claim is combined with "communicative activity or parental right."

[67] Ibid., 886-887, 890.

[68] Ibid., 888.

Scalia did not provide lengthy textual reasoning or historical grounds for its holding, but did submit that his approach was a "permissible" interpretation of the Free Exercise Clause.[69]

In subsequent Free Exercise Clause cases Scalia has not changed his approach established in *Employment Division v. Smith.* In *Church of the Lukumi Babalu Aye, Inc., v. City of Hialeah,* 508 U.S. 520 (1993) he wrote a concurring opinion joining the majority opinion of Anthony Kennedy.[70] The facts involved the Santeria religion, a minority faith that emerged in the 1800s as slaves from Africa synthesized elements of their native religion with Roman Catholicism. According to Kennedy's majority opinion this "syncretion, or fusion" resulted in a religious practice including *orishas* wherein adherents "express their devotion to spirits . . . through the iconography of Catholic saints."[71] Thus aspects of the Roman Catholic faith were merged with native spirituality, and Santeria members engaged in Roman Catholic sacraments. In addition, adherents believed that each person has an "individual" destiny which one finds by means of devotion to "the *orishas.*"[72] In order to facilitate this discovery, moreover, individuals who practice Santeria engage in animal sacrifice, and this practice was at the heart of the case.

Santeria practitioners engage in these sacrifices "at birth, marriage, and death rites, for the cure of the sick, for the initiation of new members and priests, and during an annual celebration."[73] The animals included chickens, pigeons, doves, ducks, guinea pigs, goats, sheep, and turtles. Members of this faith sacrificed the animals generally by slicing the arteries in their necks, and subsequently they became part of a celebratory meal with the exception of ceremonies related to healing and death. The majority opinion also points out that believers in Santeria suffered discrimination for their faith in Cuba and thus were forced to engage in these rituals in secret ceremonies. Santeria was

---

[69] Ibid., 878-879.

[70] *Church of the Lukumi Babalu Aye,* 508 U.S. at 557-559.

[71] Ibid., 524.

[72] Ibid.

[73] Ibid., 525.

brought to America "most often by exiles from the Cuban revolution;" the opinion also noted that the lower federal district trial court in the case "estimated that there are about 50,000 practitioners in South Florida" as of the last decade of the twentieth century.[74]

The specific church in the case was called "Church of the Lukumi Babalu Aye, Inc.," and it was incorporated pursuant to Florida law in 1973. Members of this church practiced Santeria, and their priest was named Ernesto Pichardo, who held the title "*Italero*." The position of *Italero* was almost the highest in the Santeria hierarchy, and Pichardo also served as the President for the non-profit corporation. In the late 1980s the Church of the Lukumi Babalu Aye began an effort to obtain land in the city of Hialeah, Florida, in order to build a church, a school, a cultural center, and a museum as well.[75] Their President, Pichardo, expressly declared in public that the desire of the church body was to promote Santeria in the public square, and he specified that this would include promotion of the ritual of animal sacrifice. Soon the church complied with the municipal requirements for utilities and licenses, but the process did not go smoothly.[76] Leaders in the city reacted to the presence of Santeria and the practice of animal sacrifice in the minority faith by calling an emergency City Council meeting for June 9, 1987. The council then passed a series of ordinances that effectively restricted the religious practices of the Santeria.

These ordinances accomplished several things. They documented, in part, the alarm of Hialeah residents that "certain religions may propose to engage in practices which are inconsistent with public morals, peace or safety."[77] Secondly, the city's leaders enacted an "emergency ordinance" that criminalized animal sacrifice via the incorporation of Florida state laws. Florida law prohibited cities from passing animal cruelty laws inconsistent with state law, and therefore city lawyers obtained approval from the Florida Attorney General's office before moving ahead. Once they secured an opinion that the

---

[74] Ibid. The facts of the case with reference to Santeria are set out on pages 524 and 525 of the majority opinion.

[75] Ibid., 526.

[76] Ibid.

[77] Ibid.

proposed Hialeah laws were consistent with state law, the city's leaders passed three ordinances related to animal sacrifice.

The first ordinance, Ordinance 87-52, defined animal sacrifice as "to unnecessarily kill, torment, torture, or mutilate an animal in a public or private ritual or ceremony not for the primary purpose of food consumption."[78]   Ordinance 87-52 also outlawed the ownership or keeping of these animals for eating as food. Yet, importantly, the ordinance limited this restriction to that individual or group that "kills, slaughters or sacrifices animals for any type of ritual, regardless of whether or not the flesh or blood of the animal is to be consumed," which was a reference to the practitioners of Santeria.[79] It also exempted businesses that cultivated and processed animals for sale as food products.

Another ordinance was passed subsequent to approval by the state Attorney General. It was Ordinance 87-71 that also contained language prohibiting the practice of animal as "contrary to the public health, safety, welfare and morals of the community."[80] Moreover, this ordinance also outlawed animal sacrifice within the city of Hialeah. Finally, the city adopted another ordinance which limited the slaughter of animals to locations specifically set aside by the city for slaughterhouses; it only provided exceptions for those businesses which handle hogs and cattle pursuant to already existing state laws.

All of these laws passed through the city council without any votes against them. In addition, the laws contained penalties for those who violated them such as fines up to $500 and penal confinement up to 60 days. In reaction, the Church of Lukumi Babalu Aye filed a lawsuit in federal court claiming primarily that the Hialeah laws violated their First Amendment Free Exercise Clause rights. For a remedy the Church pled for the courts to stop enforcement of the laws and to grant them a judgment, which would provide for payments to the church as compensation for their damages. Both lower federal courts ruled in favor of the city. Likewise, the District Court for the Southern District of Florida did not find any violations for the Free Exercise Clause. It

---

[78] Ibid., 527.

[79] Ibid.

[80] Ibid., 528.

reasoned that the city's laws were not directed at Santeria, but instead designed to stop animal sacrifice in all cases. Moreover, the District Court ruled that the Hialeah ordinances did not "target" Santeria textually, and even if they did, this would be permissible if the conduct in question "is deemed inconsistent with public health and welfare."[81] Finally, the lower federal trial court also found four compelling interests for the governments' actions regarding animal sacrifice: a substantial health risk, potential danger to children exposed to the practice, defense of animals from cruelty, and the need for the city to insure that slaughterhouses are properly regulated. For the court these compelling interests outweighed any religious liberty claim the adherents of Santeria had via the facts of the case.

The Eleventh Circuit Court of Appeals upheld the decision of the District Court for the Southern District of Florida in a brief summary opinion. The opinion said that the city's laws did not violate the Constitution; it did not mention the *Employment Division v. Smith* case.[82]

In the majority opinion for the Supreme Court, Anthony Kennedy overruled the lower federal courts. He distinguished *Employment Division v. Smith* by reasoning that in this case the laws were not neutral because they intended to discriminate against Santeria, even though their language was arguably "secular" on its face.[83] He concluded for the majority of the court based on a review of the facts and background of the Hialeah laws that "suppression of the central element of the Santeria worship service was the object of the ordinances."[84] Kennedy based this conclusion on several factors: the inclusion of "sacrifice" and "ritual" in the text of the laws, language therein indicating fear of Santeria among citizens and referring to public safety and morals, and "religious gerrymander" in the impact of the laws since only Santeria's conduct was regulated by them in practical reality.[85] Finally, the Court also concluded that the Hialeah

---

[81] Ibid., 529.

[82] Ibid., 530.

[83] Ibid., 534.

[84] Ibid.

[85] Ibid., 535.

ordinances involved in the case were overbroad in their regulation of Santeria, and could have achieved the government's interest of preventing animal cruelty without violating the free exercise rights of Church of Lukumi Babalu Aye.[86]

Kennedy's opinion also concluded that the ordinances failed the requirements of general applicability established in *Employment Division v. Smith* because they left out a lot of conduct which laws intended to prevent cruelty to animals should have included. Here Kennedy reasoned that the laws were designed to discriminate against Santeria and its unique form of worship. He supported his arguments with evidence from the legislative history of the ordinances wherein Hialeah residents and city council members made derogatory and inflammatory comments about Santeria's beliefs and practices. These included one instance when a member of the City Council named Martinez who favored the ordinances said that in Cuba "people were put in jail for practicing this religion," and those present clapped in approval of the religious discrimination.[87]

Scalia voted with the majority in *Hialeah*, but wrote a concurring opinion in part to explain his disagreement with Kennedy's review of the legislative history of the city's ordinances.[88] He disagreed with the majority opinion's differentiation between "neutrality" and "general applicability" with reference to the Hialeah ordinances, and he adhered to his Free Exercise Clause interpretations expressed in *Employment Division v. Smith*.

Scalia referred back to *Smith's* use of the terms "neutrality" and "general applicability" and to his majority opinion in that case that laws that are neutral and have general applicability do not violate the Free Exercise Clause even when they proscribe religiously motivated conduct indirectly. He conceded, in contradiction to his customary emphasis on textualism, that neutrality and general applicability are not mentioned in the actual language of the First Amendment but were only developed by free exercise precedent as tests for proper application of

---

[86] Ibid., 538-539.

[87] Ibid., 541.

[88] Ibid., 557f.

the First Amendment. [89]   Nonetheless, Scalia reiterated his own distinction between "neutrality" and "general applicability" by reasoning that non-neutral laws discriminate against religion textually, whereas laws that fail to be generally applicable "target the practices of a particular religion for discriminatory treatment" by means of "design, construction, or enforcement." [90] He also indicated in his short concurring opinion that laws which are either non-neutral or fail to pass muster as generally applicable would both probably violate the First Amendment, yet his opinion is ambiguous at this point. He agreed with Kennedy's evaluation of the "invalidating factors" in Part II of the majority opinion, but he did not specifically analyze any of them.

Scalia disagreed with Kennedy's use of legislative history to establish the "subjective motivation of the lawmakers, *i.e.*, whether the Hialeah City Council actually intended to disfavor the religion of Santeria."[91]   This was consistent with his aversion to the attempt to ascertain what legislative intent is when legislators come to the table with varied motives for laws they enact. He wrote:

> it is virtually impossible to determine the singular "motive" of
> a collective legislative body.[92]

Also, he argued that this is particularly true in First Amendment cases where the pertinent analysis considers "the effects of the laws enacted" and not the motives used by individual legislators when they compose legislation.[93] Near the conclusion of the opinion he added,

---

[89] Ibid., 557. Antonin Scalia, *A Matter of Interpretation: Federal Courts and the Law* (Princeton, NJ: Princeton University Press, 1997), 37-47.

[90] Ibid.

[91] Ibid., 558.

[92] Ibid., 558 referring to his critique of attempts to determine legislative intent in the Establishment Clause case, *Edwards v. Aguillard*, 482 U.S. 578, 636-639 (1987) (SCALIA, J., dissenting).

[93] In the opinion Scalia then cites the language of the First Amendment, "Congress shall make no law . . . prohibiting the free exercise [of religion] . . . ." Ibid.

"Nor, in my view, does it matter that a legislature consists entirely of the pure hearted, if the law it enacts in fact singles out a religious practice for special burdens. Had the ordinances here been passed with no motive on the part of any councilman except the ardent desire to prevent cruelty to animals . . . they would nonetheless be invalid."[94]

A subsequent free exercise case solidified Scalia's approach in Free Exercise Clause cases. The case of *City of Boerne v. Flores*, 521 U.S. 507 (1997) resolved for the time being a significant controversy between Congress and the Supreme Court over power to interpret the Constitution. The majority opinion was again authored by Anthony Kennedy and held that the Religious Freedom Restoration Act of 1993, 107 Stat. 1488, 42 U.S.C. Section 2000bb *et seq* was unconstitutional as applied to the states.[95] Congress passed the Religious Freedom Restoration Act in 1993 in response to the Court's ruling in *Smith* in 1990, which had thrown out the compelling interest test of *Sherbert v. Verner*. The Religious Freedom Restoration Act's language reinstated the compelling interest test to all levels of government action in America. The primary rationale for the *City of Boerne* ruling was therefore that Congress had overstepped its boundaries pursuant to the Fourteenth Amendment's Enforcement Clause when it passed the Religious Freedom Restoration Act, and effectively overruled *Employment Division v. Smith*. This violated separation of powers and federalist principles according to the majority opinion and infringed upon the Court's supreme role as interpreter of the Constitution.[96]

The facts of the case centered upon St. Peter's Catholic Church in Boerne, Texas, not far from San Antonio. St. Peter's founders built it in 1923, and the architectural style is that of the mission churches of western America's history. Over time the Church proved faithful to its mission and outgrew its worship center, which could accommodate 230 worshippers. Therefore, San Antonio's Archbishop authorized the church's plan to build onto the existing structure to better handle the 40 to 60 additional attendees at mass.[97]

---

[94] Ibid., 559.

[95] *Flores*, 521 U.S. at 536.

[96] Ibid., 536 citing *Marbury v. Madison*, 1 Cranch at 177.

[97] Ibid., 512.

Subsequent to the decision of the Archbishop the city of Boerne decided in its governing body to adopt a law that enabled its Historic Landmark Commission to develop a preservation plan for potential sites in the city which could serve as "historic landmarks and districts."[98] The new city law empowered the Historic Landmark Commission with control over authorization for new buildings that impacted sites, which had been set-aside as landmarks. St. Peters applied for approval of its building project, but the commission refused to permit the church to build the addition designed to accommodate more participants in worship.

After these events transpired, the Archbishop sued in the United States District Court for the Western District of Texas. One of the claims made on behalf of the church in the lawsuit was grounded in the newly passed Religious Freedom Restoration Act drafted by Congress as a reaction to the Supreme Court's *Employment Division v. Smith* decision. This claim maintained that the Historic Landmark Commission's denial of the building permit violated the Religious Freedom Restoration Act because the city's commission did not have a compelling interest for denying the church's application for a permit. The federal district court held in favor of the city at the trial level that Congress had overreached its Fourteenth Amendment Section 5 powers in the Religious Freedom Restoration Act, and thus St. Peters had no claim based on the Religious Freedom Restoration Act since it was unconstitutional in this regard.[99] The Fifth Circuit Court of Appeals reversed the federal trial court and held that the Religious Freedom Restoration Act was constitutional. The Supreme Court then granted a Petition for Certiorari and accepted the appeal.

Kennedy wrote the Supreme Court's majority opinion in *City of Boerne*, in which he agreed with the federal trial court's conclusion that Congress did not have power pursuant to Section 5 of the Fourteenth Amendment to require states to apply the compelling interest test. Kennedy's majority opinion thus struck down as unconstitutional the part of the Religious Freedom Restoration Act that applied the compelling interest test from *Sherbert* to state and local

---

[98] Ibid.

[99] Ibid., 512.

governments.[100] Justice Sandra Day O'Connor authored a dissenting opinion in *City of Boerne* that is significant because she criticized Scalia's reasoning in *Smith* on the basis of her own historical research into the intent of the Free Exercise Clause.[101]

O'Connor critiqued Scalia's *Smith* opinion in her *City of Boerne* dissent for failing to review the "early American tradition of religious free exercise."[102] She then engaged in an extensive review of early American historical sources regarding the meaning of free exercise of religion, while asserting from the outset that history does not tell us precisely what the "Framers thought the phrase signified."[103] In her historical review O'Connor began with Lord Baltimore's efforts to attain protection of religious liberty for Roman Catholics in Maryland in 1648, and concluded with a brief account of Virginia's struggle over religious liberty in the 1770s.[104] The primary conclusion O'Connor obtained from her historical examination of these early sources was that "at the time the Bill of Rights was ratified, it was accepted that government should, when possible, accommodate religious practice,"[105] which is a conclusion in direct conflict with Scalia's opinion in *Smith*.

Scalia's opinion in *City of Boerne v. Flores* did not address the issues raised in the majority opinion concerning the Fourteenth Amendment's Enforcement Clause and judicial supremacy. Rather, Scalia devoted his opinion to responding to O'Connor and to a defense of the historical foundations for his opinion in *Employment Division v. Smith*.

He criticized O'Connor's dissent in *City of Boerne* in his concurrence and sought to bolster the historical case for the finding in *Smith*, though the original *Smith* majority opinion did not discuss the history behind the Free Exercise Clause.[106] He maintained again in

---

[100] Ibid., 519-520.

[101] Ibid., 544-565.

[102] Ibid., 548.

[103] Ibid., 550.

[104] Ibid., 551, 555-557.

[105] Ibid., 557.

[106] *Employment Division v. Smith*, 494 U.S. 872, 874-890 (1990).

Flores that courts should defer to legislative rationales for laws in free exercise cases where laws were neutral as to religion and generally applicable, as he had in his concurring opinion in *Hialeah*.[107]

Most of his opinion in *Flores* was a defense against O'Connor's historical critique of *Smith*. Scalia pled that the historical evidence from the founding era supported his conclusions in *Smith* more than undermined them. He referred to the scholarship of Michael McConnell and Philip Hamburger to counter O'Connor's assertions that the founders desired legislative accommodations in deference to sectarian religious conscience when neutral and general laws, which did not directly involve religion, nonetheless impinged on religious liberty.[108] Then, he objected to O'Connor's argument that early colonial laws and constitutions contradicted the *Smith* approach. Rather, he maintained that just the opposite is true because these early laws and constitutions at least arguably applied to situations where religion was used as a wedge to discriminate against others.[109] It is more likely the historical case, Scalia concluded, that in the founding era the policy preference was as follows, "Religious exercise shall be permitted so long as it does not violate general laws governing conduct."[110]

In the conclusion of his *Flores* opinion Scalia reemphasized his confidence in the *Smith* approach to the Free Exercise Clause as the one most consistent with the historical intent of the framers and with the practicalities of concrete lawsuits. He argued:

> Who can possibly be against the abstract proposition that government should not, even in its general nondiscriminatory laws, place unreasonable burdens upon religious practices?

---

[107] *Church of the Lukumi Babalu Aye, Inc., v. City of Hialeah*, 508 U.S. 520, 557-559 (1993).

[108] Ibid., 538.

[109] Ibid., 538 citing the Maryland Act Concerning Religion of 1649, the Rhode Island Charter of 1663, the New Hampshire Constitution, and the Northwest Ordinance of 1787.

[110] Ibid., 539.

Unfortunately, however, that abstract proposition must ultimately be reduced to concrete cases.[111]

Then, he closed the opinion with language that echoed Felix Frankfurter's commitment to judicial restraint and to the American democratic system. He emphasized with regard to the *Smith* approach:

> The issue presented by *Smith* is, quite simply, whether the people, through their elected representatives, or rather this Court, shall control the outcome of those concrete cases. For example, shall it be the determination of this Court, or rather of the people, whether . . . church construction will be exempt from zoning laws? The historical evidence put forward by the dissent does nothing to undermine the conclusion we reached in *Smith*: It shall be the people.[112]

In summary, the free exercise jurisprudence of Scalia was deferential to the government and the legislative process except in the case of *Church of Lukumi Babalu Aye, Inc. v. Hialeah*, 508 U.S. 520, 557-559 (1993). His free exercise jurisprudence granted deference to local and state legislatures to protect the religious liberty enshrined in the First Amendment in the process of lawmaking while simultaneously preventing Congress from stepping in to protect the rights of religious minorities at the state level in *City of Boerne v. Flores*, 521 U.S. 507, 537-544 (1997)(concurring in part). His *Employment Division, Department of Human Services v. Smith*, 494 U.S. 872 (1990) majority opinion inured to the benefit of the religion of the majority, as he acknowledged in the opinion, and in his opinion in that case he raised the possibility that anarchy will prevail if courts apply a compelling interest test or strict scrutiny to neutral and general laws which infringe religious liberty. Felix Frankfurter also raised the possibility of anarchy in his *Barnette* opinion when he wrote that:

> The constitutional protection of religious freedom terminated disabilities; it did not create new privileges . . . otherwise each

---

[111] Ibid., 544.

[112] Ibid.

individual could set up his own censor against obedience to laws conscientiously deemed for the public good by those whose business it is to make laws.[113]

Scalia's free exercise approach established in *Smith* and defended in *Flores* was therefore similar to the approach to the Free Exercise Clause which Frankfurter applied in *Minersville School District v. Gobitis*, 310 U.S. 586 (1940). Even though Scalia did not rely as heavily upon historical references to the founders in free exercise cases as Frankfurter had, Scalia did argue in favor of judicial restraint. He warned in his *Smith* opinion against the potentially negative impact on the rule of law from conscientious religious objection to neutral or generally applicable laws. He asserted, much like Frankfurter in *Barnette*, that this could lead to anarchy.

Scalia's free exercise jurisprudence was distinct from Frankfurter's with regard to reliance on American founders as authority in that Scalia did not appeal to the founders in the *Smith* and *Hialeah* free exercise cases. Scalia did not until *City of Boerne* make historical appeals to the American founding era as authority for his approach to the Free Exercise Clause. Frankfurter relied upon the founders in his opinions in the *Gobitis* and *Barnette* free exercise cases. Frankfurter cited the founders as authority for his reasoning that the mandatory flag salute ceremony was constitutional in *Gobitis* and asserted in *Barnette* that the founders did not intend to create conscientious exemptions to neutral laws via the First Amendment.[114]

The primary difference between the religion clause jurisprudences of Scalia and Frankfurter emerged when one compared their interpretations of the Establishment Clause. The distinction between their religion clause jurisprudences was verified through analysis of the Establishment Clause jurisprudence of Scalia.

---

[113] *West Virginia State Board of Education v. Barnette*, 319 U.S. 624, 653 (1943).

[114] *Gobitis*, 310 U.S. at 594-595; *Barnette*, 319 U.S. at 651-653.

CHAPTER 6
Scalia's No Establishment Opinions

AMERICA PUBLIC RELIGION IN ANTONIN SCALIA'S
ESTABLISHMENT CLAUSE OPINIONS

Antonin Scalia's record in Establishment Clause cases demonstrates the
following:

> a consistent hermeneutical approach that relies upon
> traditional, historical, and public religious practices and
> statements traceable to some of the founding era's leaders
> from Enlightenment and Civic Republican perspectives;
> criticism of the Supreme Court's Establishment Clause
> jurisprudence including opposition to the *Lemon* test;[1] and a
> lack of references to American founders from the Evangelical
> view.[2]

The "American Evangelical tradition," according to John Witte, Jr.,
contributed to the eighteenth century debates in the colonies about
religious liberty. [3] Moreover, representatives of the Evangelical

---

[1] *Lemon v. Kurtzman*, 403 U.S. 602, 612-613 (1971).

[2] Timothy L. Hall, *Separating Church and State: Roger Williams and Religious Liberty* (Urbana, IL: University of Illinois Press, 1998), 150-151.

[3] John Witte, Jr., *Religion and the American Constitutional Experiment*, 2d ed. (Boulder, CO: Westview Press, 2005), 23, 26-29.

129

tradition, such as Isaac Backus and John Leland, emphasized the separation between church and state and sought to end government establishments of religion like the Congregational Church in New England.[4] Scalia has, in addition, never voted to find an Establishment Clause violation in a major case.[5]

SCALIA'S EARLY ESTABLISHMENT CLAUSE DISSENTS

The first Establishment Clause case Scalia dissented in was the case of *Edwards v. Aguillard*, 482 U.S. 578, 610-640 (1986). The case concerned the constitutionality of Louisiana's "Balanced Treatment for Creation-Science and Evolution-Science Act," which required public school teachers to teach creation science if the school taught evolution.[6] The Balanced Treatment Act did not require teaching of either creation science or evolution, but mandated that if schools taught evolution then they must teach creation science, too.[7] Schools in Louisiana did not have to teach either evolution or creationism, but if they taught one or the other, then the law demanded that the other be offered as well. The law was challenged as a violation of the Establishment Clause in the First Amendment, which reads:

> Congress shall make no law respecting an establishment of religion . . . .[8]

Those who defended the law against this Establishment Clause attack included state leaders given the responsibility of implementing the Balanced Treatment Act. They maintained that the Balanced Treatment Act was constitutional because it promoted "a legitimate secular

---

[4] Ibid., 27.

[5] Kathleen M. Sullivan, "Justice Scalia and the Religion Clauses," *22 U. Haw. L. Rev. 449, 449* (2000).

[6] *Edwards v. Aguillard,* 482 U.S. 578, 581 (1986).

[7] *Edwards,* 482 U.S. at 581.

[8] U.S. Constitution, Amendment I.

interest, namely, academic freedom."[9] On the other hand, a group of schoolteachers, religious citizens, and parents claimed that the Act was unconstitutional on its face because it advocated a specific religious viewpoint. Both of the lower federal courts which handled the case before the Supreme Court held that the Louisiana Balanced Treatment Act was unconstitutional because it did not have a valid secular basis, and the law impermissibly advanced creation science from a unique religious perspective. The Fifth Circuit Court of Appeals also found that the legislature had the "actual intent" to demonstrate the inaccuracy of evolutionary theory, and not merely to achieve a higher degree of academic freedom.[10]

On appeal to the Supreme Court the lower federal courts were affirmed in a majority opinion authored by William Brennan and joined by Justices Marshall, Blackmun, Powell, Stevens, and O'Connor, though O'Connor did not join Part II of the majority opinion. The Court's majority applied the three pronged Establishment Clause test from the case of *Lemon v. Kurtzman*, 403 U.S. 602, 612-613 (1971) which required:

(1) a secular legislative purpose,
(2) that the law's "principal or primary effect" does not either advance or inhibit religion, and
(3) that the law should not lead to "excessive entanglement of government with religion."[11]

The majority reasoned that the Balanced Treatment Act did not have a secular purpose, that the expressed secular purpose of academic freedom was a sham, and thus the law failed the *Lemon* test.[12] Scalia authored a dissenting opinion in *Edwards v. Aguillard*. Its primary theme was Scalia's view, joined by Chief Justice Rehnquist, that the Supreme Court should not invalidate laws under the Establishment

---

[9] *Edwards v. Aguillard*, 482 U.S. 578, 581 (1986).

[10] Ibid., 582.

[11] Ibid., 583.

[12] As noted in the majority opinion, a law was deemed to fail the *Lemon* test and therefore to be unconstitutional if it failed and of *Lemon's* three prongs.

Clause based upon legislative history and the subjective motives of legislators. The opinion expressed the view that the Court should defer to the facially expressed intent of laws since legislators swear to uphold the Constitution as well.[13] He also argued in his opinion that the case's procedural "posture" prevented the court from really knowing what the Louisiana legislature's intent was regarding the Balanced Treatment Act, and the majority was assuming the worst in its rejection of the legislature's expressed intent to promote academic freedom.

Scalia advocated the view that the purpose test had not been explained by the Court in prior cases, and was almost always satisfied.[14] Also, he maintained that a proper application of the purpose test by the Court would give broad deference to the "sincere" secular motives of legislators irrespective of the results of the law in question.[15]

Scalia wrote that any secular purpose should satisfy the *Lemon* test. He wrote:

> Our cases have also confirmed that when the *Lemon* Court referred to "a secular . . . purpose," 403 U.S. at 612, it meant "a secular purpose."[16]

In other words, almost any sincere secular legislative purpose for a law that is challenged as having the effect of establishing religion will possibly pass muster for Scalia. The only way he would find a law to violate this prong of the *Lemon* test is for the law to have been

---

[13] *Edwards*, 482 U.S. at 610-611.

[14] Ibid., 613.

[15] Ibid., 614. On pages 618-619 of the dissent Scalia echoed Frankfurter's emphasis on judicial restraint whereby reviewing courts presume legislative intent behind legislation to be constitutional. He quoted a Frankfurter opinion that: "we must have 'due regard to the fact that this Court is not exercising a primary judgment but is sitting in judgment upon those who also have taken the oath to observe the Constitution and who have the responsibility for carrying on government.'" *Joint Anti-Fascist Refugee Committee v. McGrath*, 341 U.S. 123, 164 (1951)(FRANKFURTER, J., concurring).

[16] Ibid.

"motivated wholly by religious considerations." [17] Thus, Scalia articulated reasoning sufficient to avoid the first prong of the *Lemon* test in nearly all Establishment Clause cases. His criticism directed toward the *Lemon* test on this point submitted that analysis of legislative history is too uncertain, and this might enable judges to find impermissible religious motivations in the legislative history that may not necessarily have shaped or influenced the final form of a contested law. [18]

He continued his criticism of the *Lemon* test in *Edwards* by arguing that legislators should not leave their religious convictions at the door when working on legislation. After citing examples of beneficial legislation motivated by the religious values of legislators, such as legislation enacted during the civil-rights movement in the 1950s and 1960s, he added that laws do not violate the second prong of *Lemon* regarding advancement of religion just because the law is consistent with "the tenets of some or all religions." [19] He cited Supreme Court cases regarding abortion legislation that restricted access to abortions and tax deductions for the cost of religious education as examples where laws that advanced religion more than the Balanced Treatment Act in Louisiana passed constitutional scrutiny. [20] Scalia submitted that these cases demonstrated why the Court should

---

[17] Ibid., quoting the majority opinion of Chief Justice Warren Burger in *Lynch v. Donnelly*, 465 U.S. 668, 680 (1984). The *Lynch* case serves as precedent for Scalia in several Establishment Clause cases and it relies on a historical tradition of religion in the American public square traceable to America's founders. *Lee v. Weisman*, 505 U.S. 577, 581 (1992), and *McCreary County v. ACLU*, 545 U.S. 844, 889 (2005).

[18] *Edwards*, 482 U.S. at 637-638.

[19] *Edwards*, 482 U.S. at 615 quoting *McGowan v. Maryland*, 366 U.S. 420, 442 (1961) which upheld Sunday closing laws against an Establishment Clause challenge.

[20] *Edwards*, 482 U.S. at 633-635 citing *Harris v. McRae*, 448 U.S. 297, 319 (1980)(striking down establishment challenge to restrictions on Medicaid funding for abortions) and *Mueller v. Allen*, 463 U.S. 388, 394-395 (1983) (allowing tax deductions to parents of students in private schools for tuition, transportation, and textbook expenses).

not presume that a law's purpose is advancement of religion when the legislation coincides with the religious beliefs of some or all religions or benefits religion.[21] He also stated near the end of his dissent that laws that purposefully "advance" a religion in order to remedy discrimination against it, or to "facilitate its free exercise," or "to accommodate it" might be constitutional.[22]

Part III of Scalia's dissenting opinion in *Edwards v. Aguillard* presented criticism of the Court's Establishment Clause approach as delineated in the case of *Lemon v. Kurtzman*. He began by quoting Chief Justice Rehnquist's dissent in *Wallace v. Jaffree*, an Alabama school prayer case, which claimed the *Lemon* test as a whole was:

> a constitutional theory [that] has not basis in the history of the amendment that is seeks to interpret, is difficult to apply and yields unprincipled results . . . .[23]

Then, he discussed several weaknesses he found problematic in the *Lemon* theory's first prong applied in *Edwards* to hold Louisiana's Balanced Treatment Act unconstitutional. First, he submitted that the secular purpose test was hopelessly inconsistent and confusing for legislators who had to try and figure out which motives for legislation were constitutional, and which were not. He noted:

> "We have said essentially the following: Government may not act with the purpose of advancing religion, except when forced to do so by the Free Exercise Clause (which is now and then); or when eliminating existing governmental hostility to religion (which exists sometimes); or even when merely accommodating governmentally uninhibited religious practices, except that at some point (it is unclear where)

---

[21] Ibid.

[22] *Edwards*, 482 U.S. at 635.

[23] Ibid., 636 quoting *Wallace v. Jaffree*, 472 U.S. 38, 112 (1985) (REHNQUIST, J., dissenting).

intentional accommodation results in the fostering of religion, which is of course unconstitutional.[24]

Secondly, he reasoned that finding the subjective motivations of those who author statutes in the legislative process is impossible. There are just too many different motives that could lead to the formation of a law. For example, in *Edwards* alone he noted the potential motives for legislators could have included: economic improvement, payback for legislative favors, friendship with sponsors of the law, future fundraising needs, responsiveness to pressure from either voters or fellow politicians, public relations, or even pure indifference due to being inebriated when the vote occurred.[25]

Third, he maintained that it is also hard to know exactly where to find sources of legislative intent for specific legislators. He queried whether or not speeches or documents were reliable sources for intent and motives that actually ended up in a given law because these sources are subject to manipulation and spin by both lawmakers and the press. Moreover, he stressed, this left still unanswered the issue as to the number of lawmakers who must have an unconstitutional purpose for a law. Does there need to be one or more than one legislator with the motive establishing a religion for it to become unconstitutional pursuant to the Establishment Clause, he questioned?[26]

Finally, due to the problems he found with the first element of the *Lemon* test, Scalia concluded his critique of it by writing that the test should only apply if the text of the First Amendment demanded it. He then answered his own question:

That is surely not the case.[27]

This is, for him, because the text of the Establishment Clause does not "inevitably" prohibit "all governmental action intended to advance religion."[28]

---

[24] Ibid.

[25] Ibid., 637.

[26] Ibid., 638.

[27] Ibid., 639.

The next Establishment Clause case he dissented in was *Texas Monthly, Inc., v. Bullock*, 489 U.S. 1 (1989). In *Texas Monthly* William Brennan again authored the majority opinion for the court in a case about a Texas statute that exempted religious periodicals and books from sales and use taxes between 1984 and 1987. The majority ruled that the law was unconstitutional, but the majority opinion only gained the uncritical acceptance of Thurgood Marshall and John Paul Stevens. Justices White, Blackmun, and O'Connor only concurred in the judgment, and provided different rationales for their conclusions. The Brennan majority opinion based its ruling that the statute was unconstitutional on its finding that the tax exemptions provided were not broad enough to comply with the Establishment Clause.

The tax exemption statute in *Texas Monthly* only allowed exemptions to religious publications. Also, the majority held that the exemption failed for "lack of a secular objective' that would warrant a similar preference for non-religious groups, which published similar materials. The majority's opinion also reasoned that Texas was free to broaden the exemption as long as there was a "legitimate secular purpose" for extending the benefit to the publishers included and the exemption was sufficiently broad.[29]

Scalia's dissent in this case served as the first instance of historical citation from the founding era by the justice in an Establishment Clause case in order to articulate his position. Justices Rehnquist and Kennedy joined it. He appealed to history in this case in order to demonstrate that America has an historical tradition of endorsing religion in general, and to criticize the majority's notion that American government may not "convey a message of endorsement of religion."[30]

His historical review concluded that American government could endorse religion in general. He lists the Declaration of Independence,

---

[28] Ibid. It is a matter of ongoing debate as to whether the text and history of the Establishment Clause can help to clarify the correct meaning of the Establishment Clause. See, for example, Donald L. Drakeman, "Religion and the Republic: James Madison and the First Amendment," *Journal of Church and State* 25 (Autumn 1983): 427-445.

[29] *Texas Monthly Inc., v. Bullock*, 489 U.S. 1, 8-17 (1989).

[30] *Texas Monthly, Inc.*, 489 U.S. at 29-30.

the Thanksgiving Holiday "proclaimed by every President since Lincoln," "inscriptions on our coins," the language of the national pledge to the flag, prayers which begin United States Supreme Court official activities, and the presence of the Free Exercise Clause as examples of historical American government endorsement of religion. All of these examples of American public religious traditions or references are nonsectarian, nationalist, or generic forms of government endorsement of public religion that are governmentally approved.

Later on in the opinion when he stated the reasons for his dissent the justice included "the text of the Constitution" and the "traditions of our people" as supportive of the constitutionality of the Texas tax exemptions for religious publications.[31] He spent most of the opinion, though, disagreeing with the majority's application of the Court's primary precedent for religious tax exemptions, *Walz v. Tax Commission of New York City*, 397 U.S. 664 (1970). He took the majority to task for deviating from what he discerned was a clear and unbroken tradition of providing tax exemptions going back not just to *Walz*, but to the drafting of the First Amendment and the creation of America. There had in his view been an unbroken historical tradition of accommodating, and even favoring religion as a general matter therefore since the beginning of the country, but the majority opinion achieved a "revolution in our Establishment Clause jurisprudence" overruling cases which had endorsed religion generally by granting these exemptions.[32]

He conceded in *Texas Monthly* for the first time in an Establishment Clause opinion that it is sometimes difficult to differentiate when the constitutional line is crossed between a permissible accommodation of religion and an impermissible establishment, which favors specific faiths. Nonetheless he disagreed with the majority in this instance because this case was a clear one for him. The law in this case was not unconstitutional simply because it allowed churches to evangelize without being taxed on their publications because advancing religion "is their very purpose."[33]

---

[31] Ibid., at 33.

[32] Ibid., 38.

[33] Ibid., 42.

Moreover, he reasoned that the majority's holding would do more to entangle government and religion than the exemption in that it would require government regulation of religious publications including but not limited to auditing, compliance with reporting requirements, liens, and potential seizure and sale of property owned by religious groups to satisfy government liens.

The remainder of Scalia's opinion in *Texas Monthly* evidenced his view in favor of the accommodation of religion when there was a tension between allowing an accommodation and prohibiting an establishment in Establishment Clause cases. He stated his preference for accommodations in spite of the Establishment, Speech, and Press Clauses of the First Amendment thereby demonstrating how he is distinct from Frankfurter with reference to the Establishment Clause. Scalia's Establishment Clause view allowed accommodation of theistic religion in American public life against Establishment Clause challenge based upon his reading of the First Amendment and American history, whereas Frankfurter voted to find an unconstitutional violation of the Establishment Clause in every case he participated in except for *McGowan* where Frankfurter concluded the Sunday closing laws were secular in nature.[34] Both appealed to American history, but Scalia's reliance on history was part of his distinct understanding of the Establishment Clause that allowed general endorsement of public religion in spite of Establishment Clause challenge as exemplified by his opinion in *Texas Monthly* where he concluded:

---

[34] *Everson v. Board of Education*, 330 U.S. 1, 19-74 (1947(voting with dissenting justices who found that reimbursement of cost of transportation to parochial schools violated the Establishment Clause); *McCollum v. Board of Education*, 333 U.S. 203, 212 (1948)(finding an Illinois released time program in violation of the Establishment Clause); *Zorach v. Clauson*, 343 U.S. 307, 320-323 (1952)(finding a released time program after school unconstitutional); *Kedroff v. Saint Nicholas Cathedral*, 344 U.S. 94 (1952)(concurring with a majority of the Court holding that according to the Establishment Clause states may not tell churches how to select their leaders or how to make decisions about church governance); and *McGowan v. Maryland*, 366 U.S. 420 (1961).

And it is impossible to believe that the State is constitutionally prohibited from taxing Texas Monthly magazine more heavily than the Bible . . . It is not right-it is not constitutionally healthy-that this Court should feel authorized to refashion anew our civil society's relationship with religion, adopting a theory of church and state that is contradicted by current practice, tradition, and even our own case law.[35]

AMERICAN PUBLIC RELIGION IN SCALIA'S LATER ESTABLISHMENT CLAUSE CASES

In several cases in the 1990s Scalia made more explicit his belief that the *Lemon* test ought to be overruled. Also, in these cases he articulated his view of the proper approach to the Establishment Clause. This approach involved interpretation of the clause through articulation of an American tradition allowing for endorsement of general forms of religion in public life traceable to the founding of the country. This trajectory in his Establishment Clause opinions culminated in a dissenting opinion wherein he wrote about the tradition which is necessary to interpret the Establishment Clause in *McCreary County v. ACLU*, 545 U.S. 844, 885-912 (2005). Several prior cases also contain opinions with sections that added to Scalia's emphasis on tradition in interpreting the Establishment Clause.

The Court decided the case of *Lamb's Chapel v. Center Moriches Union Free School District*, 508 U.S. 384 (1993) after the case of *Lee v. Weisman*, 505 U.S. 577 (1992), but Scalia's concurring opinion in *Lamb's Chapel* is shorter, and therefore the book will examine these cases out of chronological order. *Lamb's Chapel* was primarily a free speech case, but it did involve the Establishment Clause in part.

The case concerned a New York statute that allowed public school boards to create rules and procedures for use of school buildings and property after school. The regulations stipulated ten purposes that were acceptable for after school programs, but did not allow for groups or meetings that had religious purposes. The Center Moriches Union Free School District then developed procedures and guidelines for use of its schools. These permitted "social, civic, or recreational uses . . . and use

---

[35] *Texas Monthly Inc.*, 489 U.S. at 45.

by political organizations."[36] Another rule developed by the School District, Rule 7, prohibited the use of their schools "by any group for religious purposes" in keeping with an opinion by the Attorney General of New York, and an opinion by the Second Circuit Court of Appeals in *Deeper Life Christian Fellowship Inc. v. Sobol*, 948 F.2d 79, 83-84 (1991).

The plaintiff in the case was an evangelical church named Lamb's Chapel from Center Moriches, New York. The church's pastor was John Steigerwald, and the church sought to show a film series by James Dobson of Focus on the Family in Colorado Springs, Colorado with six segments about family values. Footnote three of the majority opinion lists the titles of the segments in the film series titled *Turn Your Heart Toward Home*, including: A Father Looks Back," "Power in Parenting: The Young Child," "Power in Parenting: The Adolescent," "The Family Under Fire," "Overcoming a Painful Childhood," and "The Heritage."[37] When the school district asked for information about the church's programs a brochure was provided to it by the church. It described Dr. Dobson's credentials as "a licensed psychologist, former associate clinical professor of pediatrics at the University of Southern California, best-selling author, and radio commentator."[38] The church applied to the school district to show the films more than once, and sought to have Sunday morning classes and worship at a school as well, but its applications were rejected with the following statement from the school district, "this film does not appear to be church related and therefore your request must be refused."[39]

Lamb's Chapel subsequently sued in federal court complaining that the denials of their requests to show the films breached the Speech, Assembly, Press, Free Exercise, and Establishment Clauses in addition

---

[36] *Lamb's Chapel v. Center Moriches Union Free School District*, 508 U.S. 384, 387 (1993).

[37] Ibid., 388-389. The last segment titled "The Heritage" had an abstract which stated, "Here he speaks clearly and convincingly of our traditional values which, if properly employed and defended, can assure happy, healthy, strengthened homes and family relationships in the years to come."

[38] Ibid., 388.

[39] Ibid., 389.

to the Equal Protection Clause. The lower courts rejected the claims of the church, and the Court accepted the case on appeal as potentially in conflict with its free speech precedent.

Scalia joined in the majority opinion's judgment which overruled the lower federal courts based on the Free Speech Clause of the First Amendment, but he wrote a separate concurring opinion to express his criticism of *Lemon*[40] and to articulate an approach to the Establishment Clause which looks to history and tradition for its interpretation. He began by pointing out that he agreed with the majority's conclusion that permitting the church to use the school did not infringe upon the Establishment Clause.[41]

Byron White wrote the majority opinion in *Lamb's Chapel*. First, White addressed the free speech claim of Lamb's Chapel and found that refusal to let the church use schoolrooms violated the First Amendment's Free Speech Clause because civic and social groups already used school buildings for social and civic purposes.[42] In addition, White stressed as to the free speech claim that no one questioned whether the films Lamb's Chapel wanted to show met the qualification of fulfilling social and civic purposes. Therefore, he reasoned that the school district denied access to the evangelical church purely because the films contained religious perspectives.[43] Secondly, White's majority opinion argued that the Establishment Clause did not apply to the church's request to show the films since the school showed them after school hours, no one had to attend, and the films were open to the public. Moreover, he emphasized that many other civic groups used the buildings in similar ways, and no one should conclude the government endorsed Lamb's Chapel or its message by allowing access

---

[40] The three part Establishment Clause test from *Lemon* inquires whether a law (1) has a secular purpose, (2) a primary effect that neither advances nor inhibits religion, and (3) leads to excessive entanglement between church and state. In *Lemon* the Court held that payments to religious schools to recoup the costs incurred from teaching secular topics breached the third prong of this test. *Lemon v. Kurtzman*, 403 U.S. 602, 612-613 (1971).

[41] *Lamb's Chapel*, 508 U.S. at 397-398.

[42] Ibid., 386-397.

[43] Ibid.

to show the films. Lastly, he found that there was no real threat of public unrest due to Lamb's Chapel's use of the school premises.[44]

Scalia's agreement with the majority opinion by White on these points in *Lamb's Chapel* was reaffirmed several years later in *Rosenberger v. University of Virginia*, 515 U.S. 819 (1995) when he joined a similar majority opinion by Anthony Kennedy. Scalia voted for the majority opinion by Kennedy in *Rosenberger*, and did not write a separate opinion. *Rosenberger* concerned payments from a fund at the University of Virginia called the Student Activities Fund. Payments went from the fund to printing businesses outside of the University on behalf of various student groups within the school. The money in the fund derived from required student fees, and the University established the fund to facilitate a wide spectrum of student groups and interests.

A Christian group at the University of Virginia named Wide Awake Productions requested money from the Student Activities Fund for printing of its newspaper. The University denied the request and Wide Awake Productions challenged the denial in court pursuant to the First Amendment's protection of freedom of speech.[45]

Both the federal trial court and the Fourth Circuit Court of Appeals held in *Rosenberger* that the Establishment Clause warranted discrimination against Wide Awake Production's free speech rights. The lower courts reasoned that the Establishment Clause prohibited direct government funding student religious groups like Wide Awake under the circumstances at the University of Virginia.[46]

Kennedy's opinion for the Supreme Court in *Rosenberger* reversed both of the lower federal courts, and rejected all arguments that the Establishment Clause justified denial of funding to Wide Awake Productions. Kennedy argued that the Establishment Clause does not prohibit indirect and neutral funding of religious groups such as the funding program in place for student groups at the University of Virginia, which he found "neutral toward religion."[47] These groups

---

[44] Ibid., 395-396.

[45] *Rosenberger v. University of Virginia*, 515 U.S. 819, 819 (1995).

[46] *Rosenberger*, 515 U.S. at 842.

[47] *Rosenberger*, 515 U.S. at 840.

were independent of the University, and the University required all student groups that benefitted from the Student Activities fund to publish written disclaimers to this effect. In addition, Kennedy submitted that the Establishment Clause does not prevent religious groups from having equal access for meetings in a government building like those at the University of Virginia. He added that this was true even if religious practices occurred during the meetings so long as access to the building is provided as part of a neutral program.[48] Kennedy stressed that ruling otherwise would require government agents to examine the content of communications by student groups to insure that religious content was minimal.[49]

For similar reasons Scalia concurred with the majority opinion's holding in the *Lamb's Chapel* case. Scalia did not agree in *Lamb's Chapel* with the majority's application of the three part Establishment Clause test from the case of *Lemon v. Kurtzman*, 403 U.S. 602 (1971). He began his concurring opinion by evaluating the three prong *Lemon* test. He wrote:

> As to the Court's invocation of the *Lemon* test: Like some ghoul in a late-night horror movie that repeatedly sits up in its graveand shuffles abroad, after being repeatedly killed and buried, *Lemon* stalks our Establishment Clause jurisprudence once again, frightening the little children and school attorneys of Center Moriches Union Free School District. Its most recent burial, only last Term, was, to be sure, not fully six feet under . . . Over the years, however, no fewer than five of the currently sitting justices have, in their own opinions, personally driven pencils through the creature's heart (the author of today's opinion repeatedly) . . . The secret of the *Lemon* test's survival, I think, is that it is so easy to kill. It is there to scare us (and our audience) when we wish it to do so, but we can command it to return to the tomb at will . . . Such a docile and useful monster is worth keeping around, at least in

---

[48] Ibid., 842-843.

[49] Ibid. 844.

a somnolent state; one never knows when one might need him.[50]

Next, he listed scholars who have criticized the *Lemon* test for its uneven application and confusing results. After this he rejected the *Lemon* approach, and noted that he had participated in earlier cases which applied *Lemon's* test, but only because there were not enough votes on the court at the time to abandon the test completely.[51]

In the remainder of the opinion Scalia responded to the majority opinion's statement that it was constitutional for Lamb's Chapel to show the films at a public school because this was not an endorsement of "religion in general."[52] Here he cited American religious tradition to argue that the Establishment Clause does not prevent the government from endorsing religion in general.

He cited the framers of the Constitution, and those who authored the Northwest Ordinance of 1787 for the general proposition "that the public virtues inculcated by religion are a public good."[53] Also, he stressed that Congress passed the Northwest Ordinance "during the summer of 1789" when it was working on the First Amendment, and the Northwest Ordinance stated specifically, "Religion, morality, and knowledge, being necessary to good government and the happiness of mankind, schools and the means of education shall forever be encouraged."[54] Lastly, his concurring opinion reasoned that this traditional endorsement of religion "in general" present in American life since the founding era is evidenced throughout Supreme Court

---

[50] Ibid., 398-399.

[51] Ibid., 400 at * where he notes this in a reference to *Corporation of Presiding Bishop of Church of Jesus Christ of Latter Day Saints v. Amos*, 483 U.S. 327 (1987). Scalia had been on the Supreme Court for barely a year at the time. Looking back to that time when the Court had different members he wrote: "Lacking a majority at that time to abandon *Lemon*, we necessarily focused on that test, which had been the exclusive basis for the lower court's judgment."

[52] Ibid.

[53] Ibid.

[54] Ibid.

precedent as well. To make this point he cited the opinion of William O. Douglas in the case of *Zorach v. Clauson*, 343 U.S. 306, 313-314 (1952) where Douglas wrote, "When the state encourages religious instruction or cooperates with religious authorities by adjusting the schedule of public events to sectarian needs, it follows the best of our traditions."[55] Then, Scalia cited more cases where the Supreme Court upheld government endorsements of religion "in general" including *Lynch v. Donnelly*, 465 U.S. 668 (1984) and *Marsh v. Chambers*, 463 U.S. 783 (1983).

Lynch and *Marsh* are both significant due to references in Chief Justice Burger's majority opinions to an American historical tradition of endorsement of religion "in general."[56] *Lynch* held that the display of a nativity scene in a public park in Pawtucket, Rhode Island was constitutional as part of a larger holiday display including a Santa Claus house, carolers, the cut-out figure of a clown, and a teddy bear.[57] *Marsh* upheld the appointment of legislative chaplains in Nebraska who prayed at the beginning of each legislative session.[58] The Nebraska legislature's Executive Board of the Legislative Council selected chaplains biennially, and compensated them with "public funds."[59] Burger's opinions in both *Lynch* and *Marsh* based their holdings on the history and tradition of America, which Burger traced back to the country's founding and such practices as the Continental Congress's beginning each of its official meetings with "a prayer offered by a paid chaplain."[60]

Scalia concluded his *Lamb's Chapel* opinion by also indicating what it would take for him to find an Establishment Clause violation. In a short statement at the very end he stated that the facts in *Lamb's Chapel* did not violate the First Amendment since showing the movies

---

[55] Ibid., 400-401.

[56] Ibid., 401.

[57] *Lynch v. Donnelly*, 465 U.S. 668, 671-672 (1984).

[58] *Marsh v. Chambers*, 463 U.S. 783, 786 (1983).

[59] *Marsh*, 463 U.S. at 784-785.

[60] Ibid., at 787; *Lynch*, 465 U.S. at 674.

"did not signify state or local embrace of a particular religious sect."[61] Thus, one way a government body can violate the Establishment Clause according to Scalia is for the government to favor one unique or particular religion. Yet, it remained unclear based upon the concurring opinion in *Lamb's Chapel* if this meant that the government could favor Christianity "in general" in his view. He cleared up this ambiguity in the *McCreary* case when he stipulated that the government couldn't embrace Christianity because of the Establishment Clause.[62]

Another Establishment Clause case emerged on the Court's docket about the same time as *Lamb's Chapel*. It was the case of *Lee v. Weisman*, and it led to a dissenting opinion in which Scalia drafted a detailed argument for interpreting the Establishment Clause.

In 1989 Deborah Weisman's father Daniel objected on her behalf to a planned graduation prayer at her middle school, Nathan Bishop Middle School in Providence, Rhode Island. The public schools in Providence had long allowed school administrators to bring ministers to graduation ceremonies both to say invocations and benedictions, and this practice occurred both in middle schools and high schools. Nonetheless, not all graduation ceremonies had prayers because discretion was given to principals as to whether or not to invite clergy to pray.[63]

In spite of Daniel Weisman's objection to the planned prayer of Rabbi Leslie Gutterman of the Temple Beth El at Deborah's graduation, the school's principal Robert E. Lee moved ahead as planned. He gave the Rabbi a pamphlet called "Guidelines for Civic Occasions" to help him prepare for the prayer at the graduation ceremony. The pamphlet had been drafted by the National Conference of Christians and Jews. It advised that prayers at ceremonies such as the one at Nathan Bishop Middle School should have language, which is fitting for "nonsectarian" occasions, and therefore be inclusive and sensitive.[64] Moreover, when Principal Lee provided the pamphlet to

---

[61] Ibid.

[62] *McCreary County v. ACLU*, 545 U.S. 844, 897 (2005).

[63] *Lee v. Weisman*, 505 U.S. 577, 581 (1992).

[64] Ibid.

Rabbi Gutterman he instructed him to pray "nonsectarian" prayers for both the prayer at the beginning and the end of the ceremony.

The prayer, which the Rabbi prayed as the Invocation, consisted of the following words:

> God of the Free, Hope of the Brave: For the legacy of America where diversity is celebrated and the rights of minorities are protected, we thank You. May these young men and women grow up to enrich it. For the liberty of America, we thank You. May these new graduates grow up to guard it. For the political process of America in which all its citizens may participate, for its court system where all may seek justice we thank You. May those we honor this morning always turn to it in trust. For the destiny of America we thank You. May the graduates of Nathan Bishop Middle School so live that they might help to share it. May our aspirations for our country and for these young people, who are our hope for the future, be richly fulfilled. AMEN.[65]

The Benediction, reproduced as well in the majority opinion, was similarly general in its language, but the content was much less civic in its orientation. To the contrary, it primarily expressed thanks for the families, graduates, school teachers, and administrators.

Daniel Weisman sought an injunction to prevent the prayers at his daughter's graduation, but the legal action was untimely. Therefore, Deborah went to the ceremony where the prayers were offered. Afterwards, her father once again took legal action by asking for a permanent injunction preventing the practice of having clergy deliver prayers at graduations in Providence. The Federal District Trial Court found in favor of the Weismans that the school graduation prayers breached the Establishment Clause after applying the three part *Lemon* test. It discerned that the prayers failed the second prong of the test that stated that a law has to have "a primary effect that neither advances nor inhibits religion." [66] It reasoned that this "effects test" prohibits government activity which not only prefers one religion over another,

---

[65] Ibid., 582.

[66] Ibid., 585.

but also that which favors religion in general, contrary to *Marsh v. Chambers,* 463 U.S. 783 (1983). The Federal Fifth Circuit Court of Appeals upheld the District Court's holding and application of the *Lemon* test.

Anthony Kennedy authored the Supreme Court's majority opinion in the case. The majority opinion affirmed the decisions of the lower federal courts, but it did so on different grounds that posed a potentially new approach to the Establishment Clause, at least in cases involving government sponsored prayer. His rationale for finding an Establishment Clause violation was not based on the three-part *Lemon* test, but rather the element of coercion present when the government supervises prayer at officially sponsored and effectively mandatory ceremonies.[67]

Scalia's *Lee* dissent stressed the tradition of government support for religion in general traceable back to the founding era that he maintained should serve as the guiding light for Establishment Clause interpretation. He wrote that the First Amendment provision needed to be "construed in the light of government policies of accommodation, acknowledgement, and support for religion [that] are an accepted part of our political and cultural heritage."[68] More specifically, he claimed the clause's meaning "is to be determined by reference to historical practices and understandings."[69] Also, he argued that a holding which struck down traditional, historical religious practices such as the prayers in *Lee* was an incorrect interpretation of the Establishment Clause because he asserted that the meaning of the clause was available in religious practices traceable to America's founders.[70] Thus, he could not join the majority decision that did not have any references to traditional religious practices, which were part of America's historical religious tradition.

Secondly, he maintained that the majority's ruling was contrary to a longstanding American tradition of nonsectarian prayer to God at

---

[67] Ibid., 586-587.

[68] Ibid., 631.

[69] Ibid.

[70] Ibid., citing Justice Kennedy's opinion in *County of Allegheny v. ACLU,* 492 U.S. 573, 657, 670 (1989).

public ceremonies, and this was tantamount to "social engineering" by judicial fiat that "bulldozed" tradition.[71] The result, Scalia warned, would be a weakened constitutional system that depended on the ever-changing beliefs and values of individual justices on the Supreme Court. A better methodology for maintaining strong protection for constitutional rights was to interpret the Establishment Clause according to principles that "have deep foundations in the historic practices of our people."[72]

Over the course of several pages in his dissent Scalia then provided an account of the public religious traditions and historic practices that have deep foundations in America's past. He cited Oliver Wendell Holmes's admonition that "a page of history is worth a volume of logic" arguing that it "applies with particular force" to Establishment Clause methodology, and emphasized that appropriate interpretations "comport with what history reveals was the contemporaneous understanding of its guarantees."[73] He allowed that the mere existence of a practice at the nation's founding did not foreclose the issue of constitutionality, but submitted that it was very important in Establishment Clause interpretation nonetheless. Additionally, he quoted Justices William Brennan and Warren Burger to support the methodology he defended with reference to Establishment Clause hermeneutics. In *Abington v. Schempp*, 374 U.S. 203, 294 (1963) Brennan wrote, "The line we must draw between the permissible and the impermissible is one which accords with history and faithfully reflects the understanding of the Founding Fathers."[74] The reference to former Chief Justice Burger in his *Weisman* dissent came from the case of *Marsh v. Chambers*, which also relied heavily on early American historical practices to uphold legislative prayers against First Amendment challenge.[75] Burger stated in *Marsh* that "[H]istorical

---

[71] Ibid., 632.

[72] Ibid., 632.

[73] Ibid., referring favorable again to the case of *Lynch v. Donnelly*, 465 U.S. 668, 673 (1984) which also based its decision upholding a government display of the nativity on a reading of American history and tradition.

[74] Ibid., 632.

[75] *Marsh v. Chambers*, 463 U.S. at 790.

evidence sheds light not only on what the draftsmen intended the Establishment Clause to mean, but also on how they thought that clause applied" to religious practices of the founding era.[76]

These public religious practices from American history were, moreover, replete with "public ceremonies featuring prayers."[77] For support of this proposition he referred to the following Supreme Court cases: *Lynch v. Donnelly*, 465 U.S. at 674-678; *Marsh v. Chambers*, 463 U.S. at 786-788; *Wallace v. Jaffree*, 472 U.S. at 100-103; and *Engel v. Vitale*, 370 U.S. at 446-450, and footnote 3. These cases documented public religious practices in the American past which Scalia looked to as support, including:

(1) prayers in the Continental Congress, Supreme Court, the Senate and House of Representatives, and presidential inauguration ceremonies; (2) statements by Presidents George Washington, John Adams, Thomas Jefferson, James Madison, Abraham Lincoln, Grover Cleveland, Woodrow Wilson, Franklin D. Roosevelt, Dwight D. Eisenhower, and John F. Kennedy;

(2) the language of the Star Spangled Banner and the 1954 Pledge of Allegiance;

(3) the National Day of Prayer;

(4) language on coins stating "IN GOD WE TRUST";

(5) language at the end of the Declaration of Independence which states "And for the support of this Declaration, with a firm reliance on the protection of divine Providence, we mutually pledge to each other our Lives, our Fortunes and our sacred Honor";

(6) the provision of paid chaplains by Congress;

(7) a national day of Thanksgiving and other national holidays with strong religious significance;

(8) art in publicly supported galleries "predominantly inspired by one religious faith";[78]

---

[76] *Lee v. Weisman*, 505 U.S. 577, 632 (1992).

[77] Ibid., 633.

[78] *Lynch*, 465 U.S. at 676.

(9) the Northwest Ordinance's provisions on religion and public virtue and religious schools; and

(10) appropriations in the eighteenth and nineteenth centuries for sectarian education of Native Americans.

He then added to these historical examples the following additional ones:

(1) President George Washington's First Inaugural Address and swearing in ceremony wherein the President placed his hands on a Bible;

(2) Thomas Jefferson's first and second inaugural addresses;

(3) James Madison's first inaugural address;

(4) President George Herbert Walker Bush's inaugural speech; and

(5) prayers at official events for all branches of the national government since the founding era.[79]

All of these historical practices, for Scalia, established a general and unbroken tradition of public prayer in official civic ceremonies. In addition to these, he found a specific tradition of public prayer in official civic ceremonies. In addition to these, he found a specific tradition of prayer at high school graduations, which dated back to the 1860s. He noted that one source shows that there was prayer at the first high school graduation at Norwich Free Academy in Connecticut. Moreover, this graduation prayer was contemporaneous with ratification of the Fourteenth Amendment.[80] Thus, graduation prayer at public schools amounted to an historical tradition widely established and recognized and consistent with the text and history of the Establishment Clause.[81]

---

[79] *Lee v. Weisman,* 505 U.S. at 633-635.

[80] Ibid., 635. Citing Brodinsky, "Commencement Rites Obsolete? Not At All. A 10 Week Study Shows," *10 Updating School Board Policies,* No. 4, p. 3 (Apr. 1979).

[81] Ibid., 636.

The next part of Scalia's dissenting opinion included a strongly worded critique of Kennedy's conclusion that psychological coercion was present in the case because the government was involved in a scenario where children were indirectly forced to pray.[82] He argued that the court was acting outside the realm of its expertise by acting like a psychologist. In a manner echoing the arguments of Frankfurter in both *Gobitis* and *Barnette* he dismissed the majority's conclusions as intolerant of the will of the legislative majority. He submitted that it was perfectly reasonable for the school district authorities to cultivate tolerance for the religious rituals of others by having the prayers. He claimed that this merely leads to inculcation of the civic virtue of tolerance, which public school administrators and leaders should encourage. In addition, Scalia argued for the development of this civic virtue of tolerance by reasoning that the government's interest in cultivating tolerance trumped the interests of those who objected to "the false appearance of participation."[83]

He further warned that the majority's conclusions would lead to an assault on one of the religious rituals present in American civic life, the Pledge of Allegiance, and its language referring to "one nation under God." He wrote, "Logically, that ought to be the next project for the Court's bulldozer."[84] He pointed out that the same students present for the prayers said the Pledge without any problems just a few moments before the objectionable prayers. Yet, he warned, the majority was not concerned about any coercion with the Pledge even though it raised the same Establishment Clause issue.

Scalia next sought to dismiss the evidence of coercion by the government in the case. He could not see how the school district officials were enforcing any kind of orthodoxy, or really violating anyone's conscience in any meaningful manner. What looked like psychological coercion to the majority amounted to "distortions of the record" for him.[85] Scalia rejected Kennedy's argument that the prayer

---

[82] Ibid., 633-639.

[83] Ibid., 638.

[84] Ibid., 639.

[85] Ibid., 640.

in *Lee* amounted to psychological coercion, and countered that the Establishment Clause was intended to prohibit:

(1) coercion of religious orthodoxy,
(2) financial support of religion by force of law and threat of penalty, (3) forced attendance at a government church,
(3) mandated use of state clergy to perform sacraments,
(4) civil disabilities for dissenters, and
(5) the national government from regulating state establishments.[86]

Thus, for example, the government clearly could not endorse specific aspects of sectarian faiths such as the divinity of Christ without violating the Establishment Clause. Yet, the prayers in *Lee* were, in Scalia's own words, "so characteristically American" that they did not amount to an unconstitutional establishment of religion, and therefore were constitutional and innocuous. For him governmentally sponsored religious speech at graduation ceremonies is relatively harmless because it is not coercive in that the listener to the prayers can respond any way they like such as refusing to listen to the prayer or sitting down. He did, however, write that legally unconstitutional coercion was present in cases such as *Barnette*, and the school prayer decisions of *Engel* and *Abington v. Schempp*, but argued that these cases were distinguishable because school classrooms in those cases created a coercive environment distinct from that present in graduation ceremonies. Moreover, in *Barnette* he stressed that there were legal sanctions involved such as expulsion, and governmentally forced payment for private schooling.[87]

The conclusion of Scalia's *Lee* dissent once again referred to examples of religion in American public life from the past, and stressed that religion by its nature is public as well as private, and thereby demands public acknowledgement. He cited the Declaration of Independence, George Washington's first Thanksgiving Proclamation,

---

[86] Ibid., 640-641.

[87] Ibid., 642-643, citing *West Virginia Board of Education v. Barnette*, 319 U.S. 624, 643 (1943); *Engel v. Vitale*, 370 U.S. 421 (1962); and *School Dist. of Abington v. Schempp*, 374 U.S. 203 (1963).

and the "age-old practices of our people" in support of allowing prayer at graduation ceremonies like those in *Lee*.[88] He criticized the majority for taking a "bold step" by thwarting the desire of the majority of the American people to solemnize public occasions by thanking God for the blessings of the country. Moreover, he submitted that the Constitution does not intend to frustrate the desire of a religious majority to have nonsectarian prayers at public school graduations. He submitted that having these prayers helps fulfill the founders' goal of avoiding sectarian strife by encouraging everyone to gather to pray in tolerant respect for one another across religious boundaries. This would lead to common affection, he asserted, one for another among citizens prayed "to the God whom they all worship and seek."[89] It would remedy the "religious bigotry and prejudice [of those present] in a manner that cannot be replicated," he claimed, leading to civic virtue and unity. He then concluded his opinion by making the following statement:

> To deprive our society of that important unifying mechanism, in order to spare the nonbeliever what seems to me the minimal inconvenience of standing or even sitting in respectful nonparticipation; is as senseless in polity as it is unsupported in law."[90]

The next Establishment Clause case that Scalia authored an opinion in was *Board of Education of Kiryas Joel Village School District v. Grumet*, 512 U.S. 687, 732-752 (1994). The facts in *Kiryas Joel* involved a school district in Monroe, New York, which was created by action of the New York legislature in 1989. The school district consisted of a village called Kiryas Joel whose citizens were all members of Satmar Hasidic Judaism, but the district only operated a program for handicapped children. The remainder of the children in Kiryas Joel continued to attend private schools. Governor Mario Cuomo signed the bill into law, and acknowledged that everyone who

---

[88] Ibid., 645-646.

[89] Ibid., 646.

[90] Ibid., 646.

lived in the district adhered to Satmar Hasidic Judaism, but he felt that this was proper. The law granted to the school district total legal authority over education in the village, but approximately 40 children participated in the handicapped program. The New York State School Board Association and its officers challenged the law in state court pursuant to the Establishment Clause. All state courts that reviewed the case agreed with the New York School Board Association that the law was an impermissible advancement of religion in violation of the Establishment Clause.[91]

David Souter's majority opinion held likewise that the law creating the school district was an impermissible establishment of religion. He submitted that the law in question violated the neutrality toward religion required by the First Amendment as announced in the cases *Committee for Public Ed. & Religious Liberty v. Nyquist*, 413 U.S. 756, 792-793 (1973) and *Epperson v. Arkansas*, 393 U.S. 97, 104 (1968). This was due to the fact that the law gave exclusive control over the public school district to one religious group with "no assurance that governmental power has been or will be exercised neutrally."[92]

Scalia disagreed with Souter's conclusions in his dissenting opinion, and stated that, "The Court's decision today is astounding."[93] He stressed that the case was one primarily about provision of secular education to the handicapped, and found the facts that the school district's authority was given exclusively to members of one religious group and that the students all were members of the same sect irrelevant. Moreover, he argued that to hold otherwise was contrary to American history in which religious groups had exercised governmental control as the nearly exclusive populations in certain parts of the country.[94] Scalia cited the Roman Catholics in New Mexico and Mormons in Utah as examples of religious groups, which were almost exclusive populations in these two states. Lastly, he urged

---

[91] *Board of Education of Kiryas Joel Village School District v. Grumet*, 512 U.S. 687, 690-696 (1994).

[92] Ibid., 696.

[93] Ibid., 752.

[94] Ibid., 735-736, n. 1-2 referring to New Mexico's Roman Catholic population and Utah's Mormon population.

that the creation of the school district was a tolerant accommodation of religion for a minority sect with a neutral, secular policy behind it-provision of special education services to a small number of students who also happened to have the same religion.[95] There was no evidence of impartiality in the case, or government favoritism for the Satmar Hasidim.

Scalia emphasized historical practices of the founding era in his *Kiryas Joel* opinion at a few points. In contrast to his *Lee* dissent, Scalia mentioned that the Establishment Clause should be interpreted with "text and history as guides," but spent most of the opinion arguing a rationale based on accommodation and toleration of minority faiths as a practical necessity.[96] He cited James Madison as authority for the proposition that government should not deprive religious people of their rights based on religious convictions. He stressed that the Court's majority opinion applied the Establishment Clause in a manner that denied religious liberty to a minority sect under the factual scenario in the case. He argued pursuant to the Establishment Clause that if the small Satmar Hasidim sect could not receive provision of government resources for education of handicapped children, then their religious liberty was violated. The better approach to the Establishment Clause in Scalia's view was to accommodate the religion of the small orthodox sect, and allow the provision of government resources in spite of Establishment Clause challenge. Therefore the *Kiryas Joel* case is analogous to the free exercise case of *Church of Lukumi Babalu Aye, Inc. v. Hialeah*, 505 U.S. 520 (1993) because in that case he voted to uphold a free exercise challenge to a law that impacted the religious liberty of members of a minority religion.

Once again, Scalia's opinion criticized the *Lemon* test. He objected to the practice of the lower courts that followed it and spent significant portions of their opinions discussing it. He called again for a moratorium on its citation, and abandonment of its unpredictable and malleable three-part test. In place of *Lemon* he offered that the court should not adopt the case-by-case approach articulated by Justice Sandra Day O'Connor, but instead seek "fidelity to the longstanding traditions of our people, which surely provide the diversity of treatment

---

[95] Ibid., 738.

[96] Ibid., 732.

that Justice O'Connor seeks, but do not leave us to our own devices."[97] Then, he closed his opinion with strong language by criticizing the majority's opinion for effectively taking a side in America's culture was in the *Grumet* case because the opinion "continues, and takes to new extremes, a recent tendency in the opinions of this Court to turn the Establishment Clause into a repealer of our Nation's tradition of religious toleration."[98]

Approximately one decade after *Kiryas Joel* the Supreme Court decided another Establishment Clause case, which Scalia authored a dissenting opinion in. This was the case *McCreary County v. ACLU*, 545 U.S. 844 (2005). Scalia's appeal to an American tradition of support for religion in general in his Establishment Clause opinions culminated in a dissenting opinion that included references to elements from the tradition, the *McCreary County v. ACLU* opinion. The case concerned a series of displays of the Ten Commandments in two different counties in Kentucky. The displays were directed and authorized by county executives. Subsequent to challenges to the displays by the American Civil Liberties Union pursuant to the Establishment Clause the counties passed resolutions with the intent of demonstrating that the Ten Commandments inspired Kentucky's law. These resolutions led to new displays that still contained the Ten Commandments, only now they were surrounded by more documentary sources with purely religious content. Soon the counties hired new lawyers in the case, and changed the displays again by eliminating some sources, editing others, and putting new ones in.[99]

The Court accepted two primary issues for review in the case: whether it was appropriate to analyze the purpose of the counties for the displays under the Establishment Clause, and whether the court should consider how the displays changed over time as part of this analysis. The majority opinion written by Souter answered both of these questions in the affirmative and ruled that the displays in the case violated the Establishment Clause. The majority therefore upheld the

---

[97] Ibid., 751. His criticism of *Lemon's* ongoing relevance is on pages 750-751.

[98] Ibid., 752.

[99] *McCreary County v. ACLU*, 545 U.S. 844, 850 (2005).

Court of Appeals for the Sixth Circuit, which had affirmed the trial court's preliminary injunction against the displays.[100]

Scalia's dissent against this holding again included a lengthy argument that proper interpretation of the Establishment Clause emerged from review of American religious tradition going back to the founders of the republic. Before doing this, though, he noted that he had attended a conference of judges in Italy in 2001 when Al Qaeda perpetrated the attacks against America on September 11. He described how almost all of the judges at the conference listened to the President of the United States as he addressed Americans, and then concluded by saying, "God bless America." Then, he noted that the next day a judge from another country approached him and complained:

> How I wish that the Head of State of my country, at a similar time of national tragedy and distress, could conclude his address 'God bless ___________.' It is of course absolutely forbidden.[101]

Then, Scalia transitioned into the heart of the opinion by comparing the American system of church and state to those in Europe, which were secular, France serving as a prime example. He noted that in these countries, "Religion is to be strictly excluded from the public forum."[102] In comparison, however, he submitted that this had never been America's approach to relations between church and state.

Then, he again cited examples of leaders from America's history that had engaged in religious practices or made public statements, which he relied upon to interpret the Establishment Clause. First, he referred to George Washington who added to the Presidential Oath of Office the phrase, "so help me God."[103] Next, he appealed to the Chief Justice of the Supreme Court John Marshall who opened sessions of the Court in the early nineteenth century with the words, "God save the United States and this Honorable Court." Third, he again cited the

---

[100] *McCreary County,* 545 U.S. at 850-851, 881.

[101] Ibid., 885.

[102] Ibid., 886.

[103] Ibid.

congressional practice of opening its sessions with prayer, just as he had in *Lee v. Weisman.* To these historical references in support of a tradition of allowing endorsement of religion in general he added: the First Congress's request for a day of Thanksgiving, the Northwest Ordinance's reference to religion and civic virtue, George Washington's inaugural prayer, John Adam's address to the Massachusetts militia, Thomas Jefferson's second inaugural address's call to prayer, and James Madison's first inaugural address.[104]

After this historical review he transitioned to the twenty-first century to conclude, "Nor have the views of our people on this matter significantly changed."[105] He found evidence for this assertion in the ongoing practice of presidents who say "so help me God" after taking the oath of office, as well as in legislative prayers, prayers "to the Almighty . . . at all levels of government," religious references on coins, the Pledge of Allegiance, and last of all in another reference to Justice Douglas's dicta in *Zorach v. Clauson*:

> We are a religious people whose institutions presuppose a Supreme Being.[106]

In light of all this historical evidence he could not agree with the majority's view that the First Amendment requires neutrality between religion and nonreligion. To the contrary, he maintained once more that neither the text of the First Amendment's Establishment Clause, or "the history and tradition that reflect our society's constant understanding of those words," or the recent unanimous Act of Congress reaffirming inclusion of "under God" in the Pledge of Allegiance supported such an

---

[104] Ibid., 887-888. He quoted language from Madison's First Inaugural which 'placed his confidence "in the guardianship and guidance of that Almighty Being whose power regulates the destiny of nations, whose blessings have been so conspicuously dispensed to this rising Republic, and to whom we are bound to address our devout gratitude for the past, as well as our fervent supplications and best hopes for the future." Ibid., 888.

[105] Ibid., 888.

[106] Ibid., 889.

approach.[107] Rather, the Supreme Court had been following a flawed approach with regard to interpretation of the Establishment Clause, which went back to the "mid-20th century."[108] He again criticized the *Lemon* test as "discredited" and subject to easy manipulation by judges who used it to read their own personal opinions into interpretation of the First Amendment. He wrote of this interpretive license applied by his peers as follows:

> What distinguishes the rule of law from the dictatorship of a shifting Supreme Court majority is the absolutely indispensable requirement that judicial opinions be grounded in consistently applied principle. That is what prevents judges from ruling now this way, now that-thumbs up or thumbs down-as their personal preferences dictate.[109]

Next, in the *McCreary* dissent, Scalia argued that the Court has not applied the "neutrality" principle consistently in its Establishment Clause precedent because religious practices historically evident in American tradition demand acknowledgement that the Constitution does not require strict neutrality between religion and nonreligion. As examples he referred to cases that preferred religion to nonreligion in the public square, including *Marsh v. Chambers* allowing legislative prayers, and *Walz v. Tax Commission of the City of New York* approving of tax exemptions for church land. In addition, Scalia criticized his peers on the Court for following an inconsistent approach to the Establishment Clause because of fear of public criticism if they did not. He charged:

> What, then, could be the genuine "good reason" for occasionally ignoring the neutrality principle? I suggest it is the instinct for self-preservation, and the recognition that the Court, which "has no influence over either sword or the purse" . . . cannot go too far down the road of an enforced neutrality

---

[107] Ibid.

[108] Ibid., 889.

[109] Ibid., 890-891.

that contradicts both historical fact and current practice without losing all that sustains it: the willingness of the people to accept its interpretation of the Constitution as definitive, in preference to the contrary interpretation of the democratically elected branches.[110]

Scalia rejected the majority's assertion that the Ten Commandments displays in the case violated the First Amendment because they favored "one religion over another."[111] He asserted that "public acknowledgment of the Creator" which favors monotheism does not violate the Establishment Clause.[112]

He began this crucial part of his argument by saying that historical tradition warranted favoritism for monotheistic public references to God. Therefore, government officials and agents could constitutionally fail to acknowledge non-monotheists in public statements by disregarding their beliefs. He submitted, "With respect to public acknowledgment of religious belief, it is entirely clear from our Nation's historical practices that the Establishment Clause permits this disregard of polytheists and believers in unconcerned deities, just as it permits the disregard of devout atheists."[113] Here again he cited George Washington's Thanksgiving Proclamation that derived from an appeal made by the First Congress, and whose content was "scrupulously nondenominational-but it was monotheistic."[114] Moreover, he added, almost ninety-eight percent of Americans are monotheists, and this fact combined with longstanding historical traditions to confirm his Establishment Clause interpretation that "there is a distance between the acknowledgment of a single creator and the establishment of a religion."[115]

---

[110] Ibid., 892-893.

[111] Ibid., 893.

[112] Ibid., 893.

[113] Ibid., 893.

[114] Ibid.

[115] Ibid., 894.

Thereafter in the dissent Scalia defended his historical methodology against the criticisms of Souter and Stevens. He maintained that his approach looked to the sources of meaning most likely to reveal the meaning of the Establishment Clause's text: the actions of the Congress who drafted it, and the first president sworn to uphold it. Then he distinguished the "Memorial and Remonstrance against Religious Assessments" of James Madison as irrelevant in this case because it was written before the idea for the constitution had been presented, and since its focus was taxation for religion, not public references to deity.

Several pages later in the opinion Scalia then made explicit that his historical methodology as applied to the Establishment Clause favored the faiths of a majority of American citizens. He wrote that his methodology did not discriminate against minority faiths, but only acknowledged the American practice of appealing to God publicly in keeping with what most Americans believed. He defended this majoritarian favoritism by writing, "Our national tradition has resolved this conflict in favor of the majority. It is not for this Court to change a disposition that accounts, many Americans think, for the phenomenon remarked upon in a quotation attributed to various authors, including Bismarck, but which I prefer to associate with Charles de Gaulle:

> God watches over little children, drunkards, and the United States of America.[116]

The conclusion of the *McCreary* opinion summarized the reasons Scalia gave in his opinion that the majority failed to apply the Establishment Clause correctly. He defended the Ten Commandments displays because they fell within an American historical tradition that publicly acknowledged God albeit in generically monotheistic terms, and at the same time he criticized the majority opinion for displaying hostility toward religion in "a revisionist agenda of secularization."[117] The displays were also relatively insignificant in his opinion because they did not highlight certain documents, or draw attention to the religious significance of the Ten Commandments. Inclusion of the

---

[116] Ibid.,900.

[117] Ibid., 910.

Magna Charta, the Declaration of Independence, the Bill of Rights, the Star Spangled Banner, the Mayflower Compact of 1620, a picture of lady Justice, "In God We Trust," and the Preamble of the Kentucky Constitution in the display not only minimized the religious content of the displays, but also provided evidence for a purely secular purpose, which was to underscore the sources which combined to produce the "foundation of our system of law and government."[118]

An individual display of the Ten Commandments should also pass muster according to Scalia since the implied purpose for the display in the courthouse was to show tolerance for Judaism, "religion in general, or for law." [119]   Moreover, again appealing to "a centuries-old tradition," Scalia argued that these displays continue the public acknowledgment of religion. He referred to "the degree to which religious belief pervaded the National Government during the founding era."[120] Then, the justice cited cases which have looked to a similar historical tradition in Establishment Clause cases to defend government recognition of public religion such as a nativity scene in a city's holiday display and prayers by governmentally selected persons in public school graduation ceremonies: *Lynch v. Donnelly*, 465 U.S. at 674-678; *Marsh v. Chambers*, 463 U.S. at 786-788; *Lee v. Weisman*, 505 U.S. at 633-636 (Scalia, J., dissenting) ; *Wallace v. Jaffree*, 472 U.S. at 100-106 (Rehnquist, J., dissenting) ; and *Engel v. Vitale*, 370 U.S. at 446-450, and n. 3.[121]

These references to traditional American public "religion in general" combined for Scalia with the display of the Ten Commandments around the Supreme Court building, and on government buildings in Washington, D.C., to establish "the popular understandings that the Ten Commandments are a foundation of the rule of law, and a symbol of the role that religion played, and continues to play, in our system of government."[122] These displays, therefore, did

---

[118] Ibid., 904.

[119] Ibid., 904 quoting Justice Stevens' opinion in *Allegheny County*, 492 U.S. at 652 (STEVENS, J., concurring in part and dissenting in part).

[120] Ibid., 906.

[121] Ibid.

[122] Ibid., 907.

not promote one religious perspective at the expense of others, or a sectarian view of Christianity, but a form of nonpreferential religion in general, or what Steven B. Epstein has defined as ceremonial deism.[123] Scalia reasoned further that because the Ten Commandments are "recognized by Judaism, Christianity, and Islam alike as divinely given" they should not offend anyone's conscience.[124]

CONCLUSION

Though he adapted an approach to the Free Exercise Clause similar to that of Felix Frankfurter, Antonin Scalia interpreted the Establishment Clause differently. Scalia appealed to an unbroken American historical tradition of government endorsement of religion generally to interpret the Establishment Clause. Moreover, this emphasis became stronger in his later Establishment Clause dissents. He argued in the *McCreary* case that the government can constitutionally favor monotheistic religions in public acknowledgments over non-monotheistic faiths, and he based this conclusion upon an American religious tradition traceable to the founders. His religion clause jurisprudence also differed from Frankfurter's because he never voted to strike down a public religious practice, custom, program or display via the Establishment Clause.

Scalia's religion clause methodology, like Frankfurter's, appealed to certain founders from the American founding era as support for his conclusions in free exercise and establishment cases. These founders

---

[123] Steven B. Epstein, "Rethinking the Constitutionality of Ceremonial Deism," *96 Columbia L. Rev. 2083, 2095* (1996). In this article Epstein defines ceremonial deism as all public religious practices that "involve 1) actual, symbolic, or ritualistic; 2) prayer, invocation, benediction, supplication, appeal, reverent reference to, or embrace of, a general or particular deity; 3) created, delivered, sponsored, or encouraged by government officials; 4) during governmental functions or ceremonies, in the form of patriotic expressions, or associated with holiday observances; 5) which, in and of themselves, are unlikely to indoctrinate or proselytize their audience; 6) which are not specifically designed to accommodate the free exercise of a particular group of citizens; and 7) which, as of this date, are deeply rooted in the nation's history and traditions." Ibid.

[124] Ibid., 909.

included George Washington, John Adams, Thomas Jefferson, James Madison, and John Marshall. Yet, Scalia and Frankfurter did not emphasize the founders in the same manner in their Establishment Clause jurisprudences, nor did their Establishment Clause opinions reveal similar conclusions about the clause's meaning.

CHAPTER 7

Frankfurter, Scalia, and Public Religion

INTRODUCTION

This concluding chapter will compare evidence from the religion clause jurisprudences of Frankfurter and Scalia in order to establish that they found different forms of American public religion constitutional. It will accomplish this by first showing that Frankfurter and Scalia interpreted the Establishment Clause differently, but adopted similar approaches in free exercise cases. Secondly, the evidence presented will demonstrate that Frankfurter and Scalia have advocated judicial restraint, and that both judges have applied originalist methodologies that relied upon some of America's founders to interpret the religion clauses. Yet, the evidence will also show that reliance on America's founders to interpret the religion clauses has not led Frankfurter and Scalia to the same conclusions when interpreting the Establishment Clause, and neither has their appeal to judicial restraint.

Rather, Frankfurter's originalist methodology stressed that the Establishment Clause was intended to separate church and state. He emphasized Thomas Jefferson and James Madison's views on religious liberty and the phrase referring to a "wall of separation" between church and state, as exemplified in his opinions in *McCollum v. Board of Education* and *McGowan v. Maryland*. [1] Scalia, in contrast,

---

[1] *McGowan v. Maryland*, 366 U.S. 420, 463-465 (1961); and *McCollum v. Board of Education*, 333 U.S. 203, 231 (1948).

emphasized the views and practices of American founders such as George Washington and John Adams in addition to those of Jefferson and Madison to argue that the Establishment Clause did not prevent government from endorsing public religion, which was theistic but generic in nature. Therefore, Scalia found some theistic forms of American public religion constitutional including a graduation prayer and a display of the Ten Commandments.[2] Frankfurter, to the contrary, only found more secular forms of American public religion constitutional such as the secular need for a day of rest, veneration of the American flag, and the need for cohesive sentiment to unify American citizens.[3]

FRANKFURTER AND SCALIA'S DIFFERENT APPROACHES TO THE ESTABLISHMENT CLAUSE

The religion clause jurisprudences of Frankfurter and Scalia differed with reference to the Establishment Clause. The evidence for this difference between the two judges was in the following cases: *McCollum v. Board of Education*, 333 U.S. 203, 212-232 (1948); *McGowan v. Maryland*, 366 U.S. 420, 463-465 (1961); *Lee v. Weisman*, 505 U.S. 577, 631-635 (1992); and *McCreary County v. ACLU*, 545 U.S. 844, 885-912 (2005).

The cases that documented Frankfurter's Establishment Clause jurisprudence included *Everson v. Board of Education*, 330 U.S. 1 (1947); *Zorach v. Clauson*, 343 U.S. 306 (1952); *McCollum v. Board of Education*, 333 U.S. 203 (1948); and *McGowan v. Maryland*, 366 U.S. 420 (1961). In these cases Frankfurter applied strict scrutiny to laws that had been challenged, and found a violation of the clause in every case except for the case of *McGowan v. Maryland*, 366 U.S. 420, 459-543 (1961). In *McGowan*, which involved both free exercise and establishment claims, his concurring opinion supported the Court's conclusion that Sunday closing laws did not unconstitutionally hinder the religious liberty of adherents of Judaism because he argued that the

---

[2] *Lee v. Weisman*, 505 U.S. 577, 631-635 (1992); and *McCreary County v. ACLU*, 545 U.S. 844, 886-889 and 893-898 (2005).

[3] *McGowan*, 366 U.S. at 463-465; and *Minersville School District v. Gobitis*, 310 U.S. 586, 591-600 (1940).

legal enforcement of a Sabbath on a Sunday was secular in nature. Frankfurter submitted that the history behind Sunday closing laws revealed a purely secular purpose by the 1950s, and this secular purpose was the government's interest in a day of rest.

Frankfurter and Scalia's distinct interpretations of the Establishment Clause become evident in their respective Establishment Clause opinions wherein Frankfurter emphasized that the clause was intended to separate church and state as well as prevent social conflict.[4] Also, Frankfurter applied the Establishment Clause strictly by voting in nearly every case he participated in to find a violation of it.[5] Scalia, to the contrary, applied the Establishment Clause weakly by never voting to find a violation of the clause in a Supreme Court case.[6] In addition, Scalia submitted that government can endorse religion generally without violating the Establishment Clause if the government's endorsement was consistent with the American historical tradition that he referred to in his dissenting opinions in *Lee v. Weisman*, 505 U.S. 577, 631-646 (1992) and *McCreary County v. ACLU*, 545 U.S. 844, 886-889 (2005). Scalia traced this American historical tradition allowing government endorsements of generic monotheism back to the speeches and public religious practices of Jefferson, Madison, Washington, Adams, and John Marshall.

Finally, Scalia's Establishment Clause opinions were distinct from Frankfurter's in that Scalia not only interpreted the Establishment Clause weakly and appealed to different founders from Frankfurter in his opinions, but also found theistic public religion constitutional. For example, the graduation prayer that Scalia deemed constitutional in *Lee v. Weisman*, 505 U.S. 577, 631-646 (1992) contained theistic, but non-specific language in its references to God. The Rabbi's prayer stated, "God of the free, Hope of the Brave: For the legacy of America where

---

[4] *McCollum v. Board of Education*, 333 U.S. 203, 231 (1948).

[5] *Everson v. Board of Education*, 330 U.S. 1, 18-63 (1947); *McCollum v. Board of Education*, 333 U.S. 203, 212-232 (1948); *Zorach v. Clauson*, 343 U.S. 307, 320-323 (1952); *Kedroff v. Saint Nicholas Cathedral*, 344 U.S. 94, 121-126 (1952); and *McGowan v. Maryland*, 366 U.S. 420, 422-453 (1961).

[6] Kathleen M. Sullivan, "Justice Scalia and the Religion Clauses," 22 *U. Haw. L. Rev.* 449, 449 (2000).

diversity is celebrated and the rights of minorities are protected, we thank You."[7] The prayer did not make any other references to God that were more specific than the second person singular reference to "You," which was repeated by the Rabbi several times.[8]

In a similar manner, in the *McCreary County* no establishment case, Scalia found another theistic example of public religion constitutional: a public display in a courthouse in Kentucky, which contained the Ten Commandments.[9] He cited a number of early American examples of public religion in *McCreary* that supported his argument that public government acknowledgment of monotheistic religion in displays, official government ceremonies, political speeches or similar practices did not violate the Establishment Clause. These included:

(1) George Washington's inclusion of the phrase, "so help me God" in the Presidential Oath of Office,
(2) John Marshall's practice of opening Supreme Court sessions in the nineteenth century with the words, "God save the United States and this Honorable Court," and
(3) the early congressional practice of opening its sessions with prayer.[10]

Also, Scalia reasoned that the Ten Commandment's display was constitutional because its content was "scrupulously nondenominational—but it was monotheistic."[11]

In contrast, in part of Frankfurter's opinion about the Establishment Clause in *McGowan v. Maryland*[12] Frankfurter relied upon Jefferson's views regarding religious liberty as the primary source for the meaning of the religion clauses. *McGowan* involved a law in

---

[7] *Lee*, 505 U.S. at 582.

[8] Ibid.

[9] *McCreary County v. ACLU*, 545 U.S. 844, 886-889 (2005).

[10] Ibid., 885-886.

[11] Ibid., 893.

[12] 366 U.S. 420 (1961).

the state of Maryland that generally prohibited the sale of all merchandise on Sundays except tobacco products, confectioners, milk, bread, fruit, gasoline, oil, various drugs and medicines, and newspapers and periodicals. Two employees of a large department store on a highway in Anne Arundel City, Maryland, were prosecuted pursuant to the law, convicted, and fined because they sold a loose-leaf binder, a can of floor wax, a stapler, staples, and a toy in violation of the law. They subsequently appealed their fines in the Court of Appeals of Maryland based upon the Equal Protection Clause of the Fourteenth Amendment, the Due Process Clauses of the First and Fourteenth Amendments, and the Establishment Clause. The case arrived at the United States Supreme Court where a majority of the Court held that the Maryland law did not violate the Constitution in an opinion by Chief Justice Earl Warren.[13]

The majority opinion in the case reasoned that the employees of the store convicted pursuant to the statute did have standing to sue under the Establishment Clause since there was direct economic injury to their interests. This direct economic injury derived from the imposition of the tenets of the Christian religion via the law, which in effect gave Christians the economic advantage of an extra day of work, Saturday. The effect of the Maryland law prevented Jewish Americans and other Saturday Sabbath worshippers from working on Sundays except in a very limited capacity, and their faith prevented them from working on Saturday.[14]

The majority's opinion concluded that the Maryland law did not violate the Establishment Clause because Sunday closing laws had "evolved" over time in America so that they were presently based on secular policy considerations.[15] Therefore, the majority found in the case that these laws were "written and administered" based on secular considerations, and thus did not amount to an establishment or religion according to the meaning of an establishment in the language of the First Amendment.[16] Rather, these laws had the intended purpose and

---

[13] *McGowan*, 366 U.S. at 422-453.

[14] Ibid., 421.

[15] Ibid., 431.

[16] Ibid., 444.

effect of providing a uniform day of rest for all citizens, a purely secular purpose, which rendered the fact that Sunday was the chosen day insignificant to the Court's majority. Moreover, this was the Court's conclusion even though the majority opinion conceded that Sunday had a peculiar meaning for the majority or dominant faith in society, Christianity. [17] The majority opinion also rejected an Establishment Clause argument that the state could have used other means to achieve its purpose of creating a uniform day of rest and recreation for all of society, which did not aid religion "remotely or incidentally." [18] The Court's majority accepted the state court's determination that the purpose and effect of the statute was to create a secular day of rest, and did not lead to government aid or preference for religion.

Frankfurter authored a concurring opinion in the *McGowan* case.[19] In his opinion he explained that he was writing in order to express the "clarity of candor which enhances the judicial process." [20] He emphasized that the history of Sunday legislation like that in the case needed careful examination so that one could more clearly see how these laws had evolved to become secular, or "the vehicle of mixed and complicated aspirations." [21] In addition, he deemed their history controlling as to the constitutional questions in the case. Yet, he also stressed that he was not relying upon the precedent set by the case of *Everson v. Board of Education* wherein Justice Hugo Black articulated a principle of strict separation between church and state, but then failed to follow the principle in the case's holding.[22]

Rather, Frankfurter looked to the *McCollum* case as primary authority for the basic principle of the separation of church and state, which he referred to as "the not rigidly precise but revealing phrase."[23]

---

[17] Ibid., 444-445.

[18] Ibid., 445-449.

[19] 366 U.S. at 459-543 (FRANKFURTER, J., concurring).

[20] Ibid., 459.

[21] Ibid., 459-460.

[22] Ibid., 460.

[23] Ibid.

He argued that this principle was fundamental for American culture and law, and then stated that it meant that "the enforcement of religious belief as such is no legitimate concern of civil government." [24] Frankfurter did not challenge the notion that the protections of the First Amendment religion clauses applied to the states through the concept of liberty enshrined in the Fourteenth Amendment's Due Process Clause. Moreover, Frankfurter denied in *McGowan* that the principle of the separation of church and state was easy to apply to cases before the Court because the principle did not have a simple meaning.

To the contrary, Frankfurter argued for a nuanced understanding of the concept of the separation of church and state consistent with his rejection of absolutes. He noted the pervasive presence of religion in American culture and how religious institutions shaped and regulated much of American activity. This led him to the conclusion consistent with his rationale in the *Gobitis* and *Barnette* free exercise cases that the liberty protections in the religion clauses do not provide religious dissenters or minorities "entire insulation from every civic obligation."[25] He grounded this assertion in the recognition that the state's interests and the interests of religion were becoming more and more intertwined as the government provided greater protection for individual rights and interests. Frankfurter submitted that due to the growth of America's government civil laws necessarily had connections with many of the religious mores of the population, but could not "always support equally the beliefs of all religious sects."[26] The Supreme Court, therefore, had to decide when the government's reasons for a law that infringed upon an individual dissenter's religious liberty warranted denial of an exemption to the law's civic obligations. He acknowledged that not all laws the infringed on religious liberty were constitutional; citing the law in *Cantwell v. Connecticut* as an example, and that in some cases the government should accomplish its goals without violating religious freedom.

---

[24] Ibid.

[25] Ibid., 461.

[26] Ibid., 462. He cited the nineteenth century Mormon polygamy cases of *Reynolds v. U.S.*, 98 U.S. 145 (1879) and *Davis v. Beason*, 133 U.S. 333 (1890) as authority for this point.

Yet, Frankfurter did not find the Maryland law at issue in the case unconstitutional because the rationale for Sunday closing laws had become thoroughly secularized and was devoid of religious content or meaning. To support this conclusion he engaged in an extensive analysis of legislative history of similar laws from the time of the English King Henry VI in 1448 through the English Commonwealth of the seventeenth century up to mid-twentieth century American law. Based upon his review of this history he claimed that by the first third of the twentieth century these laws had been denuded of most of their religious connections in England. Instead of religious purposes the laws now had the secular purpose created by the stresses of the Industrial Revolution in both England and America, which was the weekly need for a day to rest.[27]

Before he engaged in an historical review of rationales for Sunday closing laws, Frankfurter again referred to the historical tradition behind the religion clauses of the First Amendment. In this historical review he relied primarily upon the views of Thomas Jefferson and James Madison, and the events involved in the Virginia battle over religious assessments of the 1780s. After stressing that there was not a bright line between Free Exercise and Establishment Clause cases, he reviewed the history of the Virginia Act for Establishing Religious Freedom and the viewpoints of Madison and Jefferson that stood behind it. He noted some abuses of religious freedom that were prevalent in the early American colonial period, and concluded that what both Madison and Jefferson opposed was an interdependence of church and state that threatened the freedom of each.[28] Then, he stated

---

[27] *McGowan*, 366 U.S. at 470-480. Thus, Frankfurter traced the history of the Sunday closing laws from early religious moorings to a mere secular "tradition" of a weekly day of rest in the 1930s. He wrote that this history established, "the intimate relationship between civil Sunday regulation and the interest of a state in preserving to its people a recurrent time of mental and physical recuperation from the strains and pressures of their ordinary labors." Ibid., 482. In other words, the legislation was now constitutional because it had essentially been excised of any meaningful or exceptional religious connotations.

[28] Ibid., 463f. Frankfurter focuses on Madison and Jefferson on pages 464-465 of his opinion.

the conclusion that the purpose of the Establishment Clause, which derived from this historical overview, was "to assure that the national legislature would not exact its power in the service of any purely religious end; that it would not, as Virginia and virtually all of the colonies had done, make of religion, as religion, an object of legislation." [29]   Frankfurter added that the Establishment Clause prohibited an established church similar to the Church of England and the colonial American establishments. Moreover, Frankfurter submitted that the establishment provision in the First Amendment withdrew from the "legitimate sphere of legislative concern . . . man's belief or disbelief in the verity of some transcendental idea and man's expression in action of that belief or disbelief." [30]

On the other hand, Frankfurter backed away from a simple or complete separation of church and state. Just after he asserted what the Establishment Clause meant based on the Virginia struggle to disestablish the Church of England and the views of Jefferson and Madison, Frankfurter qualified his view. He reasoned that laws that do not have religious objectives or effects were not the concern of the Establishment Clause. Thus, if a law had a primary religious effect or goal as in the *McCollum* case it was unconstitutional, but if the law had a secular effect or goal as in *McGowan* it was constitutional. The crucial question in Establishment Clause cases for Frankfurter was: "What is the primary end achieved by the regulation?" [31]

Once again in the *McGowan* case Frankfurter deferred to the legislative rationale for the Sunday closing laws as rational or reasonable and thus constitutional; the secular need for a day of rest grounded in economic and health interests. According to his historical

---

[29] *McGowan*, 366 U.S. at 466.

[30] Ibid.   These prohibitions did apply to the states as well in Frankfurter's opinion.   Though he did express concerns about the doctrine of "incorporation" in other places he explicitly asserted on this page of the *McGowan* opinion that the Establishment Clause applied to the states.   Ibid., 466.   See Felix Frankfurter, "Memorandum on 'Incorporation' of the Bill of Rights into the Due Process Clause of the Fourteenth Amendment," *78 Harv. L. Rev. 746, 746-783* (1965).

[31] *McGowan*, 366 U.S. at 466.

review, cited supra, the modern reasons for a common day of rest across American society were almost exclusively secular, and should not violate the conscience of anyone who was reasonable. In addition, forty-nine states had some form of Sunday closing regulation with a great variety of restrictions and degrees of regulation, which prohibited the Supreme Court from prescribing workable constitutional exemptions to the laws. This also meant for him that the Supreme Court should defer to the reasonable argument of the states that a judicially mandated accommodation for dissenters to the legal day of rest was "unsatisfactory" and unworkable.[32]

FRANKFURTER AND SCALIA'S SIMILAR APPROACH TO THE FREE EXERCISE CLAUSE

Frankfurter's reasoning in *McGowan* resembled the same reasoning he applied to the Free Exercise Clause in the *Gobitis* and *Barnette* cases where he submitted that religious objections to the flag salute regulations in Pennsylvania and West Virginia had to yield to society's interest in cohesive sentiment as expressed in the salute to the American flag. In *McGowan* the government's expression of cohesive sentiment, which superseded religious challenge according to Frankfurter, was that society had expressed in these Sunday laws a reasonable need for a common day of rest in order to promote a healthy population and economic success.[33] Therefore, even though Frankfurter did not use the phrase cohesive sentiment in *McGowan* he did show more deference in the case to the government's interest in a common day of rest than to the Saturday Sabbatarians' religious liberty.

Frankfurter grounded his conclusion that Sunday was a secular day of rest in his historical account that showed a majority of the national community had passed reasonable laws that made Sunday a traditional American day of rest. The tradition had been accepted by societal consensus in the majoritarian legislative process and expressed across a majority of the national community in law. Thus, Frankfurter argued that minority religious objections to the law had to submit to the will of the majority. If legislators had to create exemptions it might disturb the

---

[32] Ibid., 506.

[33] Ibid., 482.

sanctity of "the atmosphere of general repose" intended by these "secular" statutes, or give Sabbatarians an uncompetitive advantage in business, or even lead to religious discrimination as employers sought to hire fellow believers.[34]

Frankfurter's Free Exercise Clause analysis expressed in *Gobitis*, *Barnette*, and *McGowan* applied judicial restraint to challenged government actions that were quasi-religious but secular in content, and his opinions in *Gobitis*, *Barnette*, and *McGowan* deferred to majority will over religious conscience. In the free exercise cases, *Gobitis* and *Barnette*, he applied an interpretation of the First Amendment, which exhibited deference to government interests and professed rationales for legislation that impinged against the religious liberty of the Jehovah's Witness claimants. His approach was based in part on Frankfurter's deference to what he saw as the government's expressed interest in the importance of societal "cohesive sentiment" or common values and beliefs, which he reasoned should receive deference from the Supreme Court.[35] If the government could express a reasonable basis for a law that may infringe upon the scruples of minority faiths it would pass judicial scrutiny according to this interpretation of the Free Exercise Clause.

Scalia's free exercise jurisprudence has also generally deferred to government interests against claims by religious litigants when the law in question was neutral with reference to religion or generally applicable.[36] He defended this approach to free exercise cases with Supreme Court precedent, his argument that the text of the Free Exercise Clause was consistent with his view, and with the historical scholarship of commentators regarding the American founders' views about religious liberty.[37] Thus, Scalia applied the Free Exercise Clause weakly in the *Smith* and *City of Boerne* cases, even though he joined in

---

[34] Ibid., 516-518.

[35] *Minersville School District v. Gobitis*, 310 U.S. 586, 595-596 (1940).

[36] Antonin Scalia, "Of Democracy, Morality, and the Majority," *Origins: CNS Documentary Service* Vol. 26, No. 6 (June 27, 1996): 81-90; *Employment Division v. Smith*, 494 U.S. 872, 874-890 (1990).

[37] *Smith*, 494 U.S. at 878-879; and *City of Boerne v. Flores*, 521 U.S. 507, 538 (1997).

the majority opinion in *Church of Lukumi Babalu Aye, Inc. v. Hialeah,* 508 U.S. 520 (1993) to find a violation of the Free Exercise Clause. In the *Hialeah* case Scalia explained his free exercise approach further, and found that the Florida law in question that prohibited animal sacrifice was not generally applicable because it targeted the Santeria religion whose adherents challenged the law under the Free Exercise Clause.[38]

FRANKFURTER AND SCALIA'S EMPHASIS ON JUDICIAL RESTRAINT AND ORIGINALISM

Frankfurter and Scalia's religion clause jurisprudences were also similar because both judges stressed judicial restraint, and applied originalist methodologies to interpret the religion clauses. Frankfurter did not make speeches or author books advocating originalism like Scalia, but he did reason in his *Gobitis* free exercise opinion that the Supreme Court's task when interpreting the religious liberty clauses required an historical inquiry into the founders' beliefs about religious liberty.[39] Scalia, moreover, has argued in speeches and in his book entitled *A Matter of Interpretation* in favor of his preferred type of originalism called textualism.[40]

In addition, both Frankfurter and Scalia stressed judicial restraint or the principle that judges should generally defer to legislatures when they review the constitutionality of laws. Frankfurter acted on this principle in the *Gobitis* and *Barnette* cases when he rejected the claim of the Jehovah's Witnesses that the mandatory flag salute ceremony forced them to violate their conscience. His opinions in *Gobitis* and *Barnette* stressed the need for "binding ties of cohesive sentiment' amongst the citizens which outweighed the religious liberty of dissenters so long as the state had some rational basis for denying a

---

[38] *Church of Lukumi Babalu Aye, Inc. v. Hialeah,* 508 U.S. 520, 557f (1993).

[39] *Minersville School District v. Gobitis,* 310 U.S. 586, 594 (1940).

[40] Antonin Scalia, "Originalism: The Lesser Evil," *57 U. Cincinnati L. Rev. 849* (1989); and Antonin Scalia, *A Matter of Interpretation: Federal Courts and the Law* (Princeton, NJ: Princeton University Press, 1997), 3-47.

religious exemption to the laws demands.[41] Plus, the judicial restraint that Frankfurter exhibited in *Gobitis* and *Barnette* derived in part from the thought of James Bradley Thayer whom Frankfurter cited in *Barnette* as support for his view in favor of judicial restraint, which Thayer traced back to the founders of America.[42]

Scalia has also emphasized judicial restraint. In a speech at the Vatican's Gregorian University in Rome in 1996 he reasoned that it was best to change bad laws in a democracy through the legislative process.[43] Then, in a subsequent interview with author Joan Biskupic, Scalia submitted that his judicial methodology better enabled judges to keep their own views from influencing their official opinions. He stated:

> This is precisely one of the reasons why I like textualism. It is an objective criterion that you can repair to, and if you find what that understanding [regarding a particular constitutional provision] was at the time, you don't have to inject your own biases and prejudices.[44]

---

[41] *Gobitis*, 310 U.S. at 595-598; and *West Virginia State Board of Education v. Barnette*, 319 U.S. 624, 647-655 (1943).

[42] *Barnette*, 319 U.S. at 667-668. Frankfurter also wrote in *Gobitis* that the best way for a democratic society such as the United States to protect religious liberty was through the legislative or political process, and not through the court system. Otherwise, he reasoned, the members of society would not value the freedom in the Bill of Rights as they should. *Gobitis*, 310 U.S. at 599. Scalia has made a similar argument in his chapter entitled, "Federal Constitutional Guarantees of Individual Rights in the United States of America," in *Human Rights and Judicial Review: A Comparative Perspective*, David M. Beatty, ed. (Boston: Martinus Nijhoff Publishers, 1994), 91.

[43] Antonin Scalia, "Of Democracy, Morality, and the Majority," *Origins: CNS Documentary Service* Vol. 26, No. 6 (June 27, 1996): 81.

[44] Joan Biskupic, *American Original: The Life and Constitution of Supreme Court Justice Antonin Scalia* (New York: Sarah Crichton Books, 2009), 209.

Frankfurter and Scalia did not, however, appeal to America's founders in the same manner in their religion clause opinions. Frankfurter relied primarily on the thought of Thomas Jefferson and James Madison for his view on religious liberty and the separation of church and state. Scalia, on the other hand, cited the speeches and public religious practices of George Washington, John Adams, and John Marshall in addition to those of Jefferson and Madison in Establishment Clause opinions. The next section of this concluding chapter will provide evidence for this distinction between the religion clause jurisprudences of the two judges.

APPEALS TO AMERICA'S FOUNDERS IN FRANKFURTER AND SCALIA'S RELIGION CLAUSE OPINIONS

Frankfurter's approach to the Establishment Clause was different from Scalia's, as noted above, and applied its language strictly. For example, in each of the following Establishment Clause cases Frankfurter voted to find an Establishment Clause violation: *Everson, McCollum, Zorach v. Clauson,* and *Kedroff v. Saint Nicholas Cathedral.*[45] Frankfurter, in addition, based all of these Establishment Clause opinions except for *Kedroff* in part on historical evidence from the American founding era, which relied primarily on the "Enlightenment" views of Thomas Jefferson that emerged in the context of the Virginia debates over religious liberty in the 1780s.[46] Frankfurter's historical emphasis did not rely on the viewpoints of the Puritans and Evangelicals who were

---

[45] *Everson v. Board of Education,* 330 U.S. 1, 18-63 (1947)(JACKSON and RUTLEDGE, J., dissenting, Frankfurter joined both opinions); *McCollum v. Board of Education,* 333 U.S. 203, 212-232 (1948)(FRANKFURTER, J., concurring); *Zorach v. Clauson,* 343 U.S. 307, 320-323 (1952) (FRANKFURTER, J., dissenting); *Kedroff v. Saint Nicholas Cathedral,* 344 U.S. 94, 121-126 (1952)(FRANKFURTER, J., concurring); and *McGowan v. Maryland,* 366 U.S. 42, 459-543 (1961)(FRANKFURTER, J., concurring).

[46] Witte, *Religion and the American Constitutional Experiment,* 29-33 where John Witte included Jefferson in this "Enlightenment" perspective, and noted that these founders emphasized the danger that religion posed to the government as well as skepticism about organized religion in some instances.

also part of the historical context behind the First Amendment according to scholar John Witte, Jr. Witte has written that at least four different viewpoints about religion influenced the First Amendment: Puritan, Evangelical, Enlightenment, and Civic Republican.[47] The early Puritans, such as John Cotton and Cotton Mather, supported a closer relationship between church and state than either the Evangelicals, such as Isaac Backus, or the Enlightenment thinkers such as Jefferson, according to Witte's research.[48]

Scalia also relied in his Establishment Clause opinions on some of the public religious practices of Jefferson and Madison.[49] For example, in *Lee v. Weisman*, 505 U.S. 577 (1992) and *McCreary County v. ACLU*, 545 U.S. 844 (2005) Scalia referred to the inaugural addresses of Jefferson and Madison in support of his argument that neither a theistic and nondenominational public school graduation prayer, nor a courthouse display including the Ten Commandments violated the Establishment Clause.[50] Yet, Scalia also referred to public religious practices by founders that Witte characterized as Civic Republicans including John Adams and George Washington, and these founders emphasized "ideals" which emerged out of the idea of a "Christian commonwealth" in Puritan and Anglican thought.[51] Scalia's explanation in *Lee* and *McCreary County* for why he referred to the public religious practices of Jefferson, Madison, Washington, and Adams did not specify the distinctions in the views of these founders. Instead, he explained that the public religious references in the official speeches and prayers of Jefferson, Madison, Washington, and Adams

---

[47] Ibid., 23-35.

[48] Ibid., 23-24 where Witte noted that the Puritans accepted a limited belief that church and state should remain separate, but sought a closer and more compact relation between the two than representatives of the Evangelical or Enlightenment views.

[49] *Lee v. Weisman*, 505 U.S. 577, 632 (1992); and *McCreary County v. ACLU*, 545 U.S. 844, 887-888 (2005).

[50] Ibid.

[51] Witte, *Religion and the American Constitutional Experiment*, 33.

supported his view that the Establishment Clause allowed government to acknowledge God in generic and nondenominational terms.[52]

Both justices' religion clause jurisprudence, therefore, referred to America's founders as a basis for their opinions, especially in Establishment Clause cases. The primary difference between the two approaches to the religion clauses, however, was that Frankfurter applied the Establishment Clause strongly, whereas Scalia applied it weakly as evidenced in *Lee* and *McCreary*, and thus Scalia's religion clause jurisprudence was more amenable to theistic public religion in the public square.

Scalia, on the other hand, did not rely on the speeches or public religious practices of Washington, Madison, Jefferson, and John Marshall in his Free Exercise Clause opinions like he did in Establishment Clause cases. For example, his opinions in the *Employment Division v. Smith*, 494 U.S. 872 (1990); *Church of Lukumi Babalu Aye, Inc. v. Hialeah*, 508 U.S. 520 (1993); and *City of Boerne v. Flores*, 521 U.S. 507 (1997) free exercise cases contained minimal references to the founding era except in *Boerne* where Scalia defended his *Smith* opinion against criticism by Sandra Day O'Connor.[53] Additionally, in the *City of Boerne* case Scalia did not refer to any founders or their writings, speeches, or involvement in religious practices, but cited two law review articles by Philip Hamburger and Michael McConnell regarding the debate about the founders' views on the free exercise of religion.[54]

---

[52] *Lee v. Weisman*, 505 U.S. 577, 631-633 (1992)(quoting in part the Burger opinions in *Marsh v. Chambers*, 463 U.S. 783, 786-788 (1983) and *Lynch v. Donnelly*, 465 U.S. 668, 676 (1984) which referred to Civic Republicans including John Adams and George Washington in support of public religion such as legislative prayers and use of religious symbols like a crèche or cross on public property); and *McCreary County v. ACLU*, 545 U.S. 844, 886-888 (2005)(citing John Marshall's practice of beginning Supreme Court sessions with prayer, George Washington's Inaugural Prayer, a d John Adams's address to the Massachusetts Militia in support of a Ten Commandments display on public property).

[53] *City of Boerne v. Flores*, 521 U.S. 507, 538-539 (1997).

[54] Ibid.

Scalia did, on the other hand, appeal to the speeches, writings, and public religious practices of Washington, Jefferson, Madison, Adams, and Marshall in Establishment Clause cases. The first Establishment Clause case in which he relied upon references like these as supporting authority for his conclusions about applications of the Establishment Clause was his opinion in *Texas Monthly, Inc. v. Bullock*, 489 U.S. 1 (1989). In *Texas Monthly* Scalia cited the Declaration of Independence, the prayers that began the Supreme Court's official activities in the early nineteenth century, and the presence of the Free Exercise Clause in the First Amendment as founding era evidence that America had a tradition of allowing government to endorse religion so long as the endorsement remained nondenominational.[55] He did not specifically cite public speeches of Jefferson or Adams in *Texas Monthly*, but he did refer to traditional religious practices, which did not trace their origins back to the founders: the Thanksgiving Holiday, religious references on coins, and the national pledge to the flag.[56]

Another Establishment Clause case where Scalia cited evidence from the American founding era in order to document an American tradition, which allowed the government to endorse religion in a nondenominational and theistic manner, was *Lamb's Chapel v. Center Moriches Union Free School District*, 508 U.S. 384, 400 (1993). Scalia referred to the Northwest Ordinance of 1787 in *Lamb's Chapel* in support for the principle that society needed religion in the public sphere to promote the common good, and stressed that the contemporaneous timing of the Northwest Ordinance and the First Amendment.[57]

Scalia's previous dissenting opinion in *Lee v. Weisman*, 505 U.S. 577 (1992) contained his first extensive use of references to the speeches and public religious practices of Washington, Adams, Jefferson, and Madison as support for his reasoning in an Establishment Clause opinion. He cited statements that George Washington, John Adams, Thomas Jefferson, and James Madison made

---

[55] *Texas Monthly, Inc. v. Bullock*, 489 U.S. 1, 29-30 (1989).

[56] Ibid., 29.

[57] *Lamb's Chapel v. Center Moriches Union Free School District*, 508 U.S. 384, 400 (1993).

while they served as president in support of his opinion that a theistic and nondenominational graduation prayer at a public middle school did not violate the Establishment Clause.[58] Similar recitations of these public religious practices and speeches were also part of previous Supreme Court opinions by Warren Burger for a majority of the Court, who also reasoned that theistic and nondenominational public religion passed constitutional scrutiny in *Lynch v. Donnelly*, 465 U.S. 668, 674-678 (1984); and *Marsh v. Chambers*, 463 U.S. 783, 786-788 (1983).

In *Lee* Scalia also cited George Washington's first inaugural swearing in ceremony when Washington placed his hands on the Bible, and Washington's first inaugural address. Then, he added citations of Thomas Jefferson's first and second inaugural addresses and James Madison's first inaugural address as more support for his reasoning that the public religious practices of the founders were analogous to the theistic graduation prayer in *Lee*.[59]

Some of the same references to public religious practices from the founding era appeared in Scalia's subsequent dissenting opinion in *McCreary County v. ACLU*, 545 U.S. 844, 886-889 (2005). In this case concerning an Establishment Clause challenge to a Ten Commandments display on public property in a courthouse he appealed to a historical tradition of nondenominational public religious practices by citing George Washington's first inaugural address and the fact that Washington added to the presidential oath of office the phrase, "so help me God."[60] Scalia's *McCreary* dissent also referred to John Marshall's practice of opening Supreme Court sessions in the nineteenth century with the words "God save the United States and this Honorable Court" in order to support his argument that government can endorse nondenominational monotheistic public religion without violating the Establishment Clause.[61]

In *McCreary* Scalia also cited the first inaugural address of James Madison in support of an American tradition, which allowed government endorsement of monotheistic public religion in spite of the

---

[58] *Lee v. Weisman*, 505 U.S. 577, 631-635 (1992).

[59] Ibid.

[60] *McCreary County v. ACLU*, 545 U.S. 844, 886 (2005).

[61] Ibid., **887-888**.

Establishment Clause. He then added to these examples of public religion John Adam's address to the Massachusetts Militia and Thomas Jefferson's second inaugural ceremony's call to prayer. These references were not the only ones from the founding era that Scalia relied upon in his *McCreary County* dissent. He also included references to the Northwest Ordinance's call for the integration of religion and civic virtue, the early congressional practice of opening sessions with prayer, and the First Congress's request for a national day of Thanksgiving.[62]

In summary, then, both Frankfurter and Scalia used references to Thomas Jefferson and James Madison as support for their reasoning in Establishment Clause cases. Frankfurter referred to Jefferson and Madison's views on religious liberty from Virginia's struggle over disestablishment of the Anglican Church in the 1770s in his Establishment Clause jurisprudence, and Scalia cited Jefferson and Madison's inaugural addresses in addition to similar references to the speeches and public religious practices of George Washington, John Adams, and John Marshall.[63]

Moreover, Frankfurter voted to find an Establishment Clause violation in all the cases he participated in except *McGowan v. Maryland*, 366 U.S. 420, 459-543 (1961), but Scalia has never voted to strike down a law pursuant to the Establishment Clause of the First Amendment. [64] Yet, in free exercise cases Scalia adopted a

---

[62] Ibid.

[63] *McCollum v. Board of Education*, 333 U.S. 203, 212-232 (1948)(FRANKFURTER, J. concurring); *Zorach v. Clauson*, 343 U.S. 307, 320-323 (1952)(FRANKFURTER, J., dissenting); *McGowan v. Maryland*, 366 U.S. 420, 459-543 (1961)(FRANKFURTER, J., concurring); *Texas Monthly, Inc. v. Bullock*, 498 U.S. 1, 29-45 (1989)(SCALIA, J., dissenting); *Lee v. Weisman*, 505 U.S. 577, 631-646 (1992)(SCALIA, J.. dissenting); *Lamb's Chapel v. Center Moriches Union Free School District*, 508 U.S. 384, 397-401 (1993); *Board of Education of Kiryas Joel v. Grumet*, 521 U.S. 687, 732-752 (1994)(SCALIA, J., dissenting); *McCreary County v. ACLU*, 545 U.S. 844, 886-898 (2005)(SCALIA, J., dissenting).

[64] Gregory O. Nies, *Religious Liberty Through the Lens of Textualism and a Living Constitution: The First Amendment Establishment Clause Interpretations of Justices William Brennan, Jr., and Antonin Scalia* (Waco,

methodology similar to Frankfurter's that was grounded in Jefferson's thinking about free exercise of religion, and the rationale for judicial restraint provided by James Bradley Thayer's Harvard Law Review article, "The Origin and Scope of the American Doctrine of Constitutional Law."[65] This similar free exercise approach grounded in Jefferson's thought was evident in Frankfurter's *Gobitis* and *Barnette* opinions, and Scalia's *Smith* and *City of Boerne* opinions.

FRANKFURTER AND SCALIA'S DIFFERENT CONCLUSIONS ABOUT
AMERICAN PUBLIC RELIGION

Lastly, Frankfurter and Scalia came to different conclusions about the constitutionality of American public religion. American public religion, as the term was outlined in chapters one and two, referred to forms of lowest common denominator public religion, which bound different groups together in a democracy. Moreover, American public religion sometimes included belief in a deity, but not always.[66]

Frankfurter's religion clause jurisprudence found a secular, quasi-religious, kind of American public religion constitutional. The flag salute ceremony that Frankfurter found constitutional in the *Gobitis* case did not include any references to God, and thus was secular in nature.[67] Yet, the mandatory flag salute in *Gobitis* was also quasi-religious. For example, the ceremony involved veneration of the American flag, and in his opinion in *Gobitis* Frankfurter submitted that

---

TX: Baylor University Press-Master's thesis, 2006), 178-180; *McGowan v. Maryland*, 366 Establishment Clause because the law had a secular rationale.

[65] *Minersville School District v. Gobitis*, 310 U.S. 586, 591-600 (1940); *West Virginia State Board of Education v. Barnette*, 319 U.S. 624, 646-672 (1943) (FRANKFURTER, J., dissenting); *Employment Division, Department of Human Services v. Smith*, 494 U.S. 872, 874-890 (1990); *City of Boerne v. Flores*, 521 U.S. 507, 538 (1997) (SCALIA, J., concurring); James B. Thayer, "The Origin and Scope of the American Doctrine of Constitutional Law," *VII Harvard L. Rev. 139* (1893).

[66] Steven B. Epstein, "Rethinking the Constitutionality of Ceremonial Deism," *96 Columbia L. Rev., 2083, 2096-2097* (1996).

[67] Epstein, *Rethinking the Constitutionality of Ceremonial Deism*, 2118.

there was a need for cohesive sentiment in America, which veneration for the flag memorialized.[68]

Therefore, Frankfurter deemed secular and metaphorical American public religion constitutional in his *Gobitis* and *Barnette* free exercise opinions. The facts of the *Barnette* case were very similar to those in *Gobitis* and Frankfurter did not alter his reasoning in *Barnette*.[69] The mandatory flag salute ceremonies in *Gobitis* and *Barnette* did not contain references to deity, but did include elements like religious faith including ritualistic veneration of the American flag and an appeal to the need for cohesive sentiment in society. In addition, Frankfurter found that a governmentally mandated day of rest on Sundays in *McGowan v. Maryland* did not violate the Establishment Clause because the government's rationale was secular. On the other hand, in the *McCollum v. Board of Education* Establishment Clause case Frankfurter voted to strike down a released time program in a public school district in Illinois.[70] He reasoned that this religious program violated the principle of the separation of church and state found in the thought of Thomas Jefferson and James Madison.[71]

Scalia, in contrast, found monotheistic American public religion constitutional in *Lee* and *McCreary County*. He reasoned that the public middle school graduation prayer in *Lee* was constitutional because America had a tradition of conducting similar public religious practices traceable back to Washington, Jefferson, and Madison.[72] In addition, the Ten Commandments display in *McCreary County* did not violate the Establishment Clause according to Scalia because the Ten Commandments' acknowledgement of deity was monotheistic in nature, and therefore nondenominational.[73]

---

[68] *Minersville School District v. Gobitis.* 310 U.S. 586. 591-600 (1940).

[69] *West Virginia State Board of Education v. Barnette.* 319 U.S. 624. 646-659 (1943) (FRANKFURTER. J., dissenting).

[70] *McCollum v. Board of Education,* 333 U.S. 203. 231 (1948).

[71] Ibid.

[72] *Lee v. Weisman,* 505 U.S. 577. 631-646 (1992) (SCALIA. J., dissenting).

[73] *McCreary County v. ACLU.* 545 U.S. 844. 886-898 (2005) (SCALIA. J., dissenting).

Scalia also submitted in his *Lee* dissenting opinion that there was an unbroken American historical tradition that allowed government endorsement of public religion, which was monotheistic and generic in nature.[74] Moreover, this emphasis became stronger in his subsequent dissenting opinion in the *McCreary* case. For example, Scalia argued in *McCreary* that the government could constitutionally favor monotheistic religions over non-monotheistic faiths in public acknowledgments of God. He based this conclusion again on an American religious tradition traceable to the American founders including Washington, Jefferson, Madison, Adams, and John Marshall.[75]

Both forms of American public religion that Scalia found constitutional in *Lee* and *McCreary* were theistic. Therefore, the theistic American public religion that Scalia found constitutional in *Lee* and *McCreary* was distinct from the secular and metaphorical public religion that Frankfurter found constitutional in *Gobitis* and *Barnette*.

In summary, then, the First Amendment religion clause jurisprudences of Frankfurter and Scalia found different forms of American public religion constitutional in *Gobitis, Barnette, McCollum, McGowan, Lee,* and *McCreary County v. ACLU.* [76] Moreover, Frankfurter applied the Free Exercise Clause weakly, but the Establishment Clause strictly as exemplified in *Minersville School District v. Gobitis,* 310 U.S. 586 (1940) and *McCollum v. Board of Education,* 333 U.S. 203 (1948).[77] Scalia, to the contrary, interpreted both clauses of the First Amendment weakly in most cases as

---

[74] *Lee,* 505 U.S. at 632.

[75] *McCreary County,* 545 U.S. at 886-889 and 893-898.

[76] *Minersville School District v. Gobitis,* 310 U.S. 586 (1940); *West Virginia State Board of Education v. Barnette,* 319 U.S. 624 (1943); *McCollum v. Board of Education,* 333 U.S. 203 (1948); *McGowan v. Maryland,* 366 U.S. 420 (1961); *Lee v. Weisman,* 505 U.S. 577 (1992); and *McCreary County v. ACLU,* 545 U.S. 844 (2005).

[77] *Gobitis* was a free exercise case, and *McCollum* was an Establishment Clause case.

evidenced by *Employment Division v. Smith*, 494 U.S. 872 (1990) and *McCreary County v. ACLU*, 545 U.S. 844 (2005).[78]

Both Frankfurter and Scalia applied originalist methodologies to the religion clauses, too. The judges both accomplished this by relying upon public statements, speeches, writings, other public documents and practices of American founders in order to interpret the meaning of the language in the religion clauses. In addition, both referred to Thomas Jefferson and James Madison for their interpretations of the religion clauses, but Frankfurter emphasized Jefferson and Madison's views on religious liberty, which emerged in the Virginia debates about disestablishment of the Anglican Church in the 1780s. Scalia, in contrast, emphasized the public speeches and practices of Jefferson and Madison in his Establishment Clause opinions in addition to the speeches and public practices of George Washington, John Adams, and John Marshall in order to support his argument that government support of generic, nondenominational public religion was constitutional. Scalia did not stress the arguments Jefferson and Madison made for the separation of church and state.

Frankfurter did not author extrajudicial books or make speeches that explained his originalist methodology for interpreting the religion clauses like Scalia did, but Frankfurter and Scalia both advocated judicial restraint. Moreover, Frankfurter and Scalia deferred to government action in Free Exercise Clause cases, and were in agreement that a democracy best protects religious liberty through the democratic process.

Lastly, the American public religion that Frankfurter found constitutional in *Gobitis, Barnette,* and *McGowan* was more secular in nature than the American public religion that Scalia found constitutional in *Lee* and *McCreary County.* The flag salute ceremonies in *Gobitis* and *Barnette* did not include references to God or belief in God, but did include elements similar to religious faith such as veneration for the flag and appeal to the need for cohesive sentiment as represented by the flag. In addition, the mandatory day of rest that Frankfurter found constitutional in *McGowan v. Maryland* had a

---

[78] *Smith* was a free exercise case, and *McCreary County* was an Establishment Clause case.

secular rationale of greater economic productivity, but the prescribed day off still resembled the religious practice of Sabbath rest.

Scalia, on the other hand, found more theistic public religious expressions such as the middle school graduation prayer in *Lee v. Weisman* and the display of the Ten Commandments in *McCreary County* constitutional. He reasoned that the type of graduation prayers evidenced in *Lee* would enhance tolerance among different religions, and that the Ten Commandments display in *McCreary* was consistent with an American tradition allowing preference for monotheistic faiths in public acknowledgments of deity.

CONCLUSIONS REGARDING AMERICAN PUBLIC RELIGION, THE RELIGION CLAUSE JURISPRUDENCES OF FRANKFURTER AND SCALIA, AND CHURCH-STATE STUDIES

Several conclusions emerge from this analysis of Frankfurter and Scalia's religion clause jurisprudences, which have meaning for church-state jurisprudence. First, Frankfurter and Scalia's appeals to the American founders in order to interpret the religion clauses in Court opinions did not lead to the same results in Establishment Clause cases. In other words, Frankfurter applied the Establishment Clause strongly, and Scalia interpreted it weakly even though they considered evidence from the same time in American history in order to interpret the establishment provision. Thus, the Supreme Court should clarify why study of the views of America's founders enhances its application of the religion clauses when reliance on the founders did not lead to consensus between Frankfurter and Scalia with regard to the Establishment Clause. Both Frankfurter and Scalia argued that the proper way to interpret the establishment provision was to examine historical evidence from the founding era, but then they came to different conclusions about what the evidence meant.[79]

---

[79] Donald L. Drakeman and John Ragosta are just two examples of scholars who continue to disagree about the original intent of the religion clauses, and the literature is vast. Donald L. Drakeman, *Church, State, and Original Intent* (New York: Cambridge University Press, 2010), 326-345; and John Ragosta, *Religious Freedom: Jefferson's Legacy, America's Creed* (Charlottesville, V.A.: University of Virginia Press, 2013), 209-222. Drakeman argues that the best conclusion from the historical evidence

Secondly, the fact that Frankfurter and Scalia appealed to the founders to interpret the religion clauses but came to different conclusions about the Establishment Clause raises questions about the degree of consensus among the founders themselves regarding religious liberty and disestablishment. Some founders emphasized the separation of church and state like Jefferson and Madison whereas others stressed the need for religious influences in public life like Washington and Adams. Some founders, such as those influenced by Enlightenment thought, seemed to fear the potential for religion to have a negative influence on the government, but others feared what might happen to America if the influence of religion was minimized or relegated to the private sphere, such as those who stressed the Puritan and Civic Republican viewpoints.[80]

This tension among the founders is significant because the tension remains in America today, but only seems more complex because of the increasing diversity of American religious life. Also, the fact that the founders did not agree about how to protect religious liberty should

---

available is that the founders wanted to prevent a single national church via the Establishment Clause. He submits that beyond this conclusion the evidence is ambiguous, and the founders compromised different competing views to pass the First Amendment. Ragosta, however, interprets the evidence differently, and argues that Thomas Jefferson's views on religious liberty remain at the center of America's creed, even though he too finds that the founders were divided about how to protect religious liberty. Arguably, the literature on the original meaning of the religion clauses has become so vast that obtaining a comprehensive understanding of it is a pyrrhic quest. Also, it does not seem possible at this point in time for a consensus to develop amongst scholars, judges, and interpreters of the religion clauses as to their meaning. This is hardly surprising, but should at least caution scholars, judges, and American citizens against making sweeping conclusions about what the First Amendment religion clauses mean.

[80] John Ragosta, though, disagrees with the conclusion that Jefferson desired a completely secular public square, and argues that some scholars and commentators have developed a false choice between secularist founders who sought to privatize religion or remove it from the public square, and others that promoted a Christian nation. Ragosta, *Jefferson's Legacy*, at 218, 220.

cause those who debate the meaning of the religion clauses today to concede that disagreement over the relationship between church and state is not a recent phenomenon. Rather, the delicate relationship between church and state requires constant negotiation, and thus it is important to continue an ongoing conversation about how to best protect religious liberty in a rapidly changing environment. A good recent example of a "healthy" conversation on the state of religious liberty in America is the symposium held at the Newseum Washington, D.C., on November 7, 2013. Participants included the Christian Legal Society, the Baptist Joint Committee for Religious Liberty, the American Jewish Committee, Religious Action Center of Reform Judaism, Union of Orthodox Jewish Congregations, Becket Fund for Religious Liberty, the Religious Freedom Center of the Newseum Institute, and scholars Douglas Laycock and Ira Lupu. The discussion was civil, and diverse views were presented.[81]

Therefore, religious liberty scholars and judges should at least acknowledge that there has never been a uniform understanding of religious liberty in America. Rather, there have been different viewpoints in dialogue on how best to protect religious liberty, and how to inculcate public virtue and cohesiveness from the very beginning of the country. Moreover, if one can trace a viewpoint on the debates about religious liberty to the founders it at least deserves respectful consideration in current debates. Otherwise, the debate will be incomplete, which is undemocratic, and protection for religious liberty may suffer because representatives of one or more viewpoints may push back against their exclusion from the debate. The author agrees with Frankfurter and Scalia, at least on this point, that protection for religious liberty in America depends upon robust respect among American citizens for the religious rights of others, and especially religious minorities. If citizens do not value religious liberty in the democratic legislative process, then courts will most likely have a difficult time protecting it. Thus, it is critical for mediating institutions and concerned groups, across the political and ideological spectrum, to

---

[81] BJC Staff Reports, "Event Examines State of Free Exercise of Religion, Landmark Legislation," *Report from the Capital* vol. 68, no. 10 (November/December 2013): 1, 6-7.

advocate for the broadest protection and respect for religious liberty for all people.

Third, the differences between Frankfurter and Scalia with reference to the Establishment Clause indicate that judicial restraint does not lead to judicial consensus or predictability, either. Moreover, if this is the case then the value of judicial restraint is diminished at least in Establishment Clause cases because legislatures may then disregard protection for religious liberty in laws without fear of any meaningful review from the courts, which could result from judicial abdication of its role of protecting the constitutional right for religious liberty. This could also lead to courts in one part of the country providing robust protection for religious liberty, but others in a different area granting deference to the legislature without regard for the impact on the religious liberty of citizens resulting in uneven levels of religious liberty across America.

This does not mean that Supreme Court judges or interpreters of the First Amendment religion clauses should refrain from considering the beliefs of the American founders about religious liberty. The fact that both Frankfurter and Scalia referred to the viewpoints and public practices of Thomas Jefferson and James Madison in their official Supreme Court opinions infers that these founders' views on religious liberty are meaningful for the ongoing debates about the meaning of the Free Exercise Clause and the Establishment Clause. Yet, the fact that Frankfurter found secular and quasi-religious American public religion constitutional, but Scalia found theistic and nondenominational public religion constitutional suggests that a tension exists between Jefferson and Madison's official practices, such as the inaugural speeches, and their views on the separation of church and state from the Virginia debates concerning disestablishment of the Anglican Church. This tension is meaningful for church-state jurisprudence because it carries within it the somewhat paradoxical result that Jefferson and Madison believed in the separation of church and state, but would not object to theistic and nondenominational public religion in official government acts or ceremonies.

The differences between the approaches of Frankfurter and Scalia in Establishment Clause cases are also meaningful because the study of Jefferson and Madison or other founders in church-state jurisprudence clearly does not lead to consensus among the judges on the Supreme Court about the Establishment Clause's meaning. Moreover, if

Frankfurter and Scalia did not reach a consensus about the Establishment Clause after reviewing the founding history, then it is reasonable to expect that references to the founding history in order to interpret the establishment provision will not lead to consensus or predictability in the Supreme Court's Establishment Clause jurisprudence.

Thus, it is fair to question whether appeals to the founders and an emphasis on judicial restraint ultimately provide secure grounding for the robust protection of religious liberty. Since religion was important enough to specifically protect it in the First Amendment then it deserves predictable constitutional protection, which is consistent throughout the United States. Courts will continue to have an important role protecting religious liberty even though I concede to Frankfurter and Scalia that courts cannot protect religious liberty without commitment to it among America's citizens. Originalist methodology combined with judicial restraint, as in the cases of Frankfurter and Scalia, seems to fall far short of guaranteeing robust, predictable, and consistent protection for religious liberty. In spite of Frankfurter and Scalia's objections to the contrary, the personal views of judges do probably influence their jurisprudence in religion clause cases, and protection for religious liberty in America needs more than courts alone to maintain its high status and broad appeal.[82]

---

[82] Drakeman, *Church, State, and Original Intent*, at 74-148 provides evidence that Justice Wiley Rutledge's personal anti-Catholic fears and bias probably influenced his interpretation of the Establishment Clause in *Everson v. Board of Education*, and therefore raises the question of the inevitability and extent that the personal biases of judges influence their interpretations of the religion clauses. See also Barry Hankins, "Supreme Court Justice Antonin Scalia, Textualism, Original Intent, and the Constitution: A Very Public Religion," *Liberty* vol. 96, no. 3 (May/June 2001): 3-7.

Bibliography

PRIMARY SOURCES

Adams, Charles Francis. ed. *The Works of John Adams.* Vol. X. Freeport, NY: Books for Libraries Press, Reprint 1969.

Cappon, Lester J. ed. *The Adams-Jefferson Letters: The Complete Correspondence Between Thomas Jefferson and Abigail and John Adams.* Vol. II. Chapel Hill, N.C.: The University of North Carolina Press, 1959.

Dillon, John F. ed. *John Marshall: Life, Character and Judicial Services As Portrayed in The Centenary and Memorial Addresses and Proceedings throughout the United States on Marshall Day, 1901.* Vol. II. Chicago: Callaghan & Company, 1903.

Elman, Philip. ed. *Of Law and Men: Papers and Addresses of Felix Frankfurter, 1939-1956.* New York: Harcourt, Brace, and Company, 1956.

Fitzpatrick, John C. *The Writings of George Washington from the Original Manuscript Sources, 1745-1799.* Vols. 26 and 33. Washington, D.C.: United States Government Printing Office, 1938 and 1940.

Frankfurter, Felix and James M. Landis. *The Business of the Supreme Court: A Study in The Federal Judicial System.* New York: The Macmillan Co., 1928.

Frankfurter, Felix. *The Public and Its Government.* New Haven, CT: Yale University Press, 1930.

———. *Mr. Justice Holmes and the Supreme Court.* Cambridge, MA: Harvard University Press, 1938.

——. "Memorandum on the 'Incorporation' of the Bill of Rights into the Due Process Clause of the Fourteenth Amendment." *78 Harvard Law Review 746* (1965).

Kurland, Philip B. ed. *Of Law and Life & Other Things That Matter: Papers and Addresses of Felix Frankfurter, 1956-1963.* Cambridge, MA: Harvard University Press, 1965.

——. *Felix Frankfurter on the Supreme Court: Extrajudicial Essays on The Court and the Constitution.* Cambridge, MA: Harvard University Press, Belknap Press, 1970.

——. *Mr. Justice Frankfurter and the Constitution.* Chicago, The University of Chicago Press, 1971.

Kurland, Philip B. and Gerhard Casper. eds. *Landmark Briefs and Arguments of the Supreme Court of the United States: Constitutional Law-Minersville School District v. Gobitis* (1940). Vol. 37. Arlington, VA: University Publications of America, Inc., 1975.

——. *Landmark Briefs and Arguments of the Supreme Court of the United States: Constitutional Law-West Virginia State Board of Education v. Barnette* (1943). Vol. 40. Arlington, VA: University Publications of America, Inc., 1975.

——. *Landmark Briefs and Arguments of the Supreme Court of the United States: Constitutional Law-Everson v. Board of Education* (1947). Vol. 44. Arlington, VA: University Publications of America, Inc., 1975.

Lash, Joseph P. ed. *From the Diaries of Felix Frankfurter.* New York: W.W. Norton & Co., Inc., 1975.

Madison, James. *Letters and Other Writings of James Madison.* Vols. I, III, IV. New York: Robert Worthington, 1884.

Marshall, John. *An Autobiographical Sketch by John Marshall.* ed. John Stokes Adams. Ann Arbor, MI: 1937.

Philips, Harlan B. *Felix Frankfurter Reminisces.* New York: Reynal & Co., 1960.

Scalia, Antonin. "Morality, Pragmatism, and the Legal Order." *Harvard Journal of Law and Public Policy 9* (1986): 123-127.

——. "Is There an Unwritten Constitution?" *Harvard Journal of Law and Public Policy* 12 (1989): 1-2.

——. "Originalism: The Lesser Evil." *57 University of Cincinnati Law Review 849* (1989).

———. "Of Democracy, Morality, and the Majority." *Origins: CNS Documentary Service* vol. 26, no. 6 (June 27, 1996): 81-90.

———. *A Matter of Interpretation: Federal Courts and the Law.* Princeton: Princeton University Press, 1997.

———. "God's Justice and Ours." *First Things: A Monthly Journal of Religion and Public Life* 123 (May 2002): 17-21.

Thayer, James Bradley, Oliver Wendell Holmes, and Felix Frankfurter. *On John Marshall.* Chicago: The University of Chicago Press, 1967.

SECONDARY SOURCES

Adams, Arlin M., and Charles Emmerich. *A Nation Dedicated to Religious Liberty: The Constitutional Heritage of the Religion Clauses.* Philadelphia: University of Pennsylvania Press, 1990.

Abraham, Henry J., and Barbara A. Perry. *Freedom and the Court: Civil Rights and Liberties in the United States,* 8th ed. Lawrence, KS: University Press of Kansas, 2003.

Abraham, Henry J. "The Status of the First Amendment's Religion Clauses: Some Reflections on Lines and Limits." *Journal of Church and State* vol. 22, no. 2 (Spring 1980): 215-231.

Adams, Dickinson W. ed. *Jefferson's Extracts from the Gospels: "The Philosophy of Jesus" and "The Life and Morals of Jesus."* Princeton, NJ: Princeton University Press, 1983.

Alley, Robert S. ed. *James Madison on Religious Liberty.* Buffalo, NY: Prometheus Books, 1985.

Audi, Robert. "The Separation of Church and State and the Obligations of Citizenship." *Philosophy and Public Affairs* vol. 18, no. 3 (Summer 1989): 278-286.

———. *Religious Commitment and Secular Reason.* New York: Cambridge University Press, 2000.

Bailyn, Bernard. *The Ideological Origins of the American Revolution.* Cambridge, MA: Belknap Press of Harvard University Press, 1992.

Baker, Leonard. *John Marshall: A Life in the Law.* New York: Macmillan, 1974.

———. *Brandeis and Frankfurter: A Dual Biography.* New York: Harper and Row, Pub., 1984.

Baker, Liva. *Felix Frankfurter.* New York: Coward-McCann, Inc., 1969.

Bellah, Robert N. "Civil Religion in America." *Daedalus* vol. 96 (Winter 1967): 1-21.

———. *The Broken Covenant: American Civil Religion in Time of Trial.* Chicago: University of Chicago Press, 1992.

Berg, Thomas C., and William G. Ross. "Some Religiously Devout Justices: Historical Notes and Comments." *81 Marquette Law Review 383* (Winter 1998).

Beschle, Donald H. "Catechism or Imagination: Is Justice Scalia's Style Typically Catholic?" *Villanova Law Review 1329* (1992).

Beveridge, Albert. *The Life of John Marshall.* Vol. IV. Boston: Houghton Mifflin Co., 1919.

Boller, Paul F., Jr., *George Washington & Religion.* Dallas, TX: Southern Methodist University Press, 1963.

Boorstin, Daniel J. *The Lost World of Thomas Jefferson.* Boston: Beacon Press, 1948.

Brisbin, Richard A. *Justice Antonin Scalia and the Conservative Revival.* Baltimore: Johns Hopkins Press, 1997.

———. "The Conservatism of Antonin Scalia." *Political Science Quarterly* 105 (1990): 2-22.

Carter, Stephen L. "The Religiously Devout Judge." *64 Notre Dame Law Review 932* (1989).

———. *God's Name in Vain: the Wrongs and Rights of Religion in Politics.* New York: Basic Books, 2000.

Chemerinsky, Erwin. "The Jurisprudence of Justice Scalia: A Critical Appraisal." *22 University of Hawaii Law Review 385* (2000).

Colby, Thomas B. "A Constitutional Hierarchy of Religions? Justice Scalia, the Ten Commandments, and the Future of the Establishment Clause." *100 Northwestern University Law Review 1097* (2006).

Collett, Teresa S. "The King's Good Servant, but God's First-The Role of Religion in Judicial Decision-making." *41 South Texas Law Review 1277* (Fall 2000).

Curry, James A., Richard B. Riley and Richard M. Battistoni. *Constitutional Government: The American Experience.* Dubuque, IA: Kendall/Hunt Publishing Company, 2009.

Curry, Thomas J. *The First Freedoms: Church and State in American to the Passage of the First Amendment.* New York: Oxford University Press, 1986.

Danzig, Richard. "How Questions Begot Answers in Felix Frankfurter's First Flag Salute Opinion." *1977 The Supreme Court Review 257* (1977).

———. "Justice Frankfurter's Opinions in the Flag Salute Cases: Blending Logic and Psychologic in Constitutional Decision-making." *36 Stanford Law Review 675* (1983-1984).

Davis, Derek H. "Editorial: Religion and the Abuse of Judicial Power." *Journal of Church and State* vol. 39, no. 2 (Spring 1997): 203-214.

———. *Religion and the Continental Congress, 1774-1789: Contributions to Original Intent.* New York: Oxford University Press, 2000.

Drakeman, Donald L. *Church, State, and Original Intent.* New York: Cambridge University Press, 2010.

———. *Church-State Constitutional Issues: Making Sense of the Establishment Clause.* New York: Greenwood Press, 1991.

———. "Religion and the Republic: James Madison and the First Amendment." *Journal of Church and State 25* (Autumn 1983): 427-445.

Edelman, Peter B. "Justice Scalia's Jurisprudence and the Good Society: Shades of Felix Frankfurter and the Harvard Hit Parade of the 1950s." *12 Cardozo Law Review 1799* (1991).

Ely, John Hart. *Democracy and Distrust: A Theory of Judicial Review.* Cambridge, MA: Harvard University Press, 1980.

Faulkner, Robert K. *The Jurisprudence of John Marshall.* Princeton, NJ: Princeton University Press, 1968.

First Amendment Center. *State of the First Amendment 2007-2010, Final Annotated Surveys*, prepared by the First Amendment Center. Nashville, TN, 2007-2010; available from http://www.freedomforum.org; Internet; accessed 11 November 2010.

Gaustad, Edwin S. *Proclaim Liberty throughout all the Land: A History of the Religion Clauses.* New York: Oxford University Press, 2003.

———. *Faith of the Founders: Religion and the New Nation, 1776-1826.* 2d ed. Waco, TX: Baylor University Press, 2004.

Gerhardt, Michael J. "A Tale of Two Textualists: A Critical Comparison of Justices Black and Scalia." *74 Boston University Law Review 26* (1994).

Green, Steven K. ""Bad History": The Lure of History in Establishment Clause Adjudication." *81 Notre Dame Law Review 1717* (2006).

Greenawalt, Kent. *Private Consciences and Public Reasons.* New York: Oxford University Press, 1995.

———. *Religion and the Constitution: Volume 1: Free Exercise and Fairness.* Princeton: Princeton University Press, 2006.

Griffen, Wendell L. "The Case for Judicial Values in Judicial Decision-Making." *81 Marquette Law Review 513* (Winter 1998).

Hall, Timothy L. "Religion and Civic Virtue: A Justification of Free Exercise." *62 Tulane Law Review 87* (1992).

———. "Sacred Solemnity: Civic Prayer, Civil Communion and the Establishment Clause." *79 Iowa Law Review 87* (1993-1994).

———. *Separating Church and State: Roger Williams and Religious Liberty.* Urbana, IL: University of Illinois Press, 1998.

Hamburger, Philip A. "A Constitutional Right of Religious Exemption: An Historical Perspective," *60 George Washington Law Review 915* (1992).

Handy, Robert T. *Undermined Establishment: Church-State Relations in America 1880-1920.* Princeton: Princeton University Press, 1991.

Hankins, Barry. "Supreme Court Justice Antonin Scalia, Textualism, Original Intent, and The Constitution: A Very Public Religion." *Liberty* vol. 96, no. 3 (May/June 2001): 3-7.

Herberg, Will. *Protestant, Catholic, Jew: An Essay in American Religious Sociology.* Garden City, NY: Anchor Books, 1960.

Hirsch, H.N. *The Enigma of Felix Frankfurter.* New York: Basic Books, Inc., 1980.

Hitchcock, James. *The Supreme Court and Religion in American Life.* 2 vols. Princeton: Princeton University Press, 2004.

Hockett, Jeffrey D. *New Deal Justice: The Constitutional Jurisprudence of Hugo L. Black, Felix Frankfurter and Robert*

Jackson. Lanham, MD: Rowman & Littlefield Publishers, Inc., 1996.

Hoffer, Peter Charles. "Frankfurter, Felix," in *The Oxford Companion to the Supreme Court of the United States*, 2d ed., Kermit L. Hall, Ed. in Chief. New York: Oxford University Press, 2005.

Holmes, David L. *The Faiths of the Founding Fathers.* New York: Oxford University Press, 2006.

Hovenkamp, Herbert. "The Political Economy of Substantive Due Process." *40 Stanford Law Review 379* (1988).

Howard, J. Woodford, Jr. *Mr. Justice Murphy: A Political Biography.* Princeton: Princeton University Press, 1968.

Hunter, James Davison. *Culture Wars: The Struggle to Define America.* New York: Basic Books, 1991.

Hunter, James Davison and Os Guinness. eds. *Articles of Faith, Articles of Peace: The Religious Liberty Clauses and the American Public Philosophy.* Washington, D.C.: Brookings Institution Press, 1990.

Hutson, James. *Forgotten Features of the Founding: The Recovery of Religious Themes in the Early American Republic.* Lanham, MD: Lexington Books, 2003.

Ickes, Harold L. *The Secret Diary of Harold Ickes, vol. III: The Lowering Clouds, 1939-1941.* New York: Simon and Schuster, 1954.

Idelman, Scott C. "The Limits of Religious Values in Judicial Decision-making." *81 Marquette Law Review 537* (Winter 1998).

———. "The Concealment of Religious Values in Judicial Decisionmaking." *91 Virginia Law Review 515* (2005).

Jackson, Robert. "Back to the Constitution." *American Bar Association Journal* 25 (1939): 748.

———. *The Supreme Court in the American System of Government.* Cambridge, MA: Harvard University Press, 1955.

Jacobs, Clyde. *Justice Felix Frankfurter and Civil Liberties.* Berkeley, CA: University of California Press, 1961.

Kannar, George. "The Constitutional Catechism of Antonin Scalia." *99 Yale Law Journal 1297* (1990).

Kelly, Alfred. "Clio and the Court: An Illicit Love Affair." *1965 Supreme Court Review 122* (1965).

Levine, Samuel J. "Law, Ethics, and Religion in the Public Square: Principles of Restraint and Withdrawal." *83 Marquette Law Review 773* (Summer 2000).

Levinson, Sanford. "Skepticism, Democracy, and Judicial Restraint: An Essay on The Thought of Oliver Wendell Holmes and Felix Frankfurter." PhD diss., Harvard University, 1969.

———. "The Democratic Faith of Felix Frankfurter." *25 Stanford Law Review 430* (February 1973).

———. *Constitutional Faith.* Princeton: Princeton University Press, 1998.

———. "The Confrontation of Religious Faith and Civil Religion: Catholics Becoming Justices." *39 DePaul Law Review 1047* (1990).

———. *Wrestling with Diversity.* Durham, N.C.: Duke University Press, 2003.

Levy, Leonard L. *The Establishment Clause: Religion and the First Amendment.* 2d ed. rev. Chapel Hill, N.C.: University of North Carolina Press, 1994.

Linder, Robert D., and Richard V. Pierard. *Twilight of the Saints: Biblical Christianity and Civil Religion in America.* Downers Grove, I.L.: Intervarsity Press, 1978.

———. *Civil Religion and the American Presidency.* Grand Rapids, M.I.: Academic Books, 1988.

Lippy, Charles H. "American Civil Religion: Myth, Reality, and Challenges," in *Faith in America: Changes, Challenges, New Directions, vol. 2, Religious Issues Today.* ed. Charles H. Lippy. Westport, Conn.: PRAEGER, 2006.

Liptak, Adam. "Some Judges Are Opting Out of Abortion Cases." *Chicago Daily Law Bulletin,* 7 September 2005, p. 2.

Maddigan, Michael M. "The Establishment Clause, Civil Religion, and the Public Church." *81 California Law Review 293* (1993).

Malone, Dumas. *Jefferson the President: First Term, 1801-1805.* Boston: Little, Brown Co., 1970.

Manwaring, David R. *Render Unto Caesar: The Flag Salute Controversy.* Chicago: University of Chicago Press, 1962.

Mapp, Alf J., Jr., *The Faiths of the Founders: What America's Founders Really Believed.* New York: Fall River Press, 2006.

Mason, Alpheus Thomas. *Security Through Freedom: American Political Thought and Practice*. Ithaca, N.Y.: Cornell University Press, 1955.

McConnell, Michael W. "The Origins and Historical Understanding of the Free Exercise of Religion." *103 Harvard Law Review 1409* (1990).

———. "Free Exercise Revisionism and the *Smith* Decision." *57 University of Chicago Law Review 1109* (1990).

———. "Religious Participation in Public Programs: Religious Freedom at a Crossroads." *59 University of Chicago Law Review 115* (1992).

Menand, Louis. *The Metaphysical Club: A Story of Ideas in America*. New York: Farrar, Straus, and Giroux, 2001.

Mendelson, Wallace. *Justices Black and Frankfurter: Conflict in the Court*. Chicago: University of Chicago Press, 1961.

Mersky, Roy M., and J. Myron Jacobstein. comps. *The Supreme Court of the United States: Hearings and Reports on Successful and Unsuccessful Nominations of Supreme Court Justices by the Senate Judiciary Committee, 1916-1986*. Vol. 13. Buffalo, N.Y.: William S. Hein & Co., Inc., 1989.

Miller, Charles A. *The Supreme Court and the Uses of History*. Cambridge, M.A.: Belknap Press of Harvard University Press, 1969.

Miller, Nicholas P. *The Religious Roots of the First Amendment: Dissenting Protestants and the Separation of Church and State*. New York: Oxford University Press, Inc., 2012.

Mirsky, Yehudah. "Civil Religion and the Establishment Clause." *95 Yale Law Journal 1237* (1986).

Murphy, Bruce Allen. *The Brandeis/Frankfurter Connection: The Secret Political Activities of Two Supreme Court Justices*. New York: Oxford University Press, 1982.

Murrin, John M. "Religion and Politics in America from the First Settlements to the Civil War." In *Religion and American Politics: From the Colonial Period to the 1980s*. ed. Mark A. Noll. New York: Oxford University Press, 1990.

———. "Fundamental Values, the Founding Fathers, and the Constitution." In *To Form a More Perfect Union: The Critical Ideas of the Constitution*. eds. Herman Belz, Ronald Hoffman, and

Peter J. Albert. Charlottesville, V.A.: The University Press of
     Virginia, 1992.
Niebuhr, H. Richard. *Radical Monotheism and Western Culture*.
     Louisville, K.Y.: Westminster/John Knox Press, 1960.
Nies, Gregory O. "Religious Liberty through the Lens of Textualism
     and a Living Constitution: The First Amendment Establishment
     Clause Interpretations of Justices William Brennan, Jr., and
     Antonin Scalia." Master's thesis, Baylor University, 2006.
Noll, Mark A. *One Nation Under God? Christian Faith and Political
     Action in America*. San Francisco: Harper and Row, 1988.
Noll, Mark A., Nathan O. Hatch and George M. Marsden. *The Search
     for Christian America*. Colorado Springs, C.O.: Helmers and
     Howard, 1989.
Novak, Michael and Jana Novak. *Washington's God: Religion,
     Liberty, and the Father of Our Country*. New York: BASIC
     BOOKS, A Member of the Perseus Books Group, 2006.
O'Reilly, David. "Scalia Opines on Faith and Justice." *The
     Philadelphia Inquirer*, 17 October 2007, sec. B, p. 5.
Osborn, Rebekah L. "Beliefs on the Bench: Recusal for Religious
     Reasons and the Model Code of Judicial Conduct." *19 Georgetown
     Journal of Legal Ethics 895* (Summer 2006).
Parrish, Michael E. *Felix Frankfurter and His Times: The Reform
     Years*. New York: The Free Press, 1982.
Perry, Michael J. "The Authority of Text, Tradition, and Reason: A
     Theory of Constitutional Interpretation." *58 Southern California
     Law Review 551* (1985).
Peters, Shawn Francis. *Judging Jehovah's Witnesses: Religious
     Persecution and the Dawn of the Rights Revolution*. Lawrence,
     K.S.: University Press of Kansas, 2000.
——. *The Yoder Case: Religious Freedom, Education, and Parental
     Rights*. Lawrence, K.S.: University Press of Kansas, 2003.
Peterson, Merrill D. *Thomas Jefferson and the New Nation, A
     Biography*. New York: Oxford University Press, 1970.
Ragosta, John. *Religious Freedom: Jefferson's Legacy, America's
     Creed*. Charlottesville, V.A.: University of Virginia Press, 2013.
Rakove, Jack N. *Original Meanings: Politics and Ideas in the Making
     of the Constitution*. New York: Vintage Books, 1996.

Rauh, Joseph L., Jr. "Felix Frankfurter: Civil Libertarian." *11 Harvard Civil Rights-Civil Liberties Law Review 496* (1976).

Rosen, Jeffrey. *The Supreme Court: The Personalities and Rivalries that Defined America.* New York: Henry Holt and Company, 2007.

Rossum, Ralph A. *Antonin Scalia's Jurisprudence: Text and Tradition.* Lawrence, K.S.: University of Kansas, 2006.

Saphire, Richard B. "Religion and Recusal." *81 Marquette Law Review 351* (Winter 1998).

Semonche, John E. *Keeping the Faith: A Cultural History of the U.S. Supreme Court.* Lanham, M.D.: Rowman and Littlefield, 1998.

Sheridan, Eugene R. *Jefferson and Religion.* Princeton, N.J.: Princeton University Press, 1983.

Shulleeta, Brandon. "At UVa. Justice Scalia warns of scholars' agendas, biases: Says Constitutional interpretation must honor framers' intent." *The Daily Progress,* April 17, 2010.

Silverstein, Mark. *Constitutional Faiths: Felix Frankfurter, Hugo Black, and the Process of Judicial Decision Making.* Ithaca, N.Y.: Cornell University Press, 1984.

Simon, James F. *The Antagonists: Hugo Black, Felix Frankfurter and Civil Liberties.* New York: Simon & Schuster, 1989.

Smith, Christopher E., and David A. Schulz. *The Jurisprudential Vision of Justice Antonin Scalia.* Lanham, M.D.: Rowman and Littlefield Publishers, Inc., 1996.

Smith, Jean Edward. *John Marshall: Definer of a Nation.* New York: Henry Holt & Company, 1996.

Smith, Steven D. *Foreordained Failure: The Quest for a Constitutional Principle of Religious Freedom.* New York: Oxford University Press, 1995.

Staab, James Brian. *The Political Thought of Justice Antonin Scalia: A Hamiltonian on the Supreme Court.* Lanham, M.D.: Rowman and Littlefield Publishers, Inc., 2006.

Stevens, Richard D. *Frankfurter and Due Process.* Lanham, M.D.: University Press of America, Inc., 1987.

Sullivan, Kathleen M. "Justice Scalia and the Religion Clauses." *22 University of Hawai'i Law Review 449* (2000).

Swanson, Wayne R. *The Christ Child Goes to Court.* Philadelphia, P.A.: Temple University Press, 1990.

Thayer, James B. "The Origin and Scope of the American Doctrine of Constitutional Law." *VII Harvard Law Review 17* (October 25, 1893).

Thomas, Helen Shirley. *Felix Frankfurter: Scholar on the Bench.* Baltimore, M.D.: The Johns Hopkins Press, 1960.

Tushnet, Mark. *A Court Divided: The Rehnquist Court and the Future of American Constitutional Law.* New York: W.W. Norton & Company, 2005.

Urofsky, Melvin I. "Conflict Among the Brethren: Felix Frankfurter, William O. Douglas and the Clash of Personalities and Philosophies on the United States Supreme Court." *1988 Duke Law Journal 71* (1988).

———. *Felix Frankfurter: Judicial Review and Individual Liberties.* Boston, M.A.: Twayne Publishers, 1991.

———. *Division and Discord: The Supreme Court Under Stone and Vinson, 1941-1953.* Columbia, S.C.: University of South Carolina Press, 1997.

White, James Boyd. "Talking About Religion in the Language of the Law: Impossible But Necessary." *81 Marquette Law Review 177* (Winter 1998).

Wick, Wendy C. *George Washington, An American Icon: The Eighteenth Century Graphic Portraits.* Charlottesville, V.A.: University of Virginia Press, 1982.

Wilson, John F. *Public Religion in American Culture.* Philadelphia, P.A.: Temple University Press, 1979.

Witte, John Jr. *Religion and the American Constitutional Experiment.* 2d ed. Boulder, C.O.: Westview Press, 2005.

———. "Facts and Fictions about the History of Separation of Church and State." *Journal of Church and State* 48, no. 1 (Winter 2006): 15-45.

Wuthnow, Robert. *Christianity and Civil Society: The Contemporary Debate.* Valley Forge, P.A.: Trinity Press International, 1996.

Zlotnick, David M. "Justice Scalia and His Critics: An Exploration of Scalia's Fidelity to His Constitutional Methodology." *48 Emory Law Journal 1377* (1999).

United States Supreme Court Cases

Establishment Clause
Reynolds v. United States, 98 U.S. 145 (1879).
Everson v. Board of Education, 330 U.S. 1 (1947).
McCollum v. Board of Education, 333 U.S. 203 (1948).
Zorach v. Clauson, 343 U.S. 307 (1952).
Engel v. Vitale, 370 U.S. 421 (1962).
Abington School District v. Schempp, 374 U.S. 203 (1961).
Epperson v. Arkansas, 393 U.S. 97 (1968).
Lemon v. Kurtzman, 403 U.S. 602 (1971).
Marsh v. Chambers, 463 U.S. 783 (1983).
Lynch v. Donnelly, 465 U.S. 668 (1984).
Wallace v. Jaffree, 472 U.S. 38 (1985).
Edwards v. Aguillard, 482 U.S. 578 (1986).
Texas Monthly, Inc. v. Bullock, 489 U.S. 1 (1989).
Allegheny County v. Greater Pittsburgh ACLU, 492 U.S. 573 (1989).
Lee v. Weisman, 505 U.S. 577 (1992).
Lamb's Chapel v. Center Moriches Union Free School District, 508 U.S. 384 (1993).
Zobrest v. Catalina Foothills School District, 509 U.S. 1 (1993).
Board of Education of Kiryas Joel v. Grumet, 521 U.S. 687 (1994).
Santa Fe Independent School District v. Doe, 530 U.S. 290 (2001).
Zelman v. Simmons-Harris, 536 U.S. 639 (2002).
McCreary County v. ACLU, 545 U.S. 844 (2005).
Van Orden v. Perry, 545 U.S. 677 (2005).
Free Exercise Clause
Cantwell v. Connecticut, 310 U.S. 296 (1940).
Minersville School District v. Gobitis, 310 U.S. 586 (1940).
West Virginia State Board of Education v. Barnette, 319 U.S. 624 (1943).
McGowan v. Maryland, 366 U.S. 420 (1961).
Sherbert v. Verner, 374 U.S. 398 (1963).
Wisconsin v. Yoder, 406 U.S. 205 (1972).
Employment Division, Department of Human Services v. Smith, 494 U.S. 872 (1990).
Church of Lukumi Babalu Aye, Inc. v. Hialeah, 508 U.S. 520 (1993).
City of Boerne v. Flores, 521 U.S. 507 (1997).

MISCELLANEOUS

Davis v. Beason, 133 U.S. 333 (1890).
Pierce v. Society of Sisters, 268 U.S. 510 (1925).
Hamilton v. Board of Regents of California, 293 U.S. 245 (1934).
Torcaso v. Watkins, 367 U.S. 488 (1967).
U.S. v. Seeger, 380 U.S. 163 (1965).
Welsh v. U.S., 398 U.S. 333 (1970).
Gillette v. U.S., 401 U.S. 437 (1971).

CPSIA information can be obtained at www.ICGtesting.com
Printed in the USA
BVOW05*1409090215

386493BV00001BA/5/P